HISTORY

OF THE

WINGATE FAMILY

IN ENGLAND AND IN AMERICA,

WITH GENEALOGICAL TABLES.

COMPILED BY CHARLES E. L. WINGATE.

PUBLISHED BY
JAMES D. P. WINGATE, EXETER, N. H.
1886.

PREFACE.

The history of the Wingate family has never been written before except in unconnected fragments, embracing one or two generations or a few individuals of one generation. Some thirty years ago Rev. Dr. A. H. Quint, of Dover, N. H., published in The Dover Enquirer four articles relating to the early Wingates of America, and these sketches formed the nucleus from which the present history has grown. Mr. John Wingate Thornton, of Boston, devoted a great deal of his time to investigating the genealogy of the family, and his unpublished work gave completeness to the story of the early American family, and also added facts relating to the English family. The work of connecting these records and of amplifying them has been carried on by the compiler of this book by researches in libraries and town records, and by correspondence with other members of the family. The genealogical tables of the earlier generations are as complete as they can be made. Those of the later generations have not in all cases been fully carried out for two reasons, first and chiefly, because repeated letters have failed to bring to hand the facts asked for, second, because a lengthened delay of years in order to hunt up a few names of present generations was not considered a sufficient reason for postponing the publication of the descriptive history, and the genealogy already obtained With the present work in the hands of members of the family it is to be hoped that interest will be aroused and more historical facts brought forward.

In arranging this work the compiler has had valuable assistance from Mr. Charles P. Bowditch, of Boston, whose records of the Pick-

ering family contain an almost complete genealogy of the Pickering-Wingate branch, from Rev. Charles Wingate of Haverhill, Mass., from Prof. Charles F. Richardson of Dartmouth College, from Mr. Dana W. Baker of Exeter, N. H., from Dr. John R. Ham of Dover, N. H., and from Rev. Jacob Chapman of Exeter, N. H.

That there may be errors in the book is to be expected. One of the greatest difficulties that has met the compiler has been the varying statements of correspondents. Members of the same immediate family have differed to an astonishing degree in matters of dates, and occasionally of names for the present generation, and in the records of generations preceding the present the difficulty in straightening out conflicting statements has, of course, been increased. In all doubtful cases the versions which seemed the most credible have been taken. Everyone who discovers what he knows to be an error, should communicate immediately with the compiler. If also each member of the Wingate family will send, as occasion calls, additional records relating to the history past or present, they will be kept on file, and when of sufficient number will be sent out to the subscribers of this book.

CHARLES E. L. WINGATE.

Boston, Mass., May 15, 1886.

CONTENTS.

CHAPTER I.

CHAPTER II.

CHAPTER III.

CHAPTER IV.

CHAPTER V.

CHAPTER VI.

CHAPTER VII.

CHAPTER VIII.

CHAPTER IX.

THE WINGATE HISTORY.

CHAPTER I.

THE ENGLISH WINGATES.

Some time in olden days a gallant English warrior was fighting with the forces of the Crown against opponents of the reign. For hours the army of which he was a member had besieged a castle, unable to force an entrance. Then suddenly the powerful and valiant soldier — than whom there was no stronger in the line — rushed to the front and under a storm of showering arrows seized the castle gate with both his hands, tore it from its fastening and bearing it away upon his shoulders, opened a way for his comrades to enter. The castle was won and England gained fresh laurels. In recognition of the event and in honor of the brave deed the hero of the day was knighted by the Crown, and to his name was added the appellation "Win-gate", symbolic of the feat.

So runs the legend that explains the origin of the family name of Wingate. Another story makes the name originate from "Wind-gate", so called from the stream of air sweeping through a chasm ; and in substantiation of this it is said that "Windgate of that ilk" is a name found in England. But the first mentioned legend finds corroboration in the crest of the Wingate family as recorded in the General Armory of England, Scotland, Ireland and Wales, (by Sir Bernard Burke, Ulster King of Arms) ;— A gate of gold with the motto Win above it. [See Chapter VII.] As to the spelling and pronunciation of the name the style has changed at various times : Wyngate, Windgate, Wyndegate we find it in the English records ; Wengett, Wendett, Windiett, Windet we find it in the American books. The spelling illustrates the looseness of early orthography, the same sound being

written in several different forms. Ninian Winzet, D. D., one of the most conspicuous, learned and respectable opponents of Knox, the Scottish Reformer, is uniformly called Wingate by Knox's Reverend biographer, the critically accurate and accomplished Dr. McCrie, while in the will of John[1] Wingate, the progenitor of the American family, the name is spelled Winget, Windiet and Windet indifferently, the g and d having, it is said, the sound of j as in James or of g as in germ. When John[3], son of Col. Joshua[2] Wingate, and grandson of the first American ancestor John[1], applied for matriculation at Harvard College in 1740, he pronounced his name "*Winjet.*" President Holyoke at once repeated his name with emphasis "*Wingate*", desiring him "no more to abuse the good and honored name of Wingate".

The syllables *zet, get, det, diet,*—giving *z* not the sibilant but the compound sound as in the Italian, and *d* the lingual sound,—are not easily distinguishable in pronunciation. *Gate* and *get* are the most anciently used and may be adopted as correct, and *zet, det, diet* be considered as accidental corruptions. *Gate, geat,* in Saxon, *gade* in Danish, and *gait* in Scottish mean "a way", "a street or passage",— thus we say the gates of Heaven, of destruction, of death, of the city, of the castle. *Winnan* in Saxon, and *Winnen* in Danish mean "to labor", "to toil", "to gain by labor", as to win a prize, a battle or a country. The name being thus divided, Win-gate, and deduced from its originals the reader can conjecture as best suits his own ingenuity or fancy the mode in which the first proprietors of the name gained their title to it.

As a local name Wingate is found early and frequently in the north of England and in Scotland. (Note *a*). Bold mountain passes, ravines, rivers *winding* between broken hills, through or over which the *wind* swept, might cause the more remarkable of these places to be called Wind-gates (or avenues), and thus the name be originated by like circumstances in different places. (Note *b*). In "Black's Picturesque Towns in England", 1847, p. 203, is stated, "For centuries the only accessible road to Buxton and Chapel-en-le-

---

NOTE (*a*). Wingate was used as a surname in both England and Scotland a long time prior to 1200.

NOTE (*b*). Wind-rush, Wynd-cliff, are names of towns in England; Wingate Grange at Newcastle in Yorkshire.

Firth was by a deep descent called the Winnets or Wind-gates from the stream of air that always sweeps through the chasm. Dark, rugged and perpendicular precipices are seen on each side of the road." The presence of the prefix *de* to the name Wingate might be, so far, evidence that the first Wingate gained his name as a designation from the accident of his residence at some place where the powers of the air held sway. But the herald's design would show that the progenitor of the family honorably *won* both name and fame at once by some gallant exploit, as the legend narrates. (Note *c*.)

In regard to the Wingate family in England, the researches of Col. Joseph L. Chester, of London, England, an antiquarian who made a specialty of genealogical study, and had the reputation of being very painstaking, and of Clutterbuck, the compiler of the History of Hertford, tell us the following : "The English family of Wingate is of great antiquity. It had existed for several generations previous to the settlement of the family at Sharpenhoe, in the parish of Streatley, in County Bedford. The Manor of the family, in the parish of Ellesborough, in Buckinghamshire, in early days called Wyngate's, is now known by the name of the Manor of Grove."

The first known individual of the family was a certain "Hemyng de Wyngate," *i. e.*, HEMYNG [1] OF WYNGATE, who was lord of that Manor about the reign of King Henry II (1154—'89.) From him descended John de Wyngate, or *John* [2] *Wingate* who died 19th Richard II (1395 — '6.) John [2] had married, 8 R. II, Agnes, the sole heiress of the family of Beleurge, or Beleverge, possessors of the estate of Sharpenhoe, County Bedford, who brought him that estate. He appears then to have changed his residence to Sharpenhoe, as the family was always afterwards called of that place. John [2] Wingate was a younger son, but the elder branches of the family appear to have died out as no trace of them remains after this period.

John [2] was succeeded by his second son *William* [3] who married

---

NOTE (*c*). " Windygate of that Ilk, a family some time with us, bears argent, a Portcullis sable, as in Workman's MS., but in Pont's MS., a Portcullis or. Portcullis, latinized Porta Cataracta, was the hereditary badge of cognizance of the sons of John of Gaunt, Duke of Lancaster, upon the account that they were born in the castle of Beaufort in France."
—[Nesbit's Heraldy, Edinburgh, 1722.

Joane, daughter of John Fitz, of Westley, in Faldhoo. Of this William[3] it is recorded in Rymer's Foedera IX, p. 249, "De protectionibus in Comitiva Regis ad partes ultra marinas", "A. D. 1415. Willielmus Wyngate de Sharpyngho in Comitatu Bedfordiæ, qui in Comitiva Carissimi Fratris Regis, Thomas, Ducis Clarenciæ, Comitis Albemarliæ et Senescalli Angliæ versus partes ultra marinas &c." William[3] died in 1452 having had three sons, *Robert*[4], *Richard*[4] and *John*[4] (the latter a Canon of the Priory of Dunstable.)

Robert[4] "dwelt at Harlington the lifetyme of his father nigh Sharpenhoe." He married Margery, daughter of Thomas Blandell. His will was made 7 H. VII, 1486, so that he probably died at about that time. He left two sons, *William*[5] and *Edmund*[5] (the latter a priest,) and a daughter *Joane*[5].

William[5], of Sharpenhoe, married Jane, daughter of Edward Morecote. His will was made 13 H. VIII, 1522, so that his death may be placed about that year. His son *Robert*[6] [by Clutterbuck called John] married Joane, daughter of John Porter, of Hartshome, Northamptonshire. He died at Harlington 1556, having had five sons and two daughters, viz., *Edmund*[7], *John*[7] (who had a son *Edward*[8] who was Serjeant of the Bear Garden to Queen Elizabeth, and died without issue, and also a daughter *Elizabeth*[8]), *Edward*[7], for thirty-three years Clerk of the Cheque to Queen Elizabeth, dying 1597, "sine exitu," and buried at St. Martins in the Fields, *Robert*[7], a merchant in London who died without issue, *William*[7], slain in the Battle of St. Quintin, *Mary*[7] and *Elizabeth*[7]. Concerning *Edward*[7], Mr. George Pease, occupant and owner of the Wingate mansion by marriage during the first of the present century, [see succeeding pages], says: "There are many ancient documents in our possession relating to the family of the Wingates, very puzzling to decipher and only interesting to a descendant of the family or to the antiquarian. The pedigree is emblazoned throughout with notices of certain members of the families and copies of wills, deeds, &c., annexed. As a sample of the former take the following, attached to Edward, grandson of Robert Wingate and his wife Joane. [This is undoubtedly an error of one generation: The Harleian MS., in the British Museum, 6113, makes Edward[7], Clerke of the Cheque a son and not grandson of Robert[6] which is the more probable as the latter died in 1556 and the former in 1597 "after a long life."] 'Edward Wingate being of a goodly prsonage and manly aspect was prferred

TABLE I.

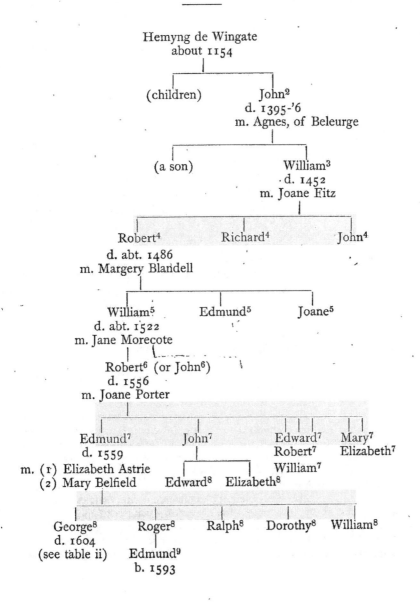

Hemyng de Wingate
about 1154

(children)   John[2]
d. 1395-'6
m. Agnes, of Beleurge

(a son)   William[3]
·d. 1452
m. Joane Fitz

Robert[4]   Richard[4]   John[4]
d. abt. 1486
m. Margery Blandell

William[5]   Edmund[5]   Joane[5]
d. abt. 1522
m. Jane Morecote

Robert[6] (or John[6])
d. 1556
m. Joane Porter

Edmund[7]   John[7]   Edward[7]   Mary[7]
d. 1559   Robert[7]   Elizabeth[7]
m. (1) Elizabeth Astrie   William[7]
(2) Mary Belfield   Edward[8]   Elizabeth[8]

George[8]   Roger[8]   Ralph[8]   Dorothy[8]   William[8]
d. 1604
(see table ii)   Edmund[9]
b. 1593

to the Service of King Edw[d] 6. He was Clerke of the Cheque of the Gard. to Queen Eliz. and he by the bountie of the Queene by his moderation, wisdome, frugalitie, celebisie and long life, gathered a plentifull estate which by his last will, dated 1596, he divided amongst those of his blood. He lies buried in ye church of St. Martins in the fields, London, at whose funeral the Heraulds at Armes assisted.'" "I am informed"—continues Mr. Pease—"there is a good engraving of this man probably taken from a clever painting in pannel in my dining room, the date thereon 1597." (Note d.)

Edmund[7], the eldest son of Robert[6], died about February, 1559 ('60.) He had married, first, Elizabeth, daughter of Thomas Astrie, of Woodend, Harlington, second, Mary, daughter of William Belfield, of Studham, Co. Hertford. By his first wife he had George[8], by his second wife he had Roger[8], Ralph[8], Dorothy[8] and William[8]. Roger[8] settled in Yorkshire, and was father of Edmund[9], the famous mathematician. Whether Roger[8] was the Roger Wingate, Esq., who received the appointment for life of King's Treasurer within the Lordship of Virginia, (mentioned in Chapter II,) is not established. It seems probable, however, on account of the distinguished services of the son. Edmund[9] has left evidence of various learning, great industry, valor and the refinements and accomplishments incident to a place at Court; but it were well for his memory that some explana-

---

NOTE (d). Rev. Dr. Ninian Wingate was born in 1518, at Renfrew, near Glasgow on the Clyde, but his connection with the direct line remains to be traced. In 1576 he was made Abbot of the Scotch monastery at Ratisbon on the Danube. He died Sept. 21, 1592, aged 74, and a monument erected to his memory recorded his exemplary life and pious death. "The name of Winzet," says Dr. David Irving in his lives of Scotish Writers "was conspicuous in the progress of those religious controversies which attended the Scotch reformation, and according to the estimate of his own party he rendered himself formidable for the strength of his talents and the extent of his theological learning." He was at first a school-master, and this is his own version, expressed in "the plain old Scotish," of the importance of such a vocation. "I ingeit the teching of the zouthed in vertew and science, nixt efter ye auctoritie with the ministeries of iustice, vnder it and efter ye angilicall office of godlie pastours, to obtene the third principal place maist commodious and necessare to the kirk of God." In 1580 his nephews John and James "Winzet" were students in Germany, as appears by a letter to them from John Lesley, the celebrated Bishop of Ross.

tion should be given, if any can be, by those who are by family ties bound to defend him, of his sudden desertion of his King and patron, Charles I, in order to assume active service with the Republicans. Edmund[9] was born in Yorkshire in 1593; he graduated at Queen's College, Oxford, about 1614, and studied law at Gray's Inn, London, cultivating at the same time his mathematical researches. He spent some years in France, from 1624, and at that time taught English to the Princess Henrietta-Marie, who was afterwards to become the Queen of Charles I of England, and to some of the ladies of her suite, also teaching mathematics at the French Court. About 1629 Edmund[9] published his Arithmetic, dedicated to Thomas, Earl of Arundel and Surrey, of which a nineteenth edition was published in 1760. He also published a table of Logarithms and other mathematical works. A diligent student in the laws as well as in mathematics, he published an abridgment of the statutes from Magna Charta until 1641, which went through several subsequent editions, by divers editors, and also a large folio volume of the maxims of the Common Law which maintained a high rank among his books. In 1655 he issued a small duodecimo volume, "The Body of the Common Laws", which was "printed by Roger Wingate at the Golden-Hinde near Lincoln's Inn in Chancery Lane." Whether he was related to the publisher does not appear. At the beginning of the Great Rebellion of Cromwell Edmund[9] was a justice of the peace and recorder at Bedford on the landed estates of his father which he had inherited. Having for some cause become alienated from King Charles I who had treated him with marked personal kindness, he became an influential member of Parliament and a supporter and friend of Cromwell when Protector. He served, too, as a commissioner for ejecting "scandalous" ministers from their benefices. Edmund[9] died at London, December, 1656. Mr. Pease says, regarding Edmund[9], "I have a basin of the Dragon pattern said to have been the breakfast cup of Prince Charles when a wanderer and for some time concealed in this house [the Wingate mansion] during the interregnum; also a ring with an admirable likeness of Charles I cut in an onyx setting, reported to have been presented to him by Edmund Wingate". (Note e.)

Note (e). John Windet was one of the Stationers Company, printers to the city of London from 1585 to 1651. His connection is not established.

George[8], eldest son of Edmund[7], moved to Harlington, Co. Bedford, and there died in 1604. He married three times : his first wife being Anne Belfield, (a niece to George[8]'s step-mother, Mary Belfield Wingate), daughter of John Belfield, of Studham ; his second wife being Anne Wiseman Fitz, daughter of John Wiseman, of Canfield, Co. Essex, and Margery, his wife, (the daughter of Sir William Waldegrace), and relict of ———— Fitz by whom she had Sir William Fitz ; his third wife being Martha, daughter of Oliver, Lord St. John. George[8] by his first wife had *Robert*[9], *George*[9] (d. s. p.), *Margery*[9] (d. s. p.), *Ralph*[9], *John*[9] (d. s. p.), *Anne*[9], *Mary*[9] and *Edward*[9]. By his second wife he had *Nicholas*[9], *Ralph*[9], *Dorothy*[9] and *Judith*[9]. George[8] was a Justice of the Peace in Bedfordshire. *Ralph*[9] had one daughter *Mary*[10] who married Sir Jerome Smithson and became ancestress to the present Duke of Northumberland. *Anne*[9] married Thomas Audley, of Houghton Conquest, Co. Bedford. *Mary*[9] married George Errswell, of Saffron Walden, Co. Essex. *Nicholas*[9], of Grays Inn, "married, Dec. 9, 1618, Lady Elizabeth Leygrosse, alias French, of Marlborough, Norfolk, widow". *Judith*[9] became the mother of the Rt. Rev. Thomas Cartwright, Bishop of Chester.

Robert[9], eldest son of George[8], married Amye, daughter of Roger Warre, Esq., Co. Somerset, by his first wife who was the daughter of Sir John Popham, Kt., Chief Justice of England. Robert[9] died in 1603 (before his father), leaving *John*[10] and *George*[10]. *George*[10], " of the Middle Temple ", died without issue. *John*[10] was born 1601 and died about August, 1642. He married Alice Smallman, daughter of Francis Smallman, Esq., of Kinnersley, Co. Hertford. John[10], "Esq." lived at Harlington and was recorded as a Justice of the Peace in 1634. He had five children, (Note *f.*), *Robert*[11] born 1627, *Francis*[11], *George*[11], *Hester*[11] and *Anne*[11]. Evidently *Robert*[11] died before his father, and left no issue, as Francis[11] succeeded to the estates. *Francis*[11] was knighted at Whitehall, April 30, 1672. Sir Francis[11] married three times, (Note *g*), his last wife being Anne, fourth daughter of Arthur Annesley, first Earl of Anglesey, the "Lord privie Seale." Sir Francis[11] had

---

Note (*f.*) According to Publications of Harleian Society, Vol. 8.

Note (*g*). It is probable that his first or second wife was Lettice, daughter of St. Pierre, D. D.

TABLE II.

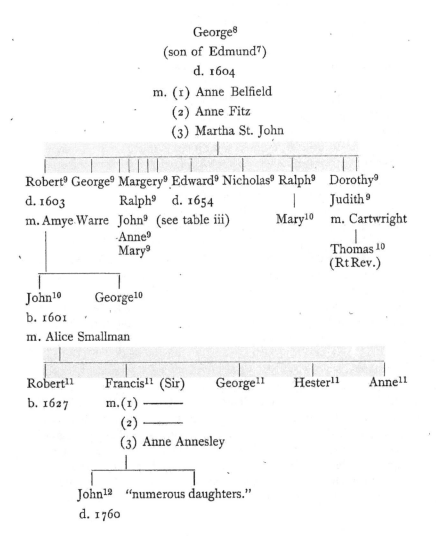

George[8]
(son of Edmund[7])
d. 1604
m. (1) Anne Belfield
(2) Anne Fitz
(3) Martha St. John

Robert[9] George[9] Margery[9] Edward[9] Nicholas[9] Ralph[9]   Dorothy[9]
d. 1603   Ralph[9]   d. 1654   Judith[9]
m. Amye Warre John[9] (see table iii)   Mary[10]   m. Cartwright
                Anne[9]
                Mary[9]   Thomas[10]
                                                        (Rt Rev.)

John[10]   George[10]
b. 1601
m. Alice Smallman

Robert[11]   Francis[11] (Sir)   George[11]   Hester[11]   Anne[11]
b. 1627   m.(1) ———
              (2) ———
              (3) Anne Annesley

John[12]   "numerous daughters."
d. 1760

numerous issue, chiefly daughters. His son *John* [12] was buried at Harlington in 1760, and with his death the name in this branch became extinct. The family at this period were divided in politics. Sir Francis [11] is immortalized in literary history by one act of his life. After the Restoration the English Government and Parliament were in ill humor with the Commonwealth men of the Milton school,—of whom even Hume says: The precious spark of liberty had been kindled and was preserved by the Puritans alone ; and it was to this sect that the English owe the whole freedom of their Constitution. The faithful applied themselves vigorously to silencing all persons disaffected to the violent measures against religious freedom, or who were disposed to worship God in any other mode than that patented by the Government which stigmatized them as " visionary, refractory fanatics." They made a law, May 16, 1664, by which all private meetings for religious exercises, including more than five persons besides the members of the family, were described as conventicles, and declared to be unlawful and seditious, punishable by penalties manifestly beyond the ability of the convicted to pay, or by the alternative of severe imprisonment. These vexatious and formidable penalties were left to be awarded wholly at the discretion of any single Justice of the Peace without the slightest check from a jury or any more competent authority. The person might be banished to any province except New England or Virginia. The persecutors well knew that the " fanatics " would find a welcome in New England and this cruel prohibition was only equalled by their prudence in keeping them from Virginia whose church-yard peace, under Berkeley's reign of no schools and no printing press, would be disturbed by these thinking men. Bishop Burnet says that this " was thought to be a great breach on the security of the English Constitution and a raising the power of Justices to a very arbitrary pitch." " The truth is," Burnet continues, " the whole face of the Government looked liker the proceedings of an inquisition than of legal courts ; and yet Sharp [the guardian of the Church] was never satisfied." During the plague the " fanatic " non-conformists went into the empty pulpits and preached to the people who were predisposed to hear good sermons, and in " many other places they began to preach openly without reflecting on the sins of the Court and on the ill-usage that they themselves had met with. This was represented very odiously at Oxford. So a severe bill was brought in requiring all the silenced

ministers to take an oath, declaring it was not lawful, on any pretence whatever, to take arms against the King or any commissioned by him, and that they would not at any time endeavor an alteration in the government of the Church or State. Such as refused this were not to come within five miles of any city or parliament borough or of the church where they had served." It is an instructive fact that · this odious law received the least opposition in the popular branch of the Parliament. Sir Francis[11] Wingate, son-in-law as he was of the Earl of Anglesey, was of course "unprejudiced" by any "abstractions" about liberty, and exercised his prerogative under the new quieting laws with becoming dignity and independence; he relieved the community from a perverse(!) and noisy(!) itinerant preacher, who feared God more than the Parliament, by imprisonment for life, and thus secured to the Christian world, from the pen of that same preacher, John Bunyan, the immortal allegory of the "Pilgrim's Progress." Of Sir Francis[11]'s son *John*[12] Mr. Pearse writes, "tradition says that he was appointed to the command of the fleet in the Mediterranean, but being laid up at Harlington with a fit of the gout which he did not survive, the appointment was transferred to Admiral Byng, the political sacrifice of the day." The importance of this command, and the outcome of that Mediterranean expedition are matters of history. The Wingate estates finally descended by marriage to the late *John Wingate Jennings*, Esq., whose only child and heiress *Elizabeth* married, Oct. 21, 1819, George Pearse, Esq., of Harlington, who was born Feb. 18, 1795. Mr. Pearse was a magistrate and Deputy Lieutenant for Bedfordshire; he also held the office of High Sheriff in 1822. They had: *George Wingate*, born Feb. 1, 1824, *Harriot Elizabeth*, and *Anna Letitia*. (Note *h.*)

Edward[9], the fifth son of George[8], removed from Harlington, Co. Bedford, to Lockley, a manor on the banks of the river Mimeran, a short distance south of the town of Welwyn, and mostly in the parish of Welwyn, about twenty-five miles from London. He married

---

Note (*h*). This Anna Letitia was probably named after another Anna Letitia, of whom it is said: "Anna Letitia Barbauld, a name long dear to the admirers of genius and the lovers of virtue, was born at the village of Kilworth, Harcourt in Leicestershire on June 20, 1743. She was the eldest child and only daughter of John Aiken, D. D., and Jane his wife, daughter of Rev. John Jennings, of Kilworth, and descended by her mother from the ancient family of Wingate, of Harlington, in Bedfordshire."

Margaret Taverner, daughter of Peter Taverner, Esq., of Hexton, Co. Hertford. Edward[9], "Esq.," was buried at Welwyn, June 19, 1654; his wife was buried there July 2, 1668. They had two daughters, Frances[10] and Jane[10], and a son Edward[10] who succeeded to the estates. Frances[10] married, Nov. 30, 1626, as second wife, Eustace Nedham, Esq., of Wymondley Priory, Co. Hertford; her husband died May, 1658. Jane[10] married, April 27, 1636, John Boteler, Gent., second son and heir to William Boteler, who was seventh son of Sir John Boteler, of Watton, Woodhall; her husband was buried at Watton, Oct. 2, 1671.

Edward[10], Esq., only son of Edward[9], was born 1606, and married Mary Allway, daughter and co-heir of Ralph Allway, Esq., of High Canons, in the parish of Sherley, Co. Hertford. He served in Parliament with Richard Jennings, Esq., for the borough of St. Albans, anno 16 Car. i., and was one of the commissioners of excise to King Charles II. He died Aug. 8, 1685. According to Sir Henry Chauney, Edward[10] "made a fair warren to this seat, [Lockley] stocked it with a choice breed of rabbits, all silver haired, and planted it with a great store of excellent wallnut trees; and, in the front of his house, raised a pleasant orchard set with the best and rarest fruit trees, where several cuts are made, through which the Mimeran passes in several streams, stored with fair trout and other fish for the provision of his table." Evidently Edward[10] was a good liver, and enjoyed the most from his wealth. (Note i.) He had eleven children: Ralph[11], Frances[11], Mary[11], Jane[11], Anne[11], Elizabeth[11], Margaret[11], Francis[11], Edward[11], William[11] and Ralph[11].

The first Ralph[11], son of Edward[10], died young, and was buried

---

Note (i). Two references in history probably refer to this Edward[10]. A copy of a book advertisement reads: "Lt. Wingate's Storming of Ghuznee and Kelat, 14 large and spirited drawings on stone, etc., £2, 2s., (pub. at £7, 7s.) 1842." Owen's History of Shrewsbury, speaking of the battle of Worcester in the time of Charles I, 1642, gives in a note the following: "This action took place on the 23d of Sept. A relation of it was published in a pamphlet entitled 'True but sad and dolefull news from Shrewsbury, &c., imprinted at Yorke and now reprinted in London Oct. 10, 1642'. The letter from Shrewsbury is subscribed B. H., Sept. 30, and says, 'We have here prisoner one Captaine Wingates burgesse for St. Albans and he fought valiently.'"

TABLE III.

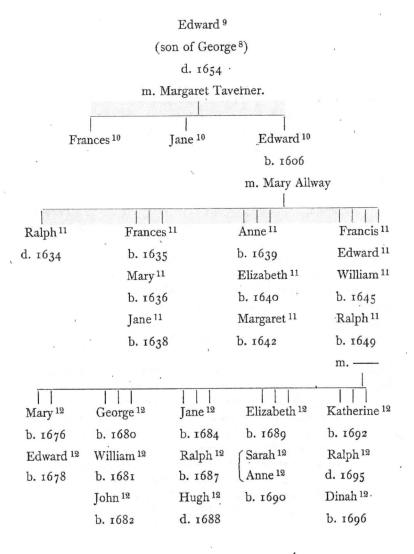

Edward [9]

(son of George [8])

d. 1654

m. Margaret Taverner.

Frances [10]	Jane [10]	Edward [10]
		b. 1606
		m. Mary Allway

Ralph [11]	Frances [11]	Anne [11]	Francis [11]
d. 1634	b. 1635	b. 1639	Edward [11]
	Mary [11]	Elizabeth [11]	William [11]
	b. 1636	b. 1640	b. 1645
	Jane [11]	Margaret [11]	Ralph [11]
	b. 1638	b. 1642	b. 1649
			m. ——

Mary [12]	George [12]	Jane [12]	Elizabeth [12]	Katherine [12]
b. 1676	b. 1680	b. 1684	b. 1689	b. 1692
Edward [12]	William [12]	Ralph [12]	⎰ Sarah [12]	Ralph [12]
b. 1678	b. 1681	b. 1687	⎱ Anne [12]	d. 1695
	John [12]	Hugh [12]	b. 1690	Dinah [12]
	b. 1682	d. 1688		b. 1696

at Welwyn, June 1, 1634. *William*[11] was born Feb. 21, 1645, and baptized March 9, the same year; he was buried at Welwyn, Dec. 21, 1650. *Frances*[11] was baptized April 5, 1635. *Mary*[11] was baptized Aug. 30, 1636. *Jane*[11] was baptized March 30, 1638, and married, Oct. 20, 1659, Andrew Clerke, Gent., of London. *Anne*[11] was baptized April 19, 1639, and married, May 24, 1670, George Margots, of London. *Elizabeth*[11] was baptized March 16, 1640, and buried May 13, 1669. *Margaret*[11] was baptized April 14, 1642, and buried Nov. 26, 1650.

The second *Ralph*[11], son of Edward[10], succeeded to the estates of Lockley. He was baptized Sept. 5, 1649, died at Greenwich and was buried at Welwyn April 14, 1727. Ralph[11] "Esq." did not retain the family estates of Lockley but sold them in the year 1715 to Edward Searle, a London merchant, and in 1814 the same estates came into the possession of George Shee, Bart. We find a record for the year 1696 which probably refers to this Ralph[11]. The "Association Rolls" from all over England are preserved in the Tower, and upon one of these, dated 1696, we read the name of R. Wingate, subscribing himself as one of the grand jury who, together with the Lord Lieutenant, Deputy Lieutenants and other officers of the county of Hertford, bound themselves to defend the right and title of King William to the crown against King James II and his adherents. Ralph[11] married Sarah ——— and had fourteen children, as follows: *Mary*[12] baptized Nov. 26, 1676, and buried May 6, 1741, *Edward*[12] baptized June 14, 1678, *George*[12] baptized Apr. 29, 1680, *William*[12] baptized Sept. 30, 1681, *John*[12] baptized Feb. 10, 1682, *Jane*[12] baptized Sept. 3, 1684, *Ralph*[12] baptized Oct. 19, 1687, and buried Nov. 22, 1693, *Hugh*[12] buried Dec. 4, 1688, *Elizabeth*[12] baptized Nov. 15, 1689, and buried Sept. 5, 1716, *Sarah*[12] and *Anne*[12] (twins), baptized Dec. 5, 1690 and buried five days later, *Katherine*[12] baptized July 6, 1692 and buried Jan. 28, 1692-3, *Ralph*[12] buried Nov. 12, 1695, *Dinah*[12] baptized July 26, 1696.

The record of later decendants remains yet to be traced out. As to the general characteristics of the English family Col. Chester says: "There are no salient features in the history of the Wingates. None of them appear to have held public positions except in one or two instances as Members of Parliament. They were simply country gentlemen and Justices of the Peace, probably preferring that quiet and healthful sort of life to the noise and bustle of statesmanship."

CHAPTER II.

JOHN[1] WINGATE OF AMERICA.

The connection between the Wingates in England and the Wingates in America cannot be traced. There are links missing in the genealogical chain which have not yet been discovered. (Note *k*). All the members of the family now in this country, however, can be traced back to one man who emigrated to America in the middle of the seventeenth century. JOHN WINGATE was born in England, and came to New Hampshire when a young man without a family. A collection of "original lists of persons of quality, emigrants, religious and political exiles," etc., compiled by John Camden Hotten, records two other Wingates coming to this land :— Charles Wyngate, age 22, conveyed to Virginia in the "Thomas C. John," Richard Lombard · master, June 1635, and John Wingatt, "received ticquetts granted out of the Secretary's office of the Barbadoes Islands for the departure off this Island," May 8, 1679, in the Ketch "Prosperous," David Fogg commander, for Virginia,—but it is probable either that these two did not long remain here or else that their lines soon became extinct. The "Patent Rolls" of England also contain an entry reading for 1640 : "6 August. Roger Wingate Esq. appointed King's Treasurer within the Lordship of Virginia for life. (15 Chas. I p. 23)," this probably refers to Roger[8], (mentioned on page 14), and as was often the custom in those days, he may never have left his home while managing affairs in the colony. The name of Wingate occurs with such frequency and dignity in the history of the early colonial enterprises to America as to afford a reasonable hope that in time the connecting links may be discovered.

Note (*k*). The fact that several of the American Wingate branches have old copies of the English Wingate coat-of arms which they hold with the tradition of their ancestors that the original came over with John[1] Wingate is, so far, a valuable link.

Thus, among many other instances, we find that Lord John Popham, Chief Justice of England, allied with the Wingate family and a leading member of the Plymouth Colony, was associated with Sir Ferdinando Gorges in sending out ships to colonize the coast of Maine in 1607, under the command of his brother, George Popham, and of Raleigh Gilbert. [Account of Gilbert Family, Vol. IV.]

In America as in England the name of Wingate was subject to varying orthography, the misspelling in many cases being due, without doubt, to the carelessness of recording clerks. Of this misspelling James Savage says, in his "Genealogical History of the First Settlers of New Hampshire," with that quaint system of abbreviations which he used: "Not the least of my causes of malediction against that usurp. Gov. [Gov. Andros] and his subord. Walter Barefoote is, that, under their admin. this name [Wingate] bec. pervert. into Windiat, to mislead honest, unskeptical Farmer. [Farmer's Register, on the basis of which the article was prepared.] Windiat John, Dover, son and jun. are introd. on the authority of Farmer in MS. note from rec. of Ct. of Quarter sess. in 1686, and without daring to propose a substitute I suggest that the name may have been mistak. for aft. sev. hours' search, I am unable to discov. it in any quarter. But aft. a week's despair unexpected. I find solution of Farmer's puzzle. Such is the spelling in the Prob. Reg. X 264 of the will of 12 Mar. 1684 with codicil 1 Dec. 1687, pro. 23 Mar. foll. bef. Walter Barefoote whereof the excors. refus. admin. was giv. to the wid. 5 April next, by Sir Edmund Andros, and I kn. from infallib. marks that the testator was Wingate, first ancest. of a much disting. fam."

JOHN[1] WINGATE was a planter at Hilton's Point, now Dover, N. H., as early as 1658. Supposing him to be not less than 21 years old when he became a land proprietor his birth year would be on or before the year 1636. Few facts are known of John[1], but enough to indicate a good standing among his fellowmen for probity, energy and success in life. John[1] was "receved inhabetant of Dover 18, 4 mo. 1660", but this must refer to citizenship and not to his settlement, as he had received land of the town 11, 11, 1658, when twenty acres were given him "at the head of Thomas laytons twenty acker lott on the west sid of the back River that joyneth to Elder nutter's 20 acker lott"; this land was bounded S. by Elder Nutters lot, E. by Thomas Layton's "for menshened lott", N. W. by John Roberds's 20 acre lott, and W. and S. E. by the Common;

.it was "laid out" 13, 5, 1662. It seems that on John [1]'s first coming to Dover he was in the service of Thomas Layton; so it would appear from a record in Dover's oldest Town Book, which states that there was conveyed him by the selectmen, 23, 10, 1658, a lot of 20 acres on the west side of back river, "at the head of the 20 acker loet given unto the afoersayd John Wingett by his master Thomas layton decesd Bounded on the North west on a twenty acker lott wich was layd out to John Roberds," laid out in 1664; and at the same time was laid out the 20 acre lot given by Thomas Layton, deceased, to John "butting at the watter sid on the south of Elder Nutters land". The records show that John [1] had other lands also: Whereas "John Wingett had tenn acres of land granted him by the Inhabetants of Dover necke" between Little John's creek and Ralph Twambleys's lot; it was laid out 3, 3, 1669, bounding on the highway going from Dover Neck to Coechechae on the W. side thereof, and in the N. E. and S. on the Common.

Apparently John[1] came over to seek his fortune, and subsequent facts show that he found it. How long he was in Layton's service, or whether he settled on the land given him by Layton, is impossible to tell. We find him soon on that homestead on Dover Neck which since the time of John[1] has ever remained in the possession of the Wingate family, having been handed down in uninterrupted descent to the sixth generation. It is now held by Joseph William[6] Wingate. (b. 1827.) As described by a sister of its present occupant the Wingate homestead, "which has the unusual characteristic of having been uninterruptedly in the possession of the family for two hundred and twenty-five years, is a beautiful farm of nearly one hundred acres very near the city. The magnificent elms which now stand before the house were planted by the late William P. M.[5] Wingate (b. 1789) in 1801. An apple tree planted with his own hand by John, the first American ancestor, survived in good condition until the great storm of 1845; it was over sixteen feet in circumference. Pieces of that tree are now in the possession of the family. We can drink from the same spring where our fore-fathers have drank for two hundred and twenty-five years, and also from a glass one hundred and twenty-five years old. The old house is full of relics. We have a flint gun carried by Moses[4] (b. 1744) in the Revolutionary war, and as grandfather Wingate handed down his fire-arms for the stalwart sons so his wife passed down her bridal robes to the daughters. The

present house was built in 1803." The 1803 house stands on the
same spot that the previous one stood upon; the original house stood
by the brook on a knoll about sixteen rods directly back of the
present dwelling.

John[1] was not early in public office; in fact he minded his
own business much more closely than the public's, and to some
purpose, inasmuch as he quietly went on amassing property. By
industry and thrift he became what Belknap says he was in 1683,
"one of the principal land holders in Dover." He served as Jury-
man and was Selectman in the years 1674, 1686 and 1687, being
chairman in the latter year. In 1675, during the sanguinary and
murderous Wars of King Philip in which the New Hampshire and
contiguous settlements of Maine suffered severely, he was in active
military service, particularly in the early months of that year.

In 1682 Robert Tufton Mason, Esq., under color of ancestral
claims, mortgaged the whole Province to Edward Cranfield and
procured his appointment as Lieutenant-Governor clothed with
extraordinary powers, the whole design of which, says Belknap, was
"to facilitate the entry of the claimant on the lands which some of the
people held by virtue of grants from the same authority and what had
all been fairly purchased of the Indians; a right which they believed
to be of more validity than any other. Having by their own labor
and expense subdued a rough wilderness, defended their families and
estates against the savage enemy, without the least assistance from
the claimant, and held possession for above fifty years, they now
thought it hard and cruel that when they had just recovered from the
horrors of a bloody war they should have their liberty abridged and
their property demanded to satisfy a claim which was at best
disputable and in their opinion groundless."

In less than a year the unprincipled Cranfield so outraged the
people as to excite civil commotions, and Edward Gove, a leading
man, with justifiable cause, but less discretion than zeal, attempted a
"revolution" under the cry of "Liberty and Reformation." A three
years' imprisonment in the Tower of London was the reward of his
spirit; by the interest of Randolph with Clarendon he was liberated
in 1686 and his estate restored to him under an order of the Parliament and the Council of New England.

Cranfield issued a notice to the inhabitants to take out leases
from Mason, of which the following evidence will indicate the result.

WINGATE HOMESTEAD, DOVER, N.H.

"17 July 1683, Waldron, John Windiat and Thomas Roberts ['three of the principal land holders in Dover'] certify that upon the Governor's summons of the 17 Feb. 1683, above, within the time set attended the Governor to know his pleasure therein, who bade them agree with Mason; in discourse with whom, in another room, the Governor overhearing came in, and told Col. Waldron that they should not hector so in his house and bade them begone, that they propounded to Mason to refer the matter to the Governor or otherwise that the Governor should state the case to his Majesty, according to the commission; which Mason refused, saying that unless they owned his title he would have nothing to do with them." (Note *l*.)

About this time Theophilus Dudley and others of Exeter, Nathaniel Bachiler, Thomas Dearborn, Henry Dearborn, Joseph Smith, Peter Weare, Anthony Stanyaw and others of Hampton, Moses Swett, Joseph Swett, John Shipway, John Cutt, Richard Waldron, William Vaughan, George Jaffrey and others of Portsmouth, *John Winget* and his brothers-in-law Anthony and John Nutter, Richard Waldron, John Gerrish and others of Dover, "loyal subjects and free holders and inhabitants" preferred an eloquent petition "To the King, Most Excellent Majesty", by their agent Nathaniel Weare, setting forth the origin of the plantations and their patient grappling "with those innumerable evils and difficulties that must necessarily accompany the settlers of new plantations, especially in such climates as these, besides the calamities of the late Indian war to the loss of many of our lives and the great impoverishment of the survivors," and praying relief from "the unreasonable demands of our pretended proprietors," etc. They were not in quiet possession until some years afterward.

John[1] married twice. His first wife was Mary, daughter of Hatevil Nutter; his second wife, whom he married about 1676, was Sarah, widow of Thomas Canney. Of John[1]'s second wife, *Sarah Canney Wingate*, little is known. James Savage in a private letter of 1857 says: The second Thomas Canney married Sarah Taylor who bore to him six children, and she afterwards married John Wingate and blessed him with five more than his first wife had left.

NOTE (*l*). This quotation is taken from the N. H. Provincial Papers, as are many others which follow in this chapter and the two succeeding chapters.

Joseph Dow, the historian of Hampton, N. H., in a private letter of
the same year says: Sarah Taylor, mother of Col. Joshua Wingate,
was a daughter of Anthony Taylor who died Nov. 4, 1687, aged 80,
and who came to Hampton probably in the Summer of 1640;
Philippa, his wife, died Sept. 20, 1683. [For genealogical record of
the Canneys see Savage's Genealogical Dictionary.]

Mary Nutter Wingate, the first wife of John¹ Wingate, was the
daughter of Elder Hatevil Nutter, one of the most enterprising, useful
and respectable planters on the Piscataqua, and as his name would
indicate, doubtless of genuine Puritan parentage. He was an occasional preacher as well as Elder. As appears from a deposition of
the Elder, when he once testified regarding some disputed land
titles, he was born in England in the year 1603 or thereabouts. He
was probably one of the company of persons " of good estates and of
some account for religion" who were induced to leave England with
Capt. Wiggans, in 1635, to found on Dover Neck a " compact town "
which was never built. He testified that he was here in 1637. He
took a lot of Capt. Wiggans in 1637 or thereabouts which was re-
bounded in 1640, thus, " Butting on ye River East [the Newicha-
wannock] and on ye west upon ye high street, on ye North upon
ye Lott of Samuel Haynes and on ye South upon ye lott of Wm.
Story." He owned also lot No. 20 on the west side of Back River
and at various times received grants of land in certain undefinable
localities. His house stood about fifteen rods N. N. E. from the
nearest corner of the lower schoolhouse [1857] on Dover Neck; in
the remnant of the old cellar two pear trees were standing as late as
that year, 1857. In 1643 the Elder had a grant of land between
Lamprill and Oyster rivers which was laid out 1662 to Anthony, his
son. He had a grant of 200 acres for a farm 2, 12 mo. 1658. In
April 1669 he gave the " Welchman's Cove " property to his grandson John, the son of Anthony. He gave to John Winget, husband
of daughter Mary, land, etc., on Dover Neck, 13 Feb. 1670. The
Elder was a very respectable man indeed. He filled various offices
in church and State, and possessed a reasonable share of this world's
goods. These considerations,—says Rev. Dr. Quint in his article
from which the most of this sketch of Hatevil Nutter is taken,—
procured for him that respect which the moral worth of a rich man
always excites. When business was slack the Elder sometimes
amused himself with the old-fashioned pastimes which a degenerate

age has abolished. That the Elder did really indulge in the manly recreations of the year of grace 1662 is inferred from a statement of the Quaker historian, Sewell. After recounting the history of some Puritanic amusements he says, " and all this [i. e. the whipping] in the presence of one Hate Evil Nutwell [Nutter], a Ruling Elder who stirred up the Constables to this wicked action, and so proved that he bore a wrong name." The Elder died in a good old age. His will, dated 28 Dec. 1674 (he being "about 71 years of age "), was proved 29 June 1675. To his "present wife Anne" he gave the use of his dwelling house, orchard, marsh in Great Bay, etc., all of it to go to his son Anthony after her decease. To his son Anthony he gave the mill grant at Lamprey river, one-third of the "movables," etc., and one-fourth of his 200 acres of land in "Cocheco Woods," marsh east of Back river, and the other third of the personal property. John Reyner and John Roberts were witnesses. The children of Hatevil Nutter were : Anthony (Note *m*), born 1630 ; Mary who married John Wingate sometime before 1670 ; Elizabeth who married Thomas Layton, Jr., son of the emigrant Thomas Layton, and who was deceased in 1674, (descendants numerous) ; Abigail who married Serjeant John Roberts, son of Thomas Roberts the emigrant, and who left descendants.

NOTE (*m.*) Anthony[2] Nutter, (Lieut.), son of the Elder and brother of Mary, the wife of John Wingate, lived for a time at Dover Neck but afterwards moved to Welchman's Cove, on Bloody Point side, (now Newington, N. H.,). He, as well as his father, was a man of note. In what particular section he lived cannot be exactly ascertained, but wherever it was, his house was his castle in the strictest sense, for it was a garrison-house of which he was commander-in-chief. He was a public man also, being Selectman for several years and Representative to the General Court for six years at least. He was otherwise noted as being engaged in the controversy with Cranfield. As a specimen of the free and easy manners which characterized this "tall big man named Antony Nutter" the reader is referred to the account of his visit with Wiggin to Mason, when the latter got his wig turned and his teeth knocked out and met with several other similar accidents. Anthony[2] Nutter married Sarah, daughter of Henry Langstaff, who outlived him. He died Feb. 19, 1686, having had four children: John[3], who lived on Bloody Point side and left issue; Hatevil[3], who lived in Newington and died 1745; Henry[3], who married July 26, 1703, Mary Shackford, and left issue; Sarah[3], who married Capt. Nathan Hill, son of Valentine and Mary (Eaton) Hill.

Hatevil[3] Nutter, son of Lieut. Anthony[2] Nutter, was twice married;

John[1] Wingate died Dec. 9, 1687. In the Spring of 1683-4, during a severe illness, he made his will which reads as follows:

In the name of God Amen the Twelfth day of March in the yeare of our Lord One Thousand Six Hundred Eighty Three foure I John Windiett of the Township of Dover in the Province of New-hampshire being of sound and pfect Memory blessed be the Almighty Godd for itt Doe heare make my Last will and Testament in manner and forme as followeth Imprimis I Commit my Soule to God who gave itt and my body to be desantly buried in some Convenient place where my Execr Hereafter named Shall appoint.

Item all such Debts as I doe by reason and Conscience owe to any person be honestly and truly satisfied and paid in Some Convenient time after my Decease My debts being paid and my funeral Charges bing Defrayed I Doe Order and Dispose of the state wch : itt hath pleased God to bestow upon me in manner as followeth Item I give to Sarah my beloved wife for Love I doe owe and bare to her and for her Comfortable Living the Lodging Room wherein we Lye and the Chamber over itt with the bed and furniture belonging to itt during her naturall Life if shee doe soe Long Remaine a Widdow; and after to Return to them; [to] whence I shall hereafter Dispose of itt and alsoe Two Cowes; and the half of the Orchard and the two acres of Land adjoyning to itt next towards Dover During her Widdowhood and no Longer.— Item I give to my Sonne John Windiett my house and Lands with the Marsh and fflats with all Appurtenances thereunto belonging One this side of the back River where my house now is And alsoe the Sixty acres of Land wch I had of my ffather [in] Law Nutter accord to Deed Scituate and lyeing att or neare a place called Rayner's brooke and the halfe of my plough Geares with half the Chaines; and of all other Implements belong theretoo And the ffeather bed and furniture in the New Roome Item I give to my Sonne Moses Windiett the ffourty acres of Land wch I had of my ffather Law Nutter Lyeing on the west side of the back River Butting on the said River with the Marsh and flatts belonging thereunto And alsoe the Twenty Acres of Land which I had by the Towne Grant as by Record may appeare Scituate and lyeing on the South east side of Zacharie ffeilds Land; and alsoe the other one halfe of the plow Geares Chains and Implements as before mentioned

---

he had by his first wife, Hatevil[4], Anthony[4], Eleanor[4] and Sarah[4]; by his second wife, John[4], Joshua[4], Abigail[4], Elizabeth[4] and Olive[4]. His son John[4] born Feb. 24, 1721, died Sept. 19, 1776, had lived in Newington, married Nov. 17, 1747 Anna Sims (born Oct. 20, 1727, died, Aug. 11, 1793) and had ten children among whom was Hatevil[5], born Dec. 1, 1748, who married Susanna Shackford (born Dec. 22, 1757) and had a son William Shackford[6] who married Ruth Wentworth.

And the ffeather bed and furniture belonging to itt whereon I have
laid in my sicknesse   Item I give to my daughter Anne Windiett all
the goods wch : I bought of Edward Allen with bedding and bed-
stead Curtaine's Vallance (?) Carpets Cupboards Chaires Stools
Tables brass pewter And Irons and two Cowes.—Item I give my
Sonne Joshuah Windiett Twenty acres of Land wch : I bought of
Lieutenant Hall Scituate & lyeing Joyning to the Twenty Acres of
Land wch : I gave to Sonne Moses Windiett on ye South East side
of itt.   Item I give to my Sonne Caleb Windiett Twenty acres of
Land wch : I bought of Thomas Leaston (?) Lyeing on the South
East side of the ffourty acres of Land wch : I gave to my Sonne
Moses Windiett butting on the back River with the Marsh and flatts
belonging to itt;   And the ffeather bed whereon John and Moses
my Sonnes doe usually lye on   Item I give to my Daughter Mary
Windiett the ffeather bed and furniture before mentoned to her
mother after her Mothers Decease :   Or doe Marry Againe.   Item
my will is yt all the remaineing of my Moveables wch : I have att the
Plantation wch : was Thomas Cannes being Two Oxen two Cows and
one younger beast wth Plow Stuffe household goods and what
besides is there I give to the five Children of Thomas Cannes wch :
are not now marryed to be equally Divided between them   As for
the household goods wch was Thomas Canies I leave it to Sarah
Windiett my wife to dispose of itt amongst them ffive of her children
wch : are not Married of Tho as Canies   I Desire mr. John Gerish
and my Brother-Law Anthony Nutter to be my Execrs in trust to see
this my will to be pformed Signed by J W the marke of John
Windiett with his Seale   And Sealed Signied in prsence of Richard
Waldern Joseph Cann [ey] and Test John Evans.

The codicil of this will was made Dec. 1, 1687, eight days
before John[1]'s death.   It reads :

In the Name of God the first day of December In the yeare of
our Lord God one Thousand Six Hundred Eighty and seaven A Cod-
icill made by me John Windiett (being att prsent of pfect Memory
Blessed be God for itt (wch doth beare date the Twelpt day of
March in the yeare of Our Lord God One Thousand Six Hundred
Eighty Three ffoure as follow Whereas I did will that all my Debts were
to be paid I doe now order them to be paid out of my whole
estate of moveables Debts and accounts which are due to me.
Second Article, I do there unto add and give to my sonne John
Windiett two oxen and the Two Cowes wch in the fourth article I
did give to my Daughter Ann Windiett.
Third Article, I doe there unto add and give to my sonne
Moses Windiett two oxen.
Item Whereas Abigail Windiett My Daughter wch was not borne
when my Will was made I doe give unto her mother One bed Tick-

ing wch is in the house and one Cow to buy feathers to fill a bed and
my Daughter Abigail to have itt when her mother Shall See itt fit
with boulster to it.   Whereas I did by my Will appoint Mr. John
Gerrish and my brother Anthony Nutter to be my Executors in trust
to see my will pformed ; and now my Brother Nutter being dead I
doe alter itt and doe appoint my very good friends and Kinsmen
John Hall Junr : and Mr. Job Clements and Zacharia field to be my
Executors in trust to See my will pformed And alsoe doe Desire Mr.
John Gerissh to be assisting to them in accounts or otherwise.   I doe
give Mr. John Gerish and Mr. Job Clements power to bind my sonnes
John Wyndiett and Moses Windiett out apprentices or otherwise to
dispose them as they Shall See meete until they be of age.   Signed
by the marke of John Windiett with his Seale and Sealed and Signed
in the presence of Richard Waldron, Joseph Canne, John Evans.

·This will was proved before Judge Walter Barefoot, 23 of March
1687-8.   The copy from which we take it is proved in the Probate
Office at Boston, where Andros required all probate business to be
done.   There is another at Exeter, [N. H.,] and possibly there are
discrepancies in spelling.

John ¹ Wingate had seven children, as follows :

     1.   Anne² b. Feb. 18, 1667.

     2.   John² b. July 13, 1670, d. 1715.

     3.   Caleb².

     4.   Moses².

     5.   Mary².

     6.   Joshua² b. Feb. 2, 1679, d. Feb. 9, 1769 N. S.

     7.   Abigail² b. between 1684 and 1687.·

CHAPTER III.

CHILDREN OF JOHN[1].

John[1] Wingate had obtained such prominence before his death that it would be natural to expect his children also to attain eminence, and the records of the Province show that such was the case. We will speak of.each in order.

I. ANNE[2].

Anne[2], the eldest daughter of John[1], was born Feb. 18, 1667. Of her life little is known. She married, before 1697, Israel *Hodgdon*, and had a son Shadrach[3], born 1709. Shadrach[3], or Deacon Shadrach[3] as he afterwards became, married Mary Ham. She was born Dec. 28, 1706, and was the daughter of Joseph Ham who in the Summer'of 1723, while getting in hay, was killed by the Indians; his daughters Tamsen and Ann were taken prisoners but were eventually ransomed; Mary escaped by flight to the garrison, although closely pursued. Shadrach[3] and Mary (Ham) Hodgdon had eight children, among whom was a son, Capt. Shadrach[4], born Feb. 4, 1742, who married, near 1765, his cousin Ann[4] Wingate, (b. 1742), daughter of John[3] and grand-daughter of John[2]. He was a shipmaster and sailed in the employ of Mark Hunking Wentworth, of Portsmouth, N. H.: he died May 3, 1776. His widow moved to the home of her father on the Dover Neck road, a little south of Pine Hill cemetery and above the old Wingate place. [For descendants of Shadrach[4] and Ann[4] (Wingate) Hodgdon, see Genealogical Tables, under Ann[4].]

II. JOHN[2].

John[2], the eldest son of John[1], was born July 13, 1670. He inherited the old homestead, and lived upon it all his life. His prominence seems to have been especially in the military line. When he was a little less than fifty years old we find him command-

ing a company in the expedition to Port Royal. The French and
the British were then at swords' points, the former having the assistance of the Indians. In 1707 the first expedition against Port
Royal, the capital of the French settlements, was carried out, but in
spite of the victory of the New Hampshire troops over the Indians,
the expedition became a failure on account of the bickering among
the officers. In 1709 a congress of delegates from all the colonies
resolved upon a second expedition, and, the British ministry approv-
ing, the colonial troops started again with an English naval force to
assist. They sailed from Boston Sept. 18, 1710, and on Sept. 24 arrived at Port Royal. The Governor of the town despairing to hold
out against such a formidable force surrendered after the firing of a
few shots. In this second expedition there were only 100 men from
New Hampshire, under the chief command of Col. Shadrach Walton.
It is not exactly clear in which expedition John[2] participated, possibly he was in both. The records of the Province for April 19, 1711
show that " Capt. John Wingett was allowed £249, 5 sh., 9d. for the
muster-roll of the company under his command upon an expedition
to Port Royal;" and for Nov. 19, 1712 show that he was "allowed
£13, 9sh., 7d. for muster-roll." Of the wife of John[2] we know
nothing except that her Christian name was Ann and that after his
death she married again, Dec. 1725, Capt. John Heard, (b. 1667).

John[2] died 1715. His will was made Dec. 28, 1714. He gave
to sons Moses[3] and Samuel[3] " all that hundred acres of land which
I had of my grandfather Nutter, lying neare Mr. Reyner's farme."
To son Edmond[3] thirty acres granted to him by the town " in barbadoes woods." To-eldest daughter Mary[3] Wingett £5 to be paid
in a year and a day after his decease. To daughter Ann[3] Drew £5
to be paid in two years and a day. To daughter Sarah[3] Wingett £5
to be paid in three years and a day. To his four other daughters,
viz., Abigail[3], Elizabeth[3], Mehitable[3] and Joanna[3] £5 each to be
paid as each comes of age. To wife Ann and eldest son John[3] the
dwelling house, barn, orchard, etc., marsh, flats, " my part of saw-mill
at Tole End, to enable them to bring up my small children," also
live stock, household goods, ready money, debts, etc.; if John[3] re-
fuse so to manage he is to have nothing until " my young children are
brought up," and what then remains to be equally divided among
the daughters. Wife Ann and son John[3] were appointed to admin-
ister. Proved in 1715.

John[2] Wingate had twelve children as follows :

    1.   Mary[3], b. Oct. 3, 1691.
    2.   John[3], b. April 10, 1693, d. Sept. 1764.
    3.   Ann[3], b. Feb. 2, 1694, d. 1787.
    4.   Sarah[3], b. Feb. 17, 1696.
    5.   Moses[3], b. Dec. 27, 1698, d. Feb. 9, 1782.
    6.   Samuel[3], b. Nov. 27, 1700.
    7.   Edmond[3], b. Feb. 27, 1702.
    8.   Abigail[3], b. March 2, 1704.
    9.   Elizabeth[3], b. Feb. 3, 1706.
   10.   Mehitable[3], b. Nov. 14, 1709.
   11.   Joanna[3], b. Jan. 6, 1711.
   12.   Simon[3], b. Sept. 2, 1713.

These children, as the records show, afterwards maintained the high standing in the community of Dover, which their father had attained.

III. CALEB[2].

Caleb[2] the second son of John[1], we know nothing of farther than is contained in the records of the Rev. and Hon. Paine[4] Wingate, (b. 1739,) as follows : "The second son of my ancestor was Caleb. He went to Maryland, or Delaware, and settled there, and I am told that there are descendants there of the name of Wingate to this day." It is possible that the Kentucky family who moved from Maryland and Delaware and who are mentioned at the end of the genealogical tables will ultimately be traced back to Caleb[2].

IV. MOSES[2].

Moses[2] without doubt is the Moses whose will was proved Aug. 7, 1705, having been made in London, England, Jan. 24, 1695, he being "of New Hampshire in New England Marriner now at London being sick." He gave to "Nicholas ffollet marriner now in London" "all my wearing Apparrell ;" to sister Ann[2] Wingate, spinster, all lands, tenements, debts, goods, chattels, etc. Nicholas ffollet and sister Ann[2] were executors. It is not probable that Moses[2] left any children.

V. MARY[2].

We have no record of *Mary*[2].

VI. JOSHUA[2].

Joshua[2], youngest son of John[1] by his second wife Sarah, "was born at Hampton where his mother casually was at the time of his birth, Feb. 2, 1679." Joshua[2] removed, when we do not know, from Dover to Hampton, (Note *n.*). Of that town he became a valued citizen, distinguished for both public and private virtues, and entrusted by his fellow citizens with positions of respectability and honor. Of his character John W. Gookin, (b. 1788), in 1850 wrote, "I have always understood that he was a very hard working, industrious man, very stern and rigid. Uncle Wingate used to say he loved his mother but did not love his father much, yet he was a man highly respected. When he wished to resign his commission as Colonel of the Hampton regiment the Royal Governor, Shute, I think, urged him not to do so as he could not find a man who would fill the office so well."

During the early residence of Joshua[2] and his family at Hampton the citizens were never without apprehensions of danger from the hostile Indians whose native suspicion and cruelty was increased by the fiendish policy of the French Romanists in Canada who ceaselessly incited them to war, to scalping parties and to the destruction of the English heretics. The following order, issued by Gov. Dudley, at Hampton, Oct. 11, 1703, shows the dangers of the times : "I do hereby direct that you forthwith order a convenient Number of Garrisons for the Town of Hampton, particularly one in the body of the Town, near the Church, to be of large contents, where the women and children may repair in case of Danger, that your soldiers may the better defend the place, and that you command all soldiers of your town to attend thereof [until] they be finished. Given under my hand" etc. In 1709, 1722, 1725 and 1740 Mr. Wingate was chosen one of the Selectmen of the town.

In Oct., 1716, Gov. Shute visited New Hampshire and "at Salisbury near the line between the two Provinces his Excellency was met by the Honorable, the Lieutenant Governor of New Hampshire, being guarded with a troop of horse from Hampton, and after that met by a troop of Horse from Exeter, and at Hampton town four

---

NOTE (*n.*) A tradition in the family has it that Joshua[2] removed his wife from Dover to a garrison house in Hampton, shortly before the birth of his eldest son, Paine[3], (Sept. 1703), for security against the Indians.

companies of foot were drawn up upon the Common before Capt.
Winget's where the Governor dined." Joshua[2] was Captain at that
date, but he received another commission next year appointing him
to the command of a company in Hampton, with the same rank.
This commission reads:

Province of New Hampshire.	SAMUEL SHUTE ESQ. CAPTAIN GENERAL *and Governor in chief in and over His Majesty's Province of New Hampshire in New England, and Vice Admiral of the same.*

To Captain Joshua Wingate.

By virtue of the Power and Authority in and by his Majesty's Royal Commission to Me Granted, to be Captain General etc.
over this His Majesty's Province of New Hampshire aforesaid I do (by
these Presents) Reposeing Especial trust and confidence in your
Loyalty, Courage and good Conduct, Constitute and Appoint you
the Said Joshua Wingate to be captain of a foot Company of Militia
in Hampton in ye regiment whereof Mark Hunking Esq. is Colonel.

You are therefore carefully and diligently to discharge the Duty
of a Captain in Leading and Ordering and Exercising said Company
in Arms, both Inferior Officers and Soldiers, and to keep them in
Good Order and Discipline both by commanding them to Obey you,
as their Captain, and yourself to observe and follow such Orders and
Instructions as you shall from time to time receive from Me or the
Commander in chief for the time being or other your Superior
Officers, for His Majesty's Service, according to Military Rules and
Discipline ; Pursuant to the trust reposed in you.

GIVEN *under my hand and seal at Portsmouth the*
twenty-seventh Day of June *in the Third* Year of His
Majesty, King GEORGE, His Reign, Annoque Domini 1717.

By his Excellency's
command   Sam'll Shute.
Richard Waldron.

This commission imposed at that period responsibilities as well
as distinction to the holder. In the winter of 1720 not long before
the birth of Joshua[2]'s daughter Love[3], (afterwards the wife of Rev.
Nathaniel Gookin) the people of Hampton were alarmed by a rumor
of an intended attack from the Indians. Mrs. Wingate fled and concealed herself in a stack of hay at a distance. A negro servant was
sent to guide her back, but in the confusion and alarm she mistook
him for an Indian and fainted. Captain Wingate sent her, guarded
by a detachment of troops, to Newburyport, about ten miles distant,
as a place of safety.

Nov. 25, 1722 Joshua[2] Wingate was chosen to represent Hampton in the Legislature, and in March 1723 he was appointed, with Thomas Marston, "a committee with the Rev. Mr. Gookin in prosecuting any person who shall encroach in the Parsonage ——." Aug. 31, 1726 he with "Capt. John Smith were chosen Agents to remonstrate against the prayer of the petition of the Falls parish to be incorporated as a town before the general assembly."

In 1727 there were eleven ordained ministers in New Hampshire, who with all the civil and military officers of the Province were required to take the oath of allegiance to His Majesty, King George II, and to swear "that from their hearts they abhorred, detested, abjured as impious and heretical that damnable doctrine that Princes excommunicated or deprived by the Pope or any authority of the See of Rome, may be deposed or murthered by their subjects or any other whatsoever." The above was signed by Richard Waldron, cler. com., Nath'l. Gookin, Minister of the Gospel, Jos'a.[2] Winget, representative, and Nath. Waire.

March 14, 1728 Mr. Wingate, Joseph Freese and twelve others "have leave to make a Pew on the Westerly end of the gallery, provided they keep the Glass in the West End of said Pew." Mr. Wingate was frequently chosen to the House of Representatives, and the following letter copied from "The New England Weekly Journal" of Monday, May 19, 1729, indicates his political sentiments :—Massachusetts refused a "fixed salary" to the Royal Governor, and both Colonies skilfully parried the position and exact commands of His Majesty in a manner which Gov. Burnet thought "better adapted to the Republic of Holland than to the British Constitution."

Sir,
I have here inserted the account of a vote passed in the House of Representatives at Portsmouth wherein they Voted to his Excellency Governor Burnet for the space of Three Years, or during his Government Two Hundred Pounds Sterling or Six Hundred Pounds in Bills of Credit for his Annual Support, etc. It was voted by a Majority of Votes as followeth : there being Fifteen Members besides the Speaker whereof Seven hold up their hands for Settling the Salary : and when the Contra was put to Vote there was Seven held up against it, and One declared he would neither Vote for it nor against it ; the Names of the Members for and against and Towns to which they belong are as follows, viz. :

Against Settling the Salary.	For Settling the Salary.

Nath. Waire ⎫
Joshua Winget ⎬ Hampton
John Sanborn ⎭
George Walker ⎫ Portsmouth
Ephraim Denit ⎭
Francis Matthews, Dover
Bartholomew King, Exeter

Joshua Peirce, Portsmouth
Theodore Atkinson, Newcastle
Richard Jeniss, Rye
Paul Gerrish ⎫ Dover
Samuel Tibbits ⎭
John Dowing, Newington
James Mackcain, Londonderry

Ebenezer Stevens, Kingstown, who declared he
would not Vote either for or against, makes up the
Fifteen besides the Speaker.

March 22, 1730-31 Gov. Belcher wrote to Secretary Waldron,
"You may remember You Urged at Hampton that Mr. Dennet might
be Major and Capt: of the Troop, but for the reasons you now mention p'rhaps it may be more prudent that Wingate have the Major's
commission. I now mention Wingate to Coll. Sherburne and if he
approves you may send a Commission for me to Sign but I will have
Him perfectly easy and satisfyed in all his officers." On the 29th
he wrote again, " Coll. Sherburne is Well satisfyed with Wingate's
being his Major so you may send Me a Commission to sign by return
of the Post. Countersign the Two Inclosed Commissions and deliver
to Mr. President Walton;" and on the 5th of April he wrote, "I
return you Wingate's Major's Commission which you must deliver to
Coll. Sherburn who desires he may be also Captain of the first Company in Hampton."

The first meeting under the act establishing the parish of North
Hampton according to the parish lines was held March 8, 1743 and
Major Wingate was chosen moderator; he with five others were
chosen Selectmen for the year.

In 1744 Major Wingate received the appointment of Colonel of
the Hampton Regiment of Militia which office he held for several
years and, on his resignation, was complimented by the Governor for
his military accomplishments. Nov. 8, 1744 Col. Wingate and
others were "chosen a Committee of the town of Hampton for a
friendly accommodation that the North parish might have some reasonable part of the parsonage land."

In 1745 came the famous siege and conquest of Louisburg, and
in this Col. Wingate took a prominent part, having command of a
company. In 1744 England had declared war against France, and

the attention of the American Colonists was early called to the city of Louisburg by the hostile excursions from that place. Louisburg, on Cape Breton, was esteemed the strongest fortress on the continent save Quebec. It had a garrison of only 600 regulars and 1000 militia but they seemed formidable when it was considered that 300 within the walls were a match for 5000 without. The New England colonies raised about 4000 men for the expedition, New Hampshire sending 500, including those whom she enlisted under Massachusetts's banners. The troops of the old Granite State, under command of William Pepperell, of Kittery, a militia Colonel, bore upon their ensigns the pious motto of Whitfield "Nil desperandum Christo duce." They led the attack on May 1, but it was not until June 17 that the siege ended and the city was surrendered. In this noted contest the army was assisted by a squadron of men-of-war.

The records indicate the lingering existence of slavery in New England, for we find mention under date of Oct. 15, 1752 "Dinah, negro of Col. Wingate's;" July 20, 1755 "George, negro man of Dr. Dearborn's;" and Oct. 3, 1779 "Peter, servant of John Wingate." On Aug. 31, 1755 "Phillis, dau. of Dr. Dearborn's negro man" was baptized.

Joshua[2] was married at Newbury, Nov. 9, 1702, to Mary Lunt, the ceremony being performed by Joseph Woodbridge, Esq. She was born at Newbury Jan. 15, 1682, being therefore 20 years old at the time of her marriage, while Joshua[2] was 23. She was the daughter of Henry Lunt, Jr., and grand-daughter of Henry Lunt, Sr., one of the first planters of Newbury. Her father was born Feb. 20, 1653 and died Oct. 15, 1709. He had two brothers and four sisters, viz.: Sarah, b. Nov. 8, 1639, Daniel, b. May 17, 1641, d. Jan. 26, 1702-3, John, b. the last of Nov. 1643, d. Sept. 17, 1678, Priscilla, b. Feb. 16, 1646, Mary, b. July 13, 1648 and Elizabeth, b. Dec. 29, 1650. Henry Lunt, Sr., the grandfather of the wife of Joshua[2] Wingate, married Anne —— who afterwards married, March 8, 1664, Joseph Hills; Henry Lunt Sr. died July 10, 1662.

The deaths of Joshua[2] and of his wife are recorded in the manuscript of his grandson Hon. Paine[4] Wingate as follows: "Feb. 9, 1769 Grandfather Wingate dyed. His descendants have been [1809] 11 children, 8 of which survive him. His Grandchildren were 79, of whc. 59 are alive. His Great Grandchildren were 66, of whc. 60 are living." "May 27, 1772, This morning about 4 o'clock

departed this life Mary the relict of Col. Joshua Wingate, aged 90 years and 4 months."

"Col. Joshua Wingate early in the morning of Feb. 9, 1769 N. Stile dyed having compleated the ninetieth year of his age wanting 4 days. He sustained for many years several respectable offices, both civil and military, with reputation. Was a steady & exemplary Christian, a faithful neighbor & friend and in domestic life was esteemed & beloved; having a well founded expectation of future blessedness he waited for death with a desireable serenity of mind and acquiescence in the Divine will. At last being worn out with the trials of life and the infirmities of age, he on a sudden fell on sleep & rested from his labors and burdens. He left a widow with whom he had lived 68 years."

Joshua² made his will March 3, 1764 but it was not probated until Feb. 22, 1769. In this he gives to his son John³ the homestead: "I give to my son John Wingate all my Farm where I now live Lying between the lands of Dr. Levi Dearborn & lands formerly belonging to Peter Jonson," etc. Furthermore he devises "I give to my daughter Love Gookin one hundred dollars. My will and meaning is that my said daughter is not to have it unless she outlives her present husband. I do give it to the children of my said daughter to be equally divided between them."

Joshua² Wingate had eleven children as follows:

1. Paine³ b. Sept. 19, 1703, d. Feb. 19, 1786.
2. Sarah³ b. Dec. 8, 1705, d. 1801.
3. Mary³ b. June 14, 1708, d. Dec. 12, 1784.
4. Joshua³ b. Sept. 7, 1710.
5. Jane³ b. July 12, 1712.
6. Abigail³ (twin) b. June 30, 1715.
7. Anna³ (twin) b. June 30, 1715, d. July 10, 1735.
8. Martha³ b. March 30, 1718, d. 1758.
9. Love³ b. April 4, 1720, d. April 1, 1809.
10. Elizabeth³ b. Nov. 21, 1722.
11. John³ b. Jan. 24, 1724-5, d. Sept. 4, 1812.

VII. ABIGAIL².

We have no record of *Abigail²*.

CHAPTER IV.

CHILDREN OF JOHN[2].

As regards the grandchildren of John[1] Wingate there still remains a record of twenty-four. The child of Anne[2] has already been mentioned. (See page 33.) This chapter is devoted to the children of John[2], the next chapter to the children of Joshua[2]. For the descendants of John[2]'s children see Chapter VIII.

I. MARY[3].

Mary[3], the eldest child of John[2], was born Oct. 3, 1691. She married Josiah *Clarke*, of Kittery, Me., and had one son, John[4].

II. JOHN[3].

John[3], the eldest son of John[2], was born April 10, 1693. He inherited the homestead, and so far as we can see lived and died upon it. The first we hear of him in public is in 1722 when the House of Representatives settled accounts for "service done the Province in cutting the road to and scouting to Winnipishoky pond," and ordered that John Wingate be paid five shillings a day for eight days' service as pilot. May 10, 1727, John[3] was appointed, by the General Assembly of the Province, one of a committee of five to "renew or perambulate the line between Barrington and Rochester." His services as pilot and "perambulator" were but stepping stones to higher offices. He had already joined the militia and in 1740 held a commission as Lieutenant of the second foot company of Dover. From 1729 to 1752 (with the exception of 1733, '39, '48 and '51) he was Selectman of the town, and was probably the Wingate who was Moderator in 1739 and 1758. It would seem that John[3] inherited an independence and firmness of opinion regarding his own good judgment for we find him, on June 4, 1745, while Selectman of Dover, refusing, together with three of his colleague

Selectmen, to take part in a town meeting which they had called, because the meeting would not carry out the order of proceedings which these four Selectmen wished. John [3] Wingate and his friends retired for awhile, but returned later on and, as the meeting again refused to alter its course, "the four Selectmen removed into a pew on the other side of the meeting house and began to carry on a meeting by themselves, altho' Silence was commanded by the Moderator." We learn nothing of the result of this division except that the opposition to Mr. Wingate and his associates elected their men and had them returned. In 1745 Captain John [3] Wingate, —for he had now risen to the command of a company—represented Dover in the House of Representatives for the Province of New Hampshire.

John [3] was twice married. His first wife, whom he married in 1717, was Dorothy Tebbets, daughter of Samuel Tebbets, of Dover. His second wife was Sarah Ricker, of Somersworth, born 1702, died March 4, 1800, aged 98. Sarah Ricker was a sister of Maturin Ricker, Jr., and a daughter of the emigrant Maturin Ricker who was killed by the Indians, and who was a brother of George Ricker, the emigrant, also killed by the Indians. Sarah herself was once carried off by the Indians.

John [3] died September, 1764. His will was made May 12, 1764, and proved September 26, 1764. He gave to "beloved wife Sarah" the use of the westerly half of his dwelling, a part of the barn, half the produce of the homestead (the produce to be gathered in by sons Moses [4] and Aaron [4]) ; if she marry she is to have only her dowry ; the sons just named are to furnish her firewood ; she is to have also during her widowhood two cows, six sheep, one swine, and the use of all household goods and furniture. To son John [4] are given seventy or eighty acres lying in Madbury "where he now lives," also forty acres in Rochester on or near Chestnut Hills. To son Samuel [4] one hundred acres in Chester "where he now lives." To son Daniel [4] one hundred acres in Rochester "where he now lives" ; also to Samuel [4] and Daniel [4] his interest in the undivided lands of Rochester. To son Joshua [4] twenty-five acres lying "where he now lives." To son Jonathan [4] sixty acres in Rochester on or near Chestnut Hills. To sons Moses [4] and Aaron [4] the "Homestead Land where I now live", reserving such part as he gives to his wife ; also all lands, salt marsh and thatch bed between the main road that leads to Cochecho

and Back river; also all live stocks, farming utensils, Black walnut desk, and brass kettle. To daughters Sarah⁴ Ham, Anna⁴, Mehitable⁴, "all my land in third division in Rochester;" also to each £200 old tenor, to be paid respectively in one, two, and three years; also such marriage portions to the last two as had been given to Sarah⁴; to them also he gave furniture.

John³ had thirteen children as follows:

1. John⁴, b. May 5, 1719, d. March 15, 1776.
2. Samuel⁴, b. Feb. 19, 1721.
3. Daniel⁴, b. Jan. 28, 1722-'23.
4. Joshua⁴, b. July 28, 1725, d. Feb. 9, 1796.
5. Jonathan⁴, bapt. Oct. 22, 1727.
6. Dorothy⁴, bapt. Sept. 23, 1733.
7. Noah⁴, bapt. Sept. 27, 1735.
8. Aaron⁴, bapt. Feb. 6, 1737.
9. Sarah⁴, bapt. Aug. 20, 1738.
10. Ann⁴, bapt. March 14, 1742, d. March 25, 1826.
11. Aaron⁴ (twin) b. Nov. 23, 1744 (bapt. Nov. 28 1744), d. Feb., 1822.
12. Moses⁴, (twin) b. Nov. 23, 1744, (bapt. Nov. 28 1744), d. April 29, 1827.
13. Mehitable⁴, bapt. Feb. 22, 1747, d. 1842-'43.

III.   ANN³.

Ann³ was born Feb. 2, 1694, and died 1787. She married, first, June 3, 1713, Francis *Drew*, of Dover, who died May 10, 1717; second, Jan. 1, 1718-'19, Daniel *Titcomb*, of Dover. She had one child by her first husband and seven by her second:

1. Joseph⁴, b. April 8, 1717.
2. Enoch⁴, b.——— d. young.
3. John⁴.
4. Abigail⁴.
5. Benjamin⁴.
6. Elizabeth⁴.
7. Sarah⁴.
8. Mary⁴.

IV.   SARAH[3].

Sarah[3] was born Feb. 17, 1696. She married, near 1717, Peter *Hayes*, of Dover, third son of the emigrant John Hayes, and lived at Tole End, Dover. She bore him eight children :

1. Benjamin[4].
2. Reuben[4].
3. John[4].
4. Joseph[4].
5. Ichabod[4].
6. Elijah[4].
7. Anna[4].
8. Mehitable[4].

V.   MOSES[3].

Moses[3], second son of John[2], was born Dec. 27, 1698. He lived in Dover, at first on the homestead, but afterwards on Silver street. As to business, he is at one time called " cooper," at another " husbandman," at a third " Lieutenant," and at last " Gentleman," which changes may be supposed to denote a steady increase of property. Records of his " buying and selling and getting gain " show us the following business transactions :

His first transaction was through his brother John[3] ; one half of a grant to Hatevil Nutter of 200 acres in 1658, lying in Cochecho woods above Tole End, was laid out " att the request of John Wingett in behalf of his 2 brothers Moses and Samuel Wingett " on the north side of Mr. Rainer's 400 acres, running from a pine north-west 120 rods, then west-south-west 100 rods to a stone near two great rocks, thence south-west to a tree, thence by Mr. Rainer's line to the first bound.

Moses[3] Wingett, of Dover, cooper, and Samuel[3] Wingett, of Kittery, blacksmith, sold, Aug. 11, 1727, to Ebenezer and John Varney a quarter of the above mentioned 200 acres given by John[2] Wingett to sons Moses[3] and Samuel[3] by will.

On Feb. 6, 1731 Moses[3] bought a piece of land of Ephraim Tebbets Jr. and Ephraim also bound himself to build a house for Moses[3] on said land.

Sept. 12, 1732 he bought of Nathaniel Hanson, carpenter, 20 acres, being part of 60 acres formerly granted and laid out to Robert

Evens, Sr., of Dover, in Cochecho Swamp or "Ash Swamp," which Hanson had by "Inheritance in fee Simple."

Another record shows: Samuel[3] Winget, blacksmith, and Andrew Spinney, ship-carpenter, both of Kittery, and Josiah Clark, of Kittery, for £12, quitclaim to Moses[3] Winget, all right in 30 acres at Barbadoes, given by Dover to John[2] Winget, late of Dover, deceased, and by him given in his last will and testament unto his son Edmund[3] Winget, late of Dover, deceased; Mary, wife of Samuel[3] Winget, Abigail, wife of Andrew Spinney, and Mary[3], wife of Josiah Clark, also sign; dated Dec. 21, 1726. Witnessed by Nathaniel Randal, Samuell Laighton.

We also find that Elizabeth Church in 1727 and Mary Church Nov. 27, 1730 each conveyed to Moses[3] Winget, of Dover, three tracts of land, one-sixth of the land where her father (deceased) lived, one-sixth of ten acres near "Campaign Rocks," and one-sixth of a lot in the Ash Swamp. Witnessed by James Hanson, Robert Evens.

On Sept. 12, 1734 he bought again: David Watson, of Dover, husbandman, conveys to Moses[3] Winget land lying "on the Southerly side of the Road that leads from Cochecho up to littleworth or Tole End where sd Wingets House now stands." Witnesses Jonathan Cushing, Elizabeth waterhous.

Two years later he bought in some family rights: Simon[3] Winget, of Biddeford, husbandman, and Joanna[3] Winget, of Dover, for £30 sell to Bro. Moses[3] Winget, of Dover, husbandman, land in Dover "at a place Commonly Called Barbadoes, on the Southerly side of the Road that leads from Barbadoes Spring in the woods, containing Six acres," it being part of thirty acres of land granted by Dover to our Hon'd. father Jno.[2] Winget late of sd Dover Deceasd; dated May 26, 1736. Witnessed by Jonathan Cushing, Eliza [beth] watterhous.

Moses[3] soon stopped buying land and went a soldiering, but before he got into actual service we find that Edmond[4] Winget, of Dover, son of Moses[3], with his father's consent, becomes apprentice to Thomas Huckins, of Durham, for three years to "the art, trade or mystery of a Joyner and chair-maker." This was Oct. 15, 1743.

Under date of July 24, 1740 we find Moses[3] Winget enrolled in ye second foot company of Dover, of which his elder brother John[3] was Lieutenant. In 1745 Moses[3] was a Lieutenant and was

seeing actual service at the Siege of Louisburg. Two letters from home doubtless interested him then, and they certainly interest us now. The first reads :

Dear and Loveing Husband

After my Love to you hoping this will fiend you in good health as we are at home god be thank for it. I have been greatly Concerned aboute your weelfare but Since I heave heard of your Safe Arriveall an Consoe, I am more satisfied in my mind but I would Intreat of you that you would not goo too Cannada if you have an opertunity but Return home as Soon as you Can thoo Edmond manneages prety well and we meak it doo as well as Can be expected. So I Send this with my Respects heaveing no more time I could Rite no more only that you would send me a Leter ye first opertunity and Send when you Shall be at home.

Dover April 29th, 1745   Abigail Winget.

Ealce Young Remembers her Love to her Husband and prays he would not goe too Cannada but if he dos She never expects to See any more.

This letter is directed thus :

For

Lieut moses winget

to Cap Briton under

Capt. Samuell Hayl in

Collo : mors Rigmant

from New Hamshear in

New England this with

Cear.

The second letter is from an old friend. It reads :

[Dover,] * * * *

Lieut. Winget my C . . . . . . to . . u hoping thes Lines will fin . . ou In . . . . helth as I am at this Riten we are . . . . . . at present the thoat Distemper Is . . . . amongst us will Twombly has lost 2 child . . . . and Joseph Twombly has lost one his only sun we have had wary wilenty thunder and Litning this year Such as you and I Never saw hardley in our Liftimes Your Brother John Drew was kild by Litning in the month of May on the Sa . . . . Day I sh . . . . say was kild at the hous of D . . . . Pitmans.

we are in Larom almost . . . . one fr . . . . men has seen . . . . . Indons at the head mill but we are . . . at much

Skeared at that you know that fr . . . . en was place . . . . . . for Seing Indions. We had a hard trial for Assembly men Such as you never saw in this town tho you are an older man than I am, but they have got thare will of . . . . but of me thaay have got John Gage Esq. Thom. Wallingford Esq. Thomas Davis.

Mager my Loving frend I have Rit the hads of all the Nuse and Concerns of ouer town   your wife has ofen bin at my hous and she bares your Absance as well as you or I can expect aney woman c . . . . . . their Surcumstances.   I Rit in short having no oportunety But this Bing from hom at Capt Hansons with [out] aney Jacket on my Back   But than [k] s be my Credet and pus I hav a good Bol of punch in my Hand and I wish you wos with me to take a part with me.

Benj. Hanson Juner

Juley 2, 1745.

How long Moses[3] was in the army we don't know; but in 1747 he was buying land again. Thus: Jonathan Watson and Winthrop Watson, both of Dover, husbandmen, for £620 old tenor, convey to Lieut. Moses[3] Winget, land joining Wiget's Homestead; land of Capt. Paul Gerrish's heirs; of Ens. Jos. Roberts heirs; and on John Randalls land. And Mary Watson, widow of David Watson, and Deborah Watson, wife of Jonathan Watson, relinquished right of dower, 22 May 1747.

In 1756 he bought more land: Solomon Hanson, Cordwainer, and Ebenezer Hanson, husbandman, both of Dover, convey to Moses[3] Winget, Gent., a lot of land at the Ash Swamp, which they had purchased 4 June 1751 of Moses Hodgdon of Berwick, 26 Mar. 1756. Jos. Hanson & Humphrey Hanson witnesses.

Moses[3] was doubtless entitled by this time to be called "Gent.," especially as he had received one important batch of property: Edward Evans, of Dover, on the 31 Oct. 1741, "being advanced in years and laboring under the infirmaties of age" gave by will "to my Kinsman Moses Winget" "My whole Estate both Real and Personal," and also makes him sole Executor. He made his mark, Jona. Cushing, Thomas Young, Jona. Cushing Jr., being his witnesses.

Five years later Moses[3] narrowly escaped assassination by an Indian. The following order of His Majesty's Superior Court of Judicature, delivered by the High Sheriff to the Governor and Council of the Province at Portsmouth, Sept. 26, 1750, explains matters: Hon. Ellis Huske, Chief Justice, said, "An Indian man of Penobscot (as he saith) by ye name of Nambrous being committed to

his Majesties goal for attempting to kill Moses Wingit, of Dover, by stabbing him with a knife in the arm and body—no evidence appearing against him, the said Indian—to convict him—It is considered by the court that the said Indian be acquitted and Discharged. And inasmuch as the Indian nations are making Warr upon his Majesties subjects in New England therefore ordered that his Excellency the Governour be Informed of this Courts order to discharge said Indian　*　*　to the intent that his Excellency may take order as shall think fit concerning him." The order was read before the Council, and " inasmuch as this tribe to which said Indian belongs having committed hostilities against his Majestys subjects of the neighboring Governments the Council advised his Excelency to give the Sheriff orders to detain the said Indian and his squaw that is now with him till further order of the Governour and Council."

Moses[3] was twice married, first, as early as 1726, to Abigail Church, second, to Deborah (Cushing) Watson, daughter of Rev. Jonathan Cushing and widow of Daniel Watson. Deborah was born Jan. 5, 1721-'2 and died Feb. 3, 1800. Her son Nathaniel, by her first husband, lived with his step-father Wingate and became heir to the estates.

Moses[3] died Feb. 9, 1782, having made his will Dec. 19, 1780, giving to wife Deborah all the furniture she brought with her, the use of the west part of dwelling, and one-third use of estate ; to daughter Abigail[4] Tebbets £5 ; to grandson Jonathan[5] Winget £10 ; to granddaughters Ann[5] Brown and Elizabeth[5] Wingate all household furniture except as above ; to Nathaniel Watson, son of my wife by a former husband, the remainder of estate. Witnessed by Caleb Hodgdon, Moses[4] Wingate and Sarah Wigglesworth. Proved April 2, 1782.

Moses[3] had seven children :

1. Deborah[4], bapt. Aug. 2, 1730.
2. Ebenezer[4], bapt. March 18, 1733.
3. Ann[4], bapt. Oct. 3, 1736.
4. Moses[4], bapt. Aug. 2, 1738, d. before June 27, 1769.
5. Benjamin[4], bapt. Sept. 28, r740.
6. Ebenezer[4], bapt. March 23, 1742.
7. Edmond[4], date of b. unknown.

VI.   SAMUEL [3].

Samuel[3] was born Nov. 27, 1700, and died before 1753. He moved from Dover to Kittery. His wife was Mary (Roberts) Hurd, widow. After the death of Samuel[3] his widow married, after 1753, as second wife, Deacon John Hayes of Dover, (b. 1686, d. July 3, 1759,) who lived at Tole End. The families were afterwards still closer united by the marriage of her daughter Mary[4] Wingate to the son of Deacon John Hayes by his first marriage, Lieut. Jonathan Hayes. Samuel[3] and Mary Wingate had one child : Mary[4].

VII.   EDMOND [3].

Edmond[3] was born Feb. 27, 1702.   [No further record.]

VIII.   ABIGAIL [3].

Abigail[3] was born March 2, 1704, and probably married Andrew *Spinney*, of Kittery.   [No further record.]

IX.   ELIZABETH [3].

Elizabeth[3] was born Feb. 3, 1706, and married a *Hodgdon*. [No further record.]

X.   MEHITABLE [3].

Mehitable[3] was born Nov. 14, 1709.   [No further record.]

XI.   JOANNA[3].

Joanna[3] was born Jan. 6, 1711. She married Ebenezer *Hill*, of Biddeford, Me., and had eight children, whose descendants, however, we do not know.

1.   Abiel[4].
2.   Mary[4].
3.   Joshua[4].
4.   Elizabeth[4].
5.   Dorothy[4].
6.   Joseph[4].
7.   Josiah[4].
8.   Jotham[4].

XII. SIMON³.

*Simon*³ was born Sept. 2, 1713. He moved to Biddeford, Me.,
was admitted to the First Church of that town, Oct. 17, 1742, and
became a deacon. He married Lydia Hill, daughter of Ebenezer
Hill and wife Abiel (Snell) Hill. She was admitted to the First
Church Nov. 25, 1744. It is probable that she married a second
time, Sept. 29, 1774, Capt. Daniel Stover. Simon³ and Lydia had
twelve children :

   1. Anna⁴.
   2. Elizabeth⁴.
   3. Hannah⁴.
   4. Snell⁴, bapt. Feb. 3, 1744.
   5. Simon⁴, bapt. June 21, 1747.
   6. John⁴, bapt. April 8, 1750.
   7. Lydia⁴, bapt. April 26, 1752.
   8. Edmund⁴, bapt. Jan. 5, 1755.
   9. ————⁴.
   10. Lucy⁴, bapt. Dec. 25, 1757.
   11. Sarah⁴, bapt. March 22, 1761.
   12. Susanna⁴.

NOTE : It is interesting to notice the comparative wealth of certain
of the grandchildren and great-grandchildren of John¹. The parish rates
of 1753, for "Cochecho Part," of Dover, where the highest rate of any
resident was £2 and the lowest 1s. 3d., show:

   Capt. John³ (son of John²), 17sh. 3d.
   Lieut. Moses³ (son of John²), 9sh. 3d.
   John⁴, Jr. (son of John³) 7sh. 9d.
   Edmond,   6sh.
   Jonathan⁴ (son of John³) 5sh. 3d.
   Joshua⁴ (son of John³) 4sh. 6d.

CHAPTER V.

CHILDREN OF JOSHUA[2].

Col. Joshua[2] Wingate had eleven children, the most noted of all being Rev. Paine[3], the eldest son. For their descendants see Chapter IX.

I. PAINE[3].*

It is not easy to over-estimate the importance of the local churches, in the history of New England during the sixteenth and seventeenth centuries. Ralph Waldo Emerson has told us that if we would see the real life of America, we must leave the city streets and look at the town-meeting. But the early New England town-meeting was closely connected with the First Church, or Second Church of Christ in the particular town. Formerly none but church-members could vote in these theocratic democracies; and the church organization remained powerful even after this restriction was removed.

The minister, in the Congregational order, was but an officiating church-member, not a priest or spiritual autocrat. Notwithstanding, he was in a true and proper sense the centre of the church and social life of his parish. By education, position, and character he was first among his equals, respected, revered, and beloved. His term of office was long: pastorates of thirty, forty, fifty, or even sixty years were not uncommon. The modern minister, too often, remains but two or three years in a place, meanwhile looking out for something better, while the pew-holders, perhaps, are wondering whether some other man would not fill the church treasury more promptly. The old-time minister grew old with his parishioners; the same persons he baptized, admitted to the church, married, and buried; he was *the* minister, not an annual peripatetic. The modern plan, it is true, sometimes gives freshness and force to pulpit

---

*Sketch of Rev. Paine[3] Wingate written by Prof. Charles F.[7] Richardson, his great-great-grandson.

ministrations, while the old plan sometimes caused stagnation ; but surely it was better on the whole. Such a head of his parish, such an influential and faithful country minister, was Rev. Paine[3] Wingate, of the Second Church (West Parish), of Amesbury, Massachusetts.

Paine[3] Wingate was born September 19, 1703. In 1719, at the age of sixteen, he entered Harvard College, where he graduated in 1723. At that time the class-lists were arranged not alphabetically, but in accordance with the supposed social standing of the family. His name, in the class of 1723 in the quinquennial catalogue, stands sixteenth in the whole number of forty-three. In those days a college education was pretty sure to be the preliminary to the minis- terial life, and three years after graduation Paine[3] entered upon his life-work. The (printed) Amesbury town-records say: "May 19, 1726, a new church was organized at Amesbury, the Second Church of Amesbury. A creed was adopted containing the embodiment of the faith, especially the Puritanical doctrine of the decrees, election, reprobation and depravity; and Mr. Pain Wingate, then a young man, chosen to be pastor." On June 15 following (the town-records erroneously say June 3) he was ordained : "Titus Wells made prayer, Mr. Gookin preached sermon from John XX, 15, Mr. Tufts offered prayer, and Mr. Cushing, of Salisbury, gave the charge. Mr. Parsons gave the right hand of fellowship." His marriage followed the next year, Dec. 12, 1727, to Mary Balch, of Wenham, Mass., a descend- ant of John Balch, of Beverly, 1630, and a member of the Beverly church. It is recorded of her that she was "a lady noted for con- siderable literary acquirements and for personal beauty."

Thenceforward until his death, Feb. 19, 1786, Paine[3] Wingate's life was that of the faithful preacher, both leader and servant of his flock. His salary was small; George Whitefield, in his journal for 1740, in speaking of New England ministers, says: "I cannot see much worldly advantage to tempt them to take upon them the sacred function. Few country ministers, as I have been informed, have sufficient allowed them to support a family." Most of them were thrifty, however, as was Paine[3] Wingate, and did, like him, support large families. Some liberal supplies were not lacking; thus Mr. Wingate, then a bachelor, received in the spring of 1727, "30 cords good wood," for his supply, and 30 cords in 1732, which, the Ames- bury historian thinks, must at least have kept him warm for a year. If revenues were small, so were expenditures; modern comforts were

lacking in great part; travel for pleasure was unknown; and the minister, who often had a little farm of his own, fared at least as well as the average parishioner. Wingate, like his fellows, worked for Christ, not for worldly comfort, and so was esteemed faithful and judicious at home and in the neighborhood. Thus, to take an early example, when but thirty-one years old, he was thought worthy to represent, as " elder," the Amesbury Second Church at an Ecclesiastical Council held at Salisbury, Mass., Aug. 13, 1734, to settle troubles in a church at Chester, N. H. Year after year went by, but his loyal work, in great things and small, did not cease. At the very last, when he had become so feeble that he could not walk, his son Joseph[4], who remained with his father at home, used to take the venerable preacher into the pulpit in his arms.

The principal memorial of Paine[3] Wingate and his work is his manuscript record of his connection with the "Second Church of Christ in Amesbury." This record, which is in perfect preservation, is contained in a book stoutly bound in mottled paper, about six by nine inches in size. The total number of written pages is 118, besides many blank leaves. Of these 118 pages, 50 are devoted to miscellaneous matters of church record; 5 to dates of administering the Lord's Supper; 4 1-2 to admissions to the church of persons previously unbaptized; 1 1-2 to admissions by letter; 2 to "persons who have renewed their baptismal covenant" (by joining the church); 11 to marriages; and 44 to baptisms. Summarizing Mr. Wingate's work, this record shows 468 administrations of the Lord's Supper; 311 admissions to the church of persons previously unbaptized; 84 admissions by letter; 321 renewals of baptismal covenant; 377 marriages; and more than 2000 baptisms. The entries, in a clear and methodical hand, are painstakingly made: "Sept. 4, 1726: Adm[rd] the Sacra: L[ds] Supper." — "Aug. 14, 1726: Rec[d]. Will[m] Harvey." — " From the first church in Almsbury, Thomas Fowler:" etc. — "Aug. 25, 1726: Married Nath[el] Tucker & Phœbe Chase." — "July 19, 1726, Baptized Abigail, y[e] Daughter of Sam[l] & Rachel Stevens." As the years go by, the handwriting, though still clear, becomes feeble. The last sacrament of the Lord's Supper noted, was "Nov. 1780"; the last marriage (recorded by his son's hand): " Octo. 23, 1785 married Joshua Chase to Molley Stokes"; and the last baptism (recorded by his own trembling pen):

"Octr 10, 1784, baptized Betty of Joseph and Judith Wingate — baptized Moses of Jacob & —— Lancaster."

The church records in the first part of the book begin with the note of the gathering of the church: —— "Amesbury [altered from Almsbury] May 19, 1726, was gathered the Second Church of Christ in Amesbury; there being then present these Revd Ministers of the Gospel, viz: Mr Wells, Mr Cushing, Mr Parsons, Mr Tufts, Mr Brown." Then follow the "Articles of faith then publicly read & Acknowledged," which embody the usual Congregational creed of that day. The articles and covenant were signed by Pain Wingate and fourteen others, and "publicly Acknowledged in the Congregation (then present) by the Subscribers, In the presence of us, Thomas Wells, John Tufts, John Brown, Pastors of ye Neighboring Churches in Almsbury, Newbury, Newtown & Haverhill." After this "Mr. P. Wingate" was unanimously chosen pastor, and arrangements for the ordination were made: "Accordingly June 15, 1726: Ordination was performed; Mr Wells made the first prayer; Mr Gookin preached from John 20. 15: Mr Tufts then prayed; & Then Mr Cushing gave the charge; after this Mr Parsons gave the right hand of fellowship: Sang Psal. 122."

The entries in the record, from this date to May 17, 1782, cover a wide range of subjects, and exhibit the usual life of a New England parish church in the eighteenth century,—the choice of deacons, the election of delegates to church councils, the raising of church funds, the discipline of offenders, etc. Aug. 8, 1726, at the start, the church bought in Boston, for £8, 10s. 10d "2 hard Mettal flaggons, 2 tankards, 2 platters, 4 beacers, 1 bason, 4 yeards of linnen cloth." Moneys were raised with some difficulty, and prices were high, especially during the Revolutionary war, toward the close of Mr. Wingate's ministry; but the church did its part in benevolent and other work. Naturally, in these pages, blemishes of life make a blacker mark than the lives of quiet rectitude unrecorded here; and the church labored faithfully with offenders, strictly carrying out the New Testament injunction to converse with the wrong-doer before disciplining him. The misdeeds were miscellaneous: Abraham Colby was called to "testify his repentance for his breach of ye Sabbath by Coming down from Chester with a Cart & ten oxen & Two horses, on L^{ds} Day;" James Sandy, Jr., made a "publick Confession before ye church, having been unawares overtaken by

Drink, & thereby so Disguised, as to be Called Drunk"; Samuel
Jewell and his wife were humbled and penitent because of "some
unhappy dissentions" between themselves; John Martin repented of
his "Rash Striking Joseph Hadley"; Samuel Hunt stayed away from
church because he felt wronged by James Sanders; Elilabeth Dow
was "very faulty in doing her part assigned towards y[e] charges of
y[e] church"; another woman was disciplined for "gadding about";
some were dealt with for absenting themselves from worship without
cause; and others, not a few, for offences against morality. All in
all, taking it for granted that a similar proportion of offences come
to light to-day, and allowing for the greater rigor of the early
churches in some things it must be admitted that the "good old
times" in New England were worse than the present, and that the
faithful and godly Paine[3] Wingate had to make an even harder fight
for Christ than most modern ministers must do.

At length, having been a father to his flock for sixty years, and
having baptized several of his grandchildren, in his own old church,
the old man laid down his staff, and died at Amesbury, Feb. 19,
1786. His widow died Oct. 10, 1788, aged 83. Of their twelve children, three died in infancy; the death of one, Sarah[4] (the second of
the name), is not recorded in the book before me; the average age
of the remaining eight was 79 3-4 years; one (Joshua[4]) died at 97,
and one (Paine[4]) at 99. To his family Paine[3] Wingate left (his
will is dated Jan. 1, 1777) his modest property.

In the last entry (May 17, 1782) in the church record, Paine[3]
Wingate writes words which may well be his memorial:

"Whatsoever is agreeable to the Word & Instructions of the
Lord Jesus Christ, I am ready thro Grace, on my Part to attend
unto." (Note o.)

Paine[3] had twelve children:

NOTE (o.) A letter written by Mary Carr[5] Wingate (b. 1797) to
William H[6]. Page says: "When Uncle 'Farmer' Wingate [Joseph[4]] came
to Maine he put on board a vessel the books and sermons of his father
[Rev. Paine[3].] Some disaster occurred and many manuscripts etc. were
lost. A few were rescued and were in your grandfather's [Joshua[4]] possession, and you know how he destroyed his papers; a few leaves of the
sermons were rescued from the fire."

1. Mary⁴, b. Dec. 28, 1728, d. March 16, 1800.
2. Elizabeth⁴, b. Sept. 17, 1730, d. Nov. 5, 1815.
3. Paine⁴, b. Aug. 21, 1732, d. Oct. 10, 1736.
4. Sarah⁴, b. Nov. 23, 1734, d. Nov. 6, 1736.
5. Sarah⁴, b. April 27, 1737, d. Aug. 28, 1824.
6. Paine⁴, b. May 14, 1739, d. March 7, 1838.
7. John⁴, b. July 4, 1741, d. March 4, 1742.
8. John⁴, b. June 25, 1743, d. July 26, 1819.
9. William⁴, b. July 9, 1745, d. Nov. 30, 1821.
10. Joshua⁴, b. March 3, 1747, d. Oct. 11, 1844.
11. Abigail⁴, b. March 27, 1749, d. Aug. 28, 1807.
12. Joseph⁴, b. July 17, 1751, d. Sept. 18, 1828.

II. SARAH³.

*Sarah*³ was born Dec. 8, 1705, and died at Hampton, 1801, aged 96. She married June 29, 1727, Dr. Edmund *Toppan*, of Hampton, son of Rev. Dr. Christopher Toppan, of Newbury, Mass. He was born Dec. 7, 1701, and died Nov. 28, 1739, H. V. 1720. [See Spalding memorial by Samuel J. Spalding, of Newburyport.] Lived in Hampton and had five children :

1. Sarah⁴, b. April 12, 1728.
2. Mary⁴, b. May 18, 1730, d. Aug. 14, 1745.
3. Ann⁴, b. Sept. 15, 1732, d. May 22, 1751.
4. Christopher⁴, b. Jan. 18, 1735, d. Feb. 28, 1818.
5. Edmund⁴, b. 1739, d. Feb. 9, 1740.

III. MARY³.

*Mary*³ was born June 7, 1708, and died Dec. 12, 1784. She married Nov. 21, 1728, Deacon Timothy *Pickering*, of Salem, Mass. He was born Feb. 10, 1702-'3, and died June 7, 1778; he was the ninth child of John Pickering (b. Sept. 10, 1658, d. June 19, 1722) who married, June 14, 1683, Sarah Burrell, (b. May 16, 1661, d. Dec. 27, 1747). This John Pickering was the first child of John Pickering (b. 1637, d. May 5, 1694) who married, 1657, Alice Flint (d. Oct. 5, 1700) and who was the son of John Pickering (b. about 1615, d. about 1657) who came from Yorkshire, England, to Salem, Mass., about 1636, and married, about that time, Elizabeth ——

(d. June 30, 1662). The arms of the Pickering family are given: "In a field ermine a lion rampant azure."

Mary[3] had nine children:

1. Sarah[4], b. Jan. 28, 1729-'30, d. Nov. 21, 1826.
2. Mary[4], b. March 29, 1733, d. Jan. 30, 1805.
3. Lydia[4], b. Feb. 27, 1735-'36, d. Oct. 21, 1824.
4. Elizabeth[4] b. Nov. 12, 1737, d. Oct. 12, 1823.
5. John[4] b. March 2, 1739-'40, d. Aug. 22, 1811.
6. Lois[4] (twin) b. April 19, 1742, d. Feb. 4, 1815.
7. Eunice[4] (twin) b. April 19, 1742, d. Jan. 7, 1843.
8. Timothy[4] b. July 6, 1745, d. Jan. 29, 1829.
9. Lucia[4] b. Nov. 12, 1747, d. Oct. 31, 1822.

IV. JOSHUA[3].

Joshua[3], was born Sept. 7, 1710, and lived and died in Wakefield. He married Dorothy Frees, and had six children:

1. Anna[4].
2. Joshua[4].
3. John[4].
4. Dorothy[4].
5. Love[4].
6. James[4].

V. JANE[3].

Jane[3] was born July 12, 1712, and married, 1732, (intentions pub. Aug. 27, 1732), Rev. Stephen *Chase*, of Newcastle, who graduated at Harvard in 1728, was ordained at Lynn, now Lynnfield, Nov. 24, 1731, and re-settled over the parish of Newcastle Dec. 5, 1750, where he died Jan. 1778. He was distinguished for great scholastic attainments and regarded as a profound theologian. (See "Chase-Townley Legacy" Chapter VII.) They had seven children:

1. Abraham[4], b. March 25, 1734, d. March 25, 1734.
2. Stephen[4], b. Feb. 22, 1735, d. Dec. 1, 1739.
3. Joshua[4], b. March, 1738.
4. Jane[4], b. Jan. 7, 1740.
5. Stephen[4], b. June 22, 1742, d. March, 1805.
6. Mary[4], b. Oct. 19, 1744.
7. John[4], b. Aug. 14, 1749.

VI.   ABIGAIL [3].

Abigail[3], (twin with Anna[3],) was born June 30, 1714,-'15, and married, Feb. 26, 1737, John *Stickney*, merchant, of Newburyport, Mass.   They had eight children :

1. John[4], b. Feb. 19, 1738, d. Dec. 5, 1803 (?).
2. Abigail[4], b. Oct. 2, 1740.
3. Anna[4], b. Feb. 26, 1742, d. Oct. 27, 1827.
4. Mary[4], b. Feb. 22, 1744.
5. William[4], b. Dec. 22, 1745, d. Aug. 25, 1823.
6. Thomas[4], b. April 7, 1748, d. Aug. 28, 1791.
7. Joseph[4], b. May 3, 1750, d. Oct. 29, 1803.
8. Mary[4], b. Nov. 24, 1752.

VII.   ANNA [3].

Anna[3], (twin with Abigail[3],) was born June 30, 1714-'15, and died July 10, 1735. She married, Jan. 31, 1733-'34, Daniel *Marston*, of Hampton, and had one child who never married. [No further record.]

VIII.   MARTHA [3].

Martha[3] was born March 30, 1718, and died at Hampton "of a violent fever" in 1758. She married, Nov. 10, 1737, Dr. John *Weeks*, of Greenland, an eminent physician who is said to have completed his studies in England. He was also a Justice of the Peace and a Colonel, presumably in the Militia. John was the son of Joshua and grandson of Leonard Weeks. Rev. Jacob[6] Chapman, their great-grandson, writes of the family, "I think the generosity in the use of property was inherited from the mother, Martha Wingate ; the father was a successful financier and accumulated a large property." After Martha[3]'s death her husband married a second wife but died in five years from the time of his first wife's decease.

Martha[3] had ten children :

1. Joshua[4], b. 1738, d. 1806.
2. Comfort[4], b. 1740, d. 1814.
3. Martha[4], b. 1742.
4. Mary[4], b. Feb. 22, 1745, d. Jan. 15, 1814.
5. Sarah[4], b. 1747, d. Nov. 22, 1818.

6.   John[4], b. Feb. 17, 1749, d. Sept. 10, 1818.
7.   William[4], b. 1751, d. Sept. 1821.
8.   Ward Cotton[4], bapt. July 15, 1753.
9.   Abigail[4].
10.   Joanna[4], b. Dec. 31, 1755, d. July 17, 1826.

IX.   LOVE [3].

Love[3] was born April 4, 1720, and died April 1, 1809. She married, Nov. 17, 1748, Rev. Nathaniel *Gookin*, (Harvard 1734) of North Hampton. He was the son of Rev. Nathaniel Gookin (Harvard 1703), of Hampton, and grandson of Rev. Nathaniel Gookin (Harvard 1675), of Cambridge, and great-grandson of Major-General Daniel Gookin, of Cambridge. He was ordained "to the pastoral office of a church at North Hill, in the town of Hampton, Oct. 31, 1739 by William Shurtleff A. M. pastor of a church in Portsmouth." After his death Mrs. Gookin with her family were welcomed by her brother John[3] to the paternal estate, and there she resided during the remainder of her life. Love[3] had eight children :

1.   ———[4].
2.   ———[4].
3.   ———[4].
4.   Elizabeth[4].
5.   Hannah[4], b. April 22, 1754, d. Aug. 4, 1797.
6.   Daniel[4], b. March 2, 1756, d. Sept. 4, 1831.
7.   Martha[4].
8.   Sarah[4].

X.   ELIZABETH [3].

Elizabeth[3] was born Nov. 21, 1722, and "dyed upward of 80 years of age." She married Dr. John *Newman*, of Newburyport, Mass., and had eleven children :

1.   Elizabeth[4].
2.   John[4].
3.   Jane[4].
4.   Wingate[4].
5.   Paine[4].
6.   Elizabeth[4].

7. Judith⁴.
8. Joshua⁴.
9. Mary⁴.
10. Timothy⁴.
11. Joanna⁴.

XI. JOHN³.

John[3], the youngest son of Joshua[2], was born at Hampton, Jan. 4, 1725. Alden's Collection of American Epitaphs thus describes him: "He was prepared for admission into Harvard College by his brother, Rev. Paine Wingate, and received his baccalaurate in 1744. In the course of the following year he made a publick profession of religion, which he adorned by his exemplary Christian deportment through a long protracted life. Meekness, humility and benevolence shone with uncommon lustre in the constellation of his virtues. He was a very conscientious and devout man. He loved the institutions of the gospel and esteemed them as most precious privileges. He delighted in the society of the pious and particularly in that of the faithful ministers of Jesus Christ, with many of whom he was well acquainted. Mr. Wingate never entered into the bonds of matrimony; yet he was esteemed, like a father, by many, who experienced his kind and watchful care. Devoid of ambition for the honors of the world, it was his constant aim to live to the glory of God and the benefit of his fellow creatures. He was never happier than when doing good to the extent of his opportunities and means, and his days were filled up with deeds of usefulness. He wept with those who wept, and rejoiced at the temporal and spiritual prosperity of all around him. He was remarkable for the simplicity and purity of his life and conversation. Of no one may it be said, with more striking propriety, that he *was an Israelite indeed in whom there was no guile.* At length bowed down with age, esteemed and revered wherever known, he closed his pilgrimage, on the 4 of September 1812, in his 88 year, to enter on the rewards of grace. *Mark the perfect man and behold the upright, for the end of that man is peace.*" It is in these words that Eliza Gookin[7] Thornton describes "Uncle John," as he looked while sitting under the trees on a Summer day: "He wore a worsted cap of many colors, a gown of purple camlet, and leather shoes adorned with an ample buckle of polished steel. His staff and tobacco-pipe lay at his side,—the former because he

was frequently 'light-headed,' the other because it was his nearest and dearest earthly friend." The same writer says of him, that, although not married, "he was an admirer of beautiful women, and it is said in his youth did actually make overtures of a very affectionate character to one whom he thought supremely so,—but he was not successful."

CHAPTER VI.

HON. PAINE[4] WINGATE.

Most prominent of all the Wingate family was Rev. and Hon. Paine[4] Wingate, the son of Rev. Paine[3] and grandson of Col. Joshua[2]. Born in Amesbury, Mass., May 14, 1739, he reached the age of full maturity at a time when the concerns of this nation were at a crisis, and when the people found need for men of the soundest judgment and wisdom to act as their representatives in conducting the affairs of the present and preparing the plans for the future. Paine[4] Wingate was called from his quiet farm life in Stratham to the Congress of the Confederation, and was afterwards one of the first Senators of New Hampshire to the Congress of the United States under the Constitution. He was later a member of the National House of Representatives, and for many years Judge of the Superior Court of New Hampshire.

As to the personal appearance of Paine[4] Wingate we know nothing, except the tradition that he "was said to look like Washington." (Note p). The character which we deduce from his life and writings as well as from the record of contemporaneous writers would lead us to think that, if appearances are in any way indicative of manner of life and strength of mind, this similarity to the features of Washington could easily exist. It is written of Paine 4, "He possessed a strong, cultivated, and well balanced mind, with great independence and decision, and with no less frankness and equanimity." In his duties at court he "sustained the character of a well informed, discerning and upright judge." His advice seems always to have been worthy of grave consideration, and his predictions,

---

NOTE (p). A letter written by Mary Carr[5] Wingate (b. 1797) to William H[6] Page says: "Your uncle Joshua once took me to Stratham to call on our aged relatives. My uncle Paine had much polish of manner, indicating his early associations. My aunt was a bright active woman though at that time passed ninety."

while he was in the public service, both regarding home and foreign affairs have proved, as we can now see, surprisingly accurate. He always had an eye to the coming history of the country, and his words ever discouraged anything for temporary benefit which might prove injurious to the United States of the future. Petty controversy between different sections of the country or between individual representatives he deprecated ; to accomplish the good of the whole people was his aim. An advocate of the strictest honesty he naturally opposed lavish expenditures in Congress, as not being a proper care of the general trust fund ; his frequent advocacy of economy was far from being an indication of selfish parsimony for he always took care, whatever the others should do, that he at least should not in his public duties cause the government the slightest unnecessary expense. It is probable that his life as a country clergyman and farmer had taught him to acquire habits of economy, but his principle was always true and generous economy. Man, he held, did not exist for self alone but owed something to society. But while entertaining this opinion he felt the utmost contempt for the low arts of the self seeking politician looking only for personal emolument.

Paine [4] Wingate's years upon the quiet farm gave him opportunity for study of national questions, and also for the peace and comfort of that home life which he enjoyed so well. He was very domestic, and in one of his letters he speaks of his own fondness for home and family. His warm friendships were a source of pleasure to all parties concerned, and his courtliness towards those friends is everywhere manifest. In his religious sentiments it is said " he was a decided Trinitarian, and accorded mainly with Henry, Watts and Doddridge." We find in his writings that he was far advanced in religious views. He was not hide-bound by prevailing customs or previous precedents, but with a clear eye saw just how far these were suited for his day and how far they could be abandoned with benefit rather than injury to the church. He was no stickler for forms, as were many clergymen of his time, but believed in the simple religion of Christ. The influence of deism among the more intelligent classes he feared, and feared equally the influence of unreasoning enthusiasm among those of less learning and less ability to self-control and self-understanding. This advanced stand in religion may perhaps account in part for the disturbing elements which entered into his pastoral life.

The boyhood and youth of Paine[4] we know nothing of, except that he graduated from Harvard College in 1759. In his later days he was for fifteen years the only one living of his class, and for several years was the oldest living graduate of the college. Being the eldest son of a Congregational clergymen it was natural, — in the eighteenth century at least, — that he also should embrace the ministerial profession. His pastorate, however, cannot be called a very successful one, though a careful and impartial study would seem to show that the parishioners and not the pastor were at fault. This leading members of his church also testify to, when they say that the "opposition was more from a disposition to make difficulty in the parish than from any reasonable objection" to Mr. Wingate ; and the fact that the contentions continued after Mr. Wingate left the pulpit is a piece of evidence. The doctrines preached and the amount of salary paid (£55 yearly) were the grounds of opposition set up.

It was on Dec. 14, 1763, when Mr. Wingate was but 24 years old, that he was ordained as pastor of the Second Church of Christ in Hampton (First Congregational Church of Hampton Falls) being the fourth minister since its organization in 1711. He was "first received by them upon his dismission and recommendation from the Second Church of Christ in Amesbury, and then elected from among them." That same year he had been called to settle in ministry at Winchester, Cheshire Co., but declined. After nearly two years of preaching, dissatisfaction was manifested by a portion of the society, by their sending, Nov. 21, 1765, a petition to Gov. Benning Wentworth for the setting off of a Presbyterian society from the old church.

It was signed by Thomas Leavitt and 55 others, who, complaining that they were assessed by the selectmen for the support of Rev. "Pain" Wingate, declare :

"The petition * * * Humbly Sheweth, that about Two years ago The Rev[d] Mr. Pain Wingate in the congregational way and manner was settled in the work of the ministry in said Town. That the Religious sentiments of and Doctrine preached by the said Rev[d] Mr. Wingate are very different from those of your Petitioners — and disagreeable to them —. That your Petitioners apprehended they could not be profited by the preaching and ministration of the s[d] Rev[d] Mr. Wingate. That the measures taken by the said Town in order to the settlement and support of the said Mr. Wingate are as your petitioners conceive unprecedented and Justly Grievous to

them, and that therefore your Petitioners and many other Inhabitants of said Town (near one half thereof) constantly opposed his settlement there and dissented therefrom," etc.

More explicit and more open is the answer of the other members of the society, when in a counter-petition to the Governor and Legislature, dated Jan. 1, 1766, they say:

"We the subscribers chosen by the Parish of Hampton Falls a committee on their behalf to make answer to a Petition, [Of Nov. 21, 1765] * * * We would therefore Inform your Excellency and Honors that Mr. Wingate Having Preached in the Parish for some months before Mr. Baileys Death and afterwards to the General Satisfaction of the People the Parish with the advice of the Neighboring ministers Proceeded to give him a call to Settle in the work of the ministry there, which call was unanimous by the Church, and General by the Parish, not more than three or four Persons opposing his Settlement. But the terms of Settlement not being agreed on he gave a Negative answer. After which the Parish heard some others on Probation and gave Mr. Micah Lawrence a call to settle, which we mention because it has been Represented as if the Parish were unreasonably set for Mr. Wingate's settlement and no other person. But the same persons who opposed Mr. Wingate's settlement opposed the settlement of Mr. Lawrence, which made the Generality of People think their opposition was more from a disposition to make Difficulty in the Parish than from any Reasonable objection they had against either of the Persons. But Mr. Lawrence also gave a Negative answer on accomp of terms of settlement. Whereupon the People in General Signified their desire to Renew their Call to Mr. Wingate, and agreed to get him to Preach for four Sabbaths, if he could be Procured. It is true this was opposed by those who had all along opposed his settlement, but this was then but three or four Persons. Mr. Wingate was accordingly Procured for four Sabbaths; after which a meeting was called. Notice being up two Sabbaths as usual, to see if the Parish would Renew their call to Mr. Wingate to settle which we mention, because it has been Represented as if there had been some unfair Proceedings as to this meeting, tho' in what Particulars we could never find. At this meeting there was again a general Vote of the Parish to Renew their call to Mr. Wingate, not more than six or seven Voting against it, and he had also again a unanimous Vote of the Church at the Same meeting also were voted terms of settlement which being five Pounds Sterling more than had been Voted before there were more Persons against the terms of settlement than against the call, tho' we think not more than ten or twelve at that time. But after wards many of these Petitioners spoke of it as an Extravagant sum (the sum is £55 Sterling in the

whole besides the Parsonage) and made this the Ground of uneasiness, and of stirring up Persons against Mr. Wingate's Settlement Representing that it was too much for such a Poor Parish to Pay, and if that were taken off they would be easy ; this was their General talk and the whole Ground of Complaint then made. With what Propriety they Desire to take off (as they say) near one half and to ￫aintain another minister when but a year or two ago the whole Pa.ʳsh were not able to pay fifty five pounds Sterling yearly, we must le￫￪c ￫o themselves to Explain. The truth is the whole Parish is not ￫￫￫￫ ￫￫￫￫ sufficient to support one minister Properly, Tho' we think ￫￫￫￫ ￫￫￫ ￫￫ Reason to find fault with what was Voted Mr. Wingate ; ￫￫￫￫ ￫￫￫￫￫￫ Rested for some time and it was Generally tho't that the u￫￫￫￫￫￫ which had arose on accomp of the Salary would subside. But s￫￫￫￫ time after some of these Persons who had all along opposed our Settlement went about, and in a very Private manner Procured a Number of Persons to Sign a Paper to signify to Mr. Wingate that there was a great Number of Persons in the Parish against his settlement, in order to Discourage him from accepting, which being accidentally heard of by one or two Persons who were for Mr. Wingate's settlement, and of the time when they Designed to carry the same to Mr. Wingate it was tho't Proper that some Person should go and meet them at Mr. Wingate's to Know what Objections there were, and Endeavor to clear up any Difficulties that might be made, accordingly three or four Persons went and met the Persons who had been Procuring Signers, and informing them of what they heard Desired to Know who were uneasy and what their Objections were, that they might clear up the Matters if they could. But they Reply'd that what they had to Say was to Mʳ Wingate Signed by a considerable Number of Persons Signifying that they were against his settling, without assigning the Least Reason, and when they were asked the Reason Declined giving any which not appearing to Mr. Wingate (after Enquiring into all circumstances) to have Equal weight with the unanimous Vote of the Church and Clear Vote of the Parish at a Legal meeting he accepted the call. After this another Paper was carried about to be signed to Request the selectmen to call a meeting 'to see if the freeholders Inhabitants of Hampton falls will Vote that all the Votes has been Past Relating to Mr Wingate call in the Work of the ministry Salary and support in this Parish of Hampton falls be Repealed and absolutely Revoked and made void &c.' Which being delivered to the select men they Denied calling a meeting, looking upon it altogether as Improper after matters had been fairly and clearly determined at fair and Legal meetings to call a meeting to Revoke the same as it would be after a minister had been settled Ever so Long to have a meeting to Revoke all that had ever been done. The absurdity and Impropriety of which they tho't must be quite Evident, with several other Reasons which they gave the Petitioners in writing in answer to their Request,

in hopes to satisfy them that their Request was unreasonable, However it had not this Effect But they proceeded to get a meeting called by two Justices at which meeting they voted all the Proceedings Relating to Mr. Wingate's settlement to be Null and Void. But not trusting to this when the Councell was convened a Committee of the above Persons appeared & Objected to Mr. Wingate's being Ordained ; But never made the Least Objection against his Doctrine, life or Conversation, but on the Contrary, being asked by the Councill whether they had any Objections of this sort, said they had not neither did they make the Least Suggestion that they were of a Different Perswasion.

We hope your Excellency and Honors will Excuse this so long a Rehearsal of the Transactions of said Parish relative to these affairs as all the Objections hitherto made were against the Proceedings of the Parish as Illegal and unfair— for that of being Presbyterians had not yet come into their minds and these Objections as in the Present Petition couched in General terms without assigning a single Instance Wherein they were to give a Particular accomp of the whole Proceedings that the Instance wherein we have failed, may be Pointed Out, for we never yet could tell wherein it was. * * * * * Moreover from the best Information we can get one Quarter part at least of these Petitioners, never heard Mr. Wingate preach in their lives and many others of them ever had the least conversation with him to Know anything of his Religious Sentiments, And they have put down the Name of one at Least in their Petition who his own father has Represented as an Idiot so wanting of understanding that he ought not to be taxed for his head and he has been accordingly omitted and many of the Other Petitioners do not own one Inch of Real Estate in the Parish. How fair these things are we leave to be Judged, and of the like sort is their assertion that near one half of the Inhabitants of said Parish Constantly opposed Mr. Wingate's settlement and dissented therefrom, the Contrary to which is Evident from the foregoing state of facts. * * * *.

That these Petitioners have the true Doctrines of Grace and Salvation preached to them according to their sense of these things we have nothing to say to and that they are so Preached by Mr. Wingate Even these Petitioners themselves after all their Endeavors, could never find the least Objection to make to the Contrary, so that the Inuendo's and suggestions against Mr. Wingate's Preaching are put in as we conceive for no other Reason then that they tho't it necessary in Order to their having any Colour for what they Ask, that there should have been in Reality what they without the least foundation Suggest."

Wherefore they prayed that the petition be dismissed " for we think that Encouraging Persons in Methods such as these Petitioners have Practised will have a direct tendency to Destroy Religious Societies of every Denomination." If, however, the petition is to be

granted they pray that the signers of said petition " be made a Dis-- trict Parish to act in all Respects by themselves. The Parish seem willing Notwithstanding the unreasonableness of all their Proceedings that they should go off as a District Parish, and their not accepting ..f this we think Shews their Disposition more to keep the Parish in Diffic·lties than that Religious Principles are the foundation of their Proceedings."

Signed   Meshech Weare ⎫
Richard Nason ⎪
Jonathan Tilton ⎬ Committee
Caleb Sanborn ⎪
Nathaniel Gove ⎪
Abner Sanborn Jr ⎭

The petition for the Presbyterian society was renewed July 3, 1767, and a bill was passed allowing the separation. This was one of the first steps towards forming a Presbyterian church in Seabrook, then a part of Hampton Falls. When Seabrook became a separate parish a proposition was made to change the location of the old meeting-house. This met with strenuous opposition. But a new house was built "near the centre of the inhabitants." Jan. 30, 1770 a majority of the parish "voted that the Rev. Mr. Paine Wingate shall go to the new meeting-house and preach and dedicate the said house to the public worship of God as soon as conveniently may be." This he declined to do, for what reason is not recorded but presumably on account of the niggardness of the parish regarding conveyance, as a subsequent legislative act shows. On June 11, 1770 the special committee of the Legislature, asked for by the people of Hampton Falls to settle their dispute regarding the new meeting-house which was placed two miles farther from the parsonage house than the old church, decided "that those persons who are better accommodated by the new Meeting-House and assisted in building the same should present the Rev. Mr. Pain Wingate with the sum of Sixty pounds, in order to provide Suitable carriage etc. for Travel of himself and family to and from Meeting."

The Legislative committee had decided that Mr. Wingate was in the right, but the malecontents in the church were still determined to keep up the trouble. In December of this year (1770) they refused to pay his salary for the year, so that in 1771 the town had to make an attempt to collect the back pay. But those who had removed to the Presbyterian society of Seabrook demurred. April

23, 1771 an ecclesiastical council was called to advise and assist in reference to the difficulties existing in the parish. In September the parish voted his dismission, giving him £50 and the use of the parsonage for four years. Preaching was hired for several years, Mr. Wingate still retaining his connection with the church and parish. His voice was heard in other pulpits if not in his own for we learn that the selectmen of North Hampton paid Mr. Wingate for preaching in 1774, £3, 18sh, 2d.

In Nov. 1774 a committee was appointed "to go and treat with the lower end of the parish concerning the difficulties that subsist in the parish," and another to go to the Association for advice respecting a minister. For several years there was preaching in both meeting-houses, and it was not until Nov. 17, 1780, over four years and a half after Mr. Wingate left the church entirely, that the "members that withdrew from the ordinances under Mr. Wingate's ministry contrary to order, and also put themselves under the care of the Presbyterian church, returned, made confession and were restored."

Mr. Wingate resigned his office as pastor March 12, 1776, and six days later requested a dismission from his pastoral relation to the church. His request was duly complied with. Rev. Paine[4] Wingate's active ministry in Hampton Falls had continued about eight years, but his pastoral connection with the church and parish extended through a little more than twelve years. Baptisms during this time were, 184; marriages of parties belonging to Hampton Falls, 45, and of others, 274. Many came from Massachusetts and were married in virtue of a license from the Governor rather than be published in the old form at home.

It was sometime before 1766 that Paine[4] Wingate married his cousin Eunice[4] Pickering, the daughter of Deacon Timothy and Mary[3] (Wingate) Pickering, the latter being the sister of Rev. Paine[3] Wingate, Sr. The couple moved from Hampton Falls to Stratham after the pastorship resignation and settled upon a farm, the same farm which has remained a homestead for this branch of the family ever since, having descended to John[5], the son of Paine[4], and then to Joseph Charles Augustus[6], the present owner. It is a large and handsome estate extending from the main road to Exeter back to the Swampscott river and having its buildings located at the foot of the hill upon whose crest stands the Congregational church of

PAINE WINGATE'S HOMESTEAD, STRATHAM, N. H.

the town. At Stratham Rev. Paine[4] Wingate preached some, but in a few years the stirring events incident to the formation of our nation called him to public duties. In May, 1775, Mr. Wingate, while still at Hampton Falls, had been appointed one of two deputies who should represent the towns-people at the Fourth Provincial Congress holden at Exeter. Some weeks before that time, as we learn from a letter written April, 1775 to Paine[4] Wingate by Col. Timothy Pickering, Mr. Wingate had expressed an opinion that a pacification with England upon honorable terms was practicable, and that he had conceived a plan by which he thought it could be attained. We have no clue, however, to the plan itself. Between Mr. Wingate and Col. Pickering, a brother of Eunice[4], the wife of Paine[4] Wingate, and one of the prominent figures in the history of that time, the closest intimacy and most affectionate friendship always existed.

In June, 1781, Mr. Wingate was one of the leading members of a convention held at Concord to form a constitution in principles more comprehensive and determinate than the Plan of Government which had been hastily prepared in 1776 as a temporary expedient to continue only during the war. The convention, after a discussion, adjourned until September and then drew up a constitution and submitted it to the people. After nine meetings in two years and after sundry alterations the constitution (the present one) was adopted and sent out for final decision by the people. In 1783 Mr. Wingate was Stratham's representative in the State Legislature, as he was also in 1795, after having finished his more important national duties.

It was March 12, 1782, that Col. Pickering wrote a letter to his friend and brother-in-law, in which he said: "Since I had the pleasure of seeing you and my sister you have had a son born, whom you have named George, as I understand; but that it was problematical whether you meant thereby to honor that name on this or the other side of the Atlantic. I presume, however, that you value your own dignity, and that of human nature, too highly to idolize either."

The concise reason for giving this name Mr. Wingate states in a letter to Col. Pickering in 1784. The letter reads:

Dear Sir: STRATHAM, January 1st, 1784.
By a letter I received from you, dated last April, I find that mine by Col. Dearborn to you has miscarried. When, or by what

conveyance, this will reach you, I am uncertain, as my situation is such that I know of no opportunity for sending. You will perceive by this that I still live at Stratham. I principally employ myself in the concerns of husbandry, and, I believe, enjoy as much contentment and happiness as is common to humanity. I have five children : two of whom you once knew, my two next are sons, named George and John, which names I think I gave them purely because they were agreeable, and convenient to pronounce while they were young, and would be short for them to use when grown up. My youngest child is a daughter, near nine months old, called Elizabeth. You know enough of our family not to doubt of my fondness for my children, nor to think it strange that I take singular pleasure in my two boys, one of which is three and the other almost five years old. We have a good share of health in general, and particularly at this time. My farm affords me something more than a bare subsistence. I have an agreeable neighborhood and extensive acquaintance. I have leisure to look upon the affairs of public life ; and if I would practice the low arts of some, I suppose I might have a share in them : perhaps I may sometime or other without. It is likely you will think it trifling to give you thus so long a detail of my domestic concerns, but I have nothing at present more interesting to inform you of.

In your last letter but one, you made some inquiries regarding Siberia wheat. It is probable that, since that time, you have heard the fate of it. That grain (as is common to most if not all exotics) has become naturalized to the climate, and subject to the disasters of other wheat. I suppose that a new importation of that kind of seed might answer the purpose again as it did heretofore. I have nothing new in husbandry to communicate. I go on pretty much in the old track of culture. By attention, neatness and labor, the products of a farm may be greatly increased : but I do not expect, by any kind of magic, to cause the earth to bring forth plentifully and durably.

I join with you in welcoming the happy event of peace, and hope the Independency of the United States will conduce to an increased freedom and happiness. It would have been an addition to my satisfaction to have had the return of peace returned you and family to your native town and connections again. You are not insensible that you have a large share in the esteem and affections of your relations and friends ; and I cannot think but that you might have gratified them, and, at the same time, have provided for yourself in your return. But I do not pretend to be judge of your prospects in business at Philadelphia. I would not attempt to dissuade you from your interest, so far as is consistent with your own ease and enjoyment of life, and that extensive usefulness which you owe to society. You may depend upon every cheerful aid in my power in whatever situation you are, and my most ardent wishes will ever attend you of prosperity and happiness. I rejoice in your domestic

welfare, the restored health of your wife, and increase of children. I hope that you will find leisure to visit us, with your family, before long, although you should think it best to fix your stated residence at the southward. In the mean time, any opportunity of writing to me of your welfare, if you will embrace it, it will afford me the greatest pleasure.

I desire that my affectionate regard to your wife and children may be mentioned, and be assured that with particular esteem and friendship, I am yours, etc.

PAINE WINGATE.

Mr. Timothy Pickering.

The people of Stratham recommended Paine [4] Wingate for a Justice of the Peace with the following words addressed to the Governor and Council :

STRATHAM, March 15, 1785.

We the subscribers beg leave to Acquaint your Excellency and Honours, that from our particular Acquaintance for a Considerable Number of years with mr. Pain Wingate ; and from his general character amonst us ; we apprehend he is a very suitable Gentleman for the office of a Justice of the Peace ; and will be likely to be very serviceable to the Town and Publick in that office —— therefore beg the favour of your Excellency and Honour, that he may be appointed to that office. (Signed) Moses Clark, and 84 others.

In 1787 Paine [4] Wingate was sent as a member of the Congress under the Confederation, and at this time began his eight years of continuous service in the national Legislative halls. A number of letters written by him during these years to two intimate friends, Col. Pickering and Samuel Lane, of Stratham, give us a very interesting and connected history not only of Mr. Wingate's individual action but also of the course of the nation. The Second Federal Convention adopted the Constitution September 17, 1787, but it was not until Sept. 13, 1788, that Congress (eleven States having at last ratified it) appointed the first Wednesday in June, 1789, for the choice of electors of President and the first Wednesday in March following as the time for commencing at New York proceedings under the Constitution. During the entire year of 1788 the American States were all kept in painful uncertainty and feverish excitement. The Confederacy was felt to be falling to pieces by its own inadequacy and weakness, and no man could tell whether the

Constitution of the United States then under consideration would be adopted by the requisite nine States or whether any other plan of union would ever be devised and established. The difficulty, irregularity and tardiness of communication left all in the dark. It was known that everywhere there was an active and determined opposition to the new system of Government submitted to the Conventions, gathering and to be gathered in the several States, for ratification or rejection. Many distinguished leaders of the people, having exaggerated fears that the proposed Constitution in some way would endanger the public liberty, were arrayed against it. In most of the States the relative strength of parties could not be ascertained, and in several of the most important ones the question was finally decided by an extremely close vote. So highly were the people wrought up that the news of ratification by State after State, arriving after the lapse of long intervals of time, was welcomed by the ringing of bells and every form of expressing gratified joy.

During this year Hon. Paine[4] Wingate wrote the first five letters herewith given. The first letter, written to Col. Pickering, reads as follows :

NEW YORK, March 29th, 1788.

Dear Sir,

Mr. Hodgdon, who is now in this city, informs me that he can frequently transmit letters to you from Philadelphia, and by him I improve this opportunity of writing to you. The distance of your situation from New Hampshire, and the difficulty of an intercourse between us, has prevented my giving, and, I suppose, receiving from you any direct intelligence for a long time. But this separation has not obliterated my remembrance of, or lessened my affection for you. It is with particular satisfaction that I sometimes hear of your welfare by our friends at Salem. This pleasure I had in the beginning of February, when your brother told me that he had received a letter from you, dated the first of January, at which time you were setting out for your new settlement ; and Mr. Hodgdon tells me that you have since been down, and returned again very lately, and that the last intelligence was that your family were all well, and that your situation was very agreeable. I rejoice in every circumstance that contributes to your domestic happiness and extensive usefulness in life ; but could wish that you had believed these two objects obtainable somewhere within the circle of your family connections and former friends. Your brother was remarkably well when I was there in February. I think he appeared to enjoy as good health and spirits as I have known him for several years. All the other

branches of the family were well. Your son came with me from
Salem to Boston in a sleigh for the sake of a ride, and to see the
bridges &c., and returned again the same day with a lad who brought
me on. Master John is sensible, and after some acquaintance is
sufficiently sociable, though with strangers rather reserved. He has
those qualities which, I think, will render him, with the advantages
of education that he will enjoy, both amiable and useful, and in
whom a parent will have great satisfaction. Your other children I
have not seen ; but I dare say they afford you the pleasing hopes of a
fond father. I have received a letter from my family, dated March
17th, when they were all well. Polly is married, and I hope and
believe to a worthy and agreeable husband. She will live about one
mile from me. Sally is a woman grown. George and John are two
good boys, and Betsy, my youngest, is about five years old, which I
suppose will finish our complement of children. My wife enjoys
uninterrupted health, and changes with the succession of years as
little as almost anybody. I shall write to her by the post to-day,
and let her know that I have heard of you by Mr. Hodgdon, which
will make a letter very welcome to her, on your account if not on
mine.

I have been in New York since February 10th, and find my
situation as agreeable as I could expect, considering that I am very
domestic, and habituated to an active life. I have nothing very
important to communicate to you. The subject which engages the
general attention at this time is the new Constitution. What will be
the fate of it is yet uncertain ; but those who are well wishers to their
country, and best know the situation we are in, are the most sensible
of the necessity of its adoption, and great pains are taken to obtain
the end. On the other hand, there are powerful opposers to it, who
avail themselves of some popular objections, and they are too successful with the less knowing part of the country. In New Hampshire, when the Convention met, there was a majority prejudiced
against the plan. They were chiefly from the interior parts of the
State, and many of the delegates were instructed to vote against it.
The most distinguished characters were in favor of it, and, after
debating it for some time, there were a few converts made, who did
not think themselves at liberty to go against their instructions, and
therefore obtained an adjournment. There is, I think, a probability
that it will finally be adopted in New Hampshire, although considerable danger that it will not. New York is very doubtful, but it is
not despaired of. Virginia and North Carolina much in the same
situation. Maryland and South Carolina are supposed to be Federal.
These two states will decide before the others, and, if they should
agree to adopt, there will be but one of the doubtful cases necessary
to make up the nine. The important decision upon the subject cannot be known before the last of July ; and, at any rate, I do not see
that the new Constitution can be got to go as early as December

next. Nothing but the hope of a new, can, I fear, keep the old Constitution from dissolution long. "Sed nunquam de Republica desperandum." The newspapers are so filled with lies that no dependance can be put on any account you receive in them respecting the Constitution.

I hope I shall soon have the pleasure of hearing from you by letter, which direct to me, in Congress, at New York. If you have any letters which you wish at any time to forward to Salem, or to any friends eastward, I will take the care of them, and send them, without hazard or expense, to the place of destination. If Congress should not adjourn, which yet is uncertain, it is likely that I shall remain in this place until October next.

I am, dear Sir, with sentiments of particular esteem and affection, your friend and brother,

PAINE WINGATE.

N. B. I desire my love to Mrs. Pickering.

Col. Timothy Pickering.

Two weeks later Mr. Wingate, writing to Mr. Lane, shows the importance which Congress placed on the ratification vote of the New Hampshire Convention, and gives the knowledge and opinion which men held of that then almost unknown land, Kentucky. In view of the freshets of recent years along the banks of the Ohio, it is also interesting to notice that the same phenomena were observed and commented on a hundred years ago.

NEW YORK, April 12, 1788.

Dear Sir,

I received your favor of March 17 and was much gratifyed with your particular information respecting the Convention, and your relation of sundry other historical events. Your account was the most minute & authentic which I had received at so early a date, concerning the debates & decisions of the convention. Tho' I was disappointed & sorry for the event, yet was glad to have the true state of the facts. I suppose as the Delegates then viewed the matter, it was fortunate that the issue was no worse. But the ill impression on the minds of people by the adjournment is more extensive & mischievous than you would imagine. It is complained of as far as Virginia, and believed that if New Hampshire had adopted, there would not have been one dissenting state. Whereas, there is now some danger that the whole plan will miscarry. I say some danger, for Virginia & New York, are, I suppose, nearly divided, and that from selfish views & their influence is considerable over other states. But upon the whole, the probability is in favor of its being adopted. You know my opinion of the necessity &

importance of this, for the safety & welfare of the country under
our present circumstances. I shall trouble you no more on this
subject. Congress have had application made to them from Kentucky, to be made an independent state. This is a large tract of
Country on the westward part of Virginia. It is situated between
the Alligany Mountains & the river Ohio, on the East of that
river. Those mountains lie in a chain from North to South & are
impassable except in two places. It is six hundred miles from the
centre of this Country, to the seat of government in Virginia, and
cannot be travelled in less than 21 days, & that with great peril in
fording or rafting over the rivers, & climing over the rocks & mountains, where there is no road, & never can be inhabitted for the distance of 5 days journey. Notwithstanding those difficulties, so
tempting is the soil that there are said to be not less than 60 thousand souls settled there already. There is a member in Congress
from that Country, a Clergymans son, who gave me this account.
He says that the winters are so mild, that the cattle in the spring will
be as fat as at any time, without the trouble of feeding them. That
it is a very healthy climate. That there are a number of salt springs
where the people can boil the water & make salt as we do out of
sea water. It is only crossing over the river & there is the western country where the Ohio company & others are about to make
their settlement. It is said that where the Ohio emptieth itself into
the Mississippi so flat is the country & such floods come down in
the spring season, that there is a space of forty miles distance laid
under water. Which forms the appearance of a sea, out of which a
forest of trees rises. The vast country northwest of the Ohio was
ceeded by Virginia to the united states upon condition that they
should be reimbursed for their expences in defending of it during the
late war. This Congress agreed to & commissioners were appointed
by mutual consent to assertain the sum. The commissioners have
not yet reported, & cannot easily agree either two of them. One
supposes that 60 Thous^d pounds P. M. would be eno', another 150
Thous^d pounds & the other would give them 220 Thous^d pounds for
their expences. This would be a dear purchase of that country to
the united states. I intended to have given you some account of the
City of New York in this letter, but have dwelt so long on the New
Constitution, & the western country, that I find I shall not have room.
Boston is not more than two-thirds as large as this city in buildings
& numbers, and I suppose are much the same in proportion of com-
merse & wealth. The continual increase is very great, & I think its
situation is very favorable to its being the centre of business & wealth
in the union. As for news, I will enclose a paper to give you that.
We have nothing remarkable in Congress. Shall be glad to hear
from you when it is convenient. I cannot take much pains in
writing, having considerable of it to do. If you can read it & find

any amusement therefrom my end is answered, especially if you will
consider it as a token of that esteem and friendship with which I am
yours &c.   PAINE WINGATE.
P. S.   If I should not write by this post
to my family please let them know that I
am well & desire my affectionate regard
to all friends.

The subjects discussed in the foregoing letter were continued
in another to Mr. Lane, later on.   It reads :

NEW YORK, June 2d, 1788.
        Dear Sir,
                I had the satisfaction of receiving your favor of the
fifteenth of May.   I can assure you that it gives me particular
pleasure to receive fresh tokens of your friendship & such communications as may serve to revive the remembrance of our former
intimacy.   At this time I am rather more in a hurry than is common,
& therefore shall give you but an imperfect letter which I desire
you will receive as a token of my esteem & respect.   I am exceeding glad to hear from you that the prospect of the new constitution
being adopted is so favorable, & that any converts have been made
to that side *.   I am fully persuaded that wise and honest men if
they knew the situation of our public affairs, would without hesitation
agree with me.   I have nothing which I am sensible of to byass my
mind in this matter but a hearty Desire for the general good.   We
are in expectation every day of receiving an account from S°
Carolina of their ratifying the new plan as we have information from
their convention since met that there is a large majority in favor of
it.   Much depends now upon New Hampshire.   Their example
will have great weight, more than many are sensible of.   If New
Hampshire should come into the plan, which from the best accounts
we rely upon, we have a good degree of probability that all the
states will eventually unite.   Our latest accounts from Europe are
that our credit begins [to] revive there already, upon the presump-
tion that our government will soon be upon a more respectable
footing.   We have now a pretty full Congress & expect soon to
have all the States represented.   We are at this time engaged in a
matter of considerable consequence, that is, whether Kentucky which
is the western part of Virginia & which I think I gave you some
account of heretofore, shall be erected into a distinct state.   This
will be an affair not easily settled †.   There are great difficulties on

---

* The New Hampshire convention 'adopted the Constitution shortly
after this was written.

† Kentucky was not admitted to the Union until June 1, 1792.

all sides. The commissioners who were appointed to judge how much the united states should pay Virginia for their expences in defending the western country during the war, have reported half a million of dollars for us to pay. This is no inconsiderable sum. Georgia have also made a cession to the united states of their Western lands on condition of their being paid one hundred thousand dollars. If we should have a few more such presents we should not know how to pay them. The expences of these purchases together with the expences of the Indian treaties & of surveying and disposing of those lands will create a very large debt. It is true the country is immensely large, is an excellent soil, & capable of supporting a vast number of inhabitants, but I think they will draw off our most valuable and enterprising young men & will impede the population of our old states & prevent the establishment of manufactures. Upon the whole I doubt whether in our day that country will not be a damage to us rather than an advantage. We seem to be overstocked with lands & I believe it had been as well for the Indians to have kept their own territory.

For what news we have I must refer you to the papers enclosed. Should be obliged to you to give that which contains some account of bees to my wife with the letters to her directed. I hope you smoke your pipe with her sometimes. I am as well contented here as I expected, & enjoy good health. I am yet among strangers & should be more in my own element at home. I shall be glad to have any intelligence from you which you shall think fit to write. I have written to Capt. Jonᵃ Wiggin as you proposed & hope it may have some effect. You will excuse my cursory writing. If you are able to read it & can derive any satisfaction from it my end is answered. I desire my respects to Mrs. Lane & wishing your health and prosperity, I am Dʳ Sir your friend & humble Servᵗ.

P. WINGATE.

The third letter from the Hon. Paine [4] Wingate to Samuel Lane, was written, apparently, in the spirit of prophecy for it gives most accurate conjectures concerning the approaching Revolution in France, and the tide of immigration towards the United States thenceforth to ensue. It is interesting to note the slow transit of news in the eighteenth century. The news from Virginia of date June 18th, important as it was, did not reach Congress at New York until the 26th.

NEW YORK, June 26, 1788.

Dear Sir,

By your favor of June 9th I recived the first intelligence from the General Court of New Hampshire after their meeting, and am much obliged to you for the trouble you took in giving me that early

information. My wife informs me that you took particular pains to convey to me the letter; I am very much gratifyed by knowing how the elections have issued. I have since seen a New Hampshire paper in which there was a list of the court &c. I now Sir with particular satisfaction, congratulate [you] upon the adoption of the new constitution in your State, and which has ensured its taking place. The latest news we have from Virginia is dated the 18th instant. By a letter from Gov. Randolph we are told that then there had no question been taken to decide the sense of the convention, but his calculation was that there were 82 for, 76 against & 10 doubtful. Another letter which is from an antifederalist of the same date says, that there are reckoned 80 on each side as certain & 8 as doubtful. The event therefore is yet very dubious. It is supposed that they would come to a determination on Saturday or Wednesday last. Of New York convention you will have as good an account as I am able to give you by the newspaper which I enclose. I hope that the spirit of lying & controversy upon this important subject will soon be done away, & that harmony and prosperity will attend the united states. We have no later intelligence from Europe than what has been in the papers. By them we have accounts of very distressing wars & other calamities. It is not unlikely that other nations may be involved. The disturbances in France between the King & his Parliament & other powerful subjects is very considerable. Perhaps it may be a fortunate time for them to regain some of their ancient liberties. The spirit of American liberty which he cherished at a distance seems to have crossed the Atlantic & is not a little troublesome to him. It may perhaps be thot wrong to suggest any thing to the reproach of our magnanimous & most christian ally, but I suppose the truth of the case is that he is a very weak & sottish prince. The latter infirmity, if he had not the former, you know will disqualify very soon a man from being active & enterprising. The Dutch are in a much worse condition than when they began their struggle & thousands of them have been obliged to fly their country & are ruined. It is very probable that those confusions in Europe may be the means of sending emigrants to America. Whether this will conduce to the real comfort & happiness of its present inhabitants I cannot say, but it will hasten on our population & make us a great if not a happy people. The western country which is yet to people is immense & I do believe it is a country in [which] the inhabitants can subsist themselves as easy as in any part of the world but they have many disadvantages. They are now settled in that country some of them a thousand miles from the sea. The Spaniards are on their West & South & tribes of Savages in the midst of them & they will I believe have wars with both of them sooner or later. Congress have agreed to sell large tracts of that country & others are applying. I hope that it will yield some emoluments to the united states. The Congress will I suppose pretty soon take up the new System & pre-

pare to put in motion. I hope that by the latter end of August we shall be able to adjourn. For my own part I am not for tarrying here any longer than is indispensable. I have my health & find my situation more agreeable than I expected. We have agreed that Kentucky should be independent in a mode comfortable to the Confederation, but it cannot take place in the present situation of affairs. I can add no more at this time but best wishes to attend you and yours and am your obliged friend and humble servant,

PAINE WINGATE.

The fourth letter of the series written to Mr. Lane, during the formative period of our government, is short, but alludes to various interesting subjects, particularly to the reason for choosing the dates for appointing electors and assembling Congress.

NEW YORK, July 29, 1788.

Dear Sir,

For the sake of giving you the latest intelligence I can, I shall now give you a short letter in great hurry. I congratulate you on the favorable and unexpected determination of New York respecting the new Constitution; an account of which I will enclose. This was a most desirable event especially to the Eastern States. North Carolina convention is now in Session & we expect to hear of their adoption within a fortni't.[*] Rhode Island yet remains anti-federal.[†] All the States are now represented in Congress, but I expect the members will many of them return home as soon as some necessary business shall be dispatched. I wish to tarry no longer than necessity shall require, out of principle of Oeconomy to the state, as well as a fondness for home. I therefore purpose to return as soon as the other members are scattering, which probably may be in about a month. My wife can inform you of some news respecting her brother Tim°. Pickering which I cannot here relate. It is said that the insurgents have put him into the hands of some Indians to keep in the woods, lest he should be retaken by the force sent to apprehend the rioters. But M^r. Pickering has desired that government would make no dishonorable concessions to those people for his sake. Tho' I do not think that M^r. Pickering will be injured personally further than by the hardship of his imprisonment, yet I desire not the above circumstance should be mentioned to my wife. I expected this day to have been able to inform you of the place in which the new Congress will meet, but the President was so unwell that he could not attend & the business was postponed. Congress

---

* North Carolina ratified Nov. 21, 1789.

† Rhode Island ratified May 29, 1790.

have agreed that the Electors of President shall be appointed on the first wednesday of Jan^y., the President be chosen the first wednesday of Feb., & Congress assemble the first wednesday of March next. Those periods may be tho't by Some to be very late but earlier dates could not suit the situation of some of the Southern States. I believe notwithstanding the meeting of the new Congress is so late there will not be necessity of another Congress under the present confederation after Novr. next. There are great struggles between Philadelphia & New York which shall be the place of Congress. I think the former most likely to pervail, but this is only mere conjecture. I thank you for your information in your last letter & shall be glad to receive communications from you whenever it is convenient. You will please give my compliments to Col. Simon Wiggin & let him know the contents of this, which I think he will be very glad to receive notice of. I am your affectionate friend & humble Servant,

PAINE WINGATE.

Deacon Lane.

In December 1788 we find Paine [4] Wingate receiving at the town election in Stratham 64 votes, while Pierce Long received 59 and Samuel Livermore 53 as Representative of the State to Congress. But Mr. Wingate was placed in the higher branch of Congress, being chosen Senator with John Langdon as his colleague, to the Congress of 1789, the First Congress of the Federal Government. May 14th of that year the Senators were divided into three divisions, and lots drawn to determine the length of service of each. Senator Wingate drew for his division and settled that he and associates should vacate their seats at the expiration of the fourth year. Senator Langdon drew for his division and obtained a six years term. So we find Mr. Wingate in both the First and Second Congresses.

Of the letters written by Mr. Wingate during three years to Col. Pickering and Mr. Lane the following are preserved. The first one written to Col. Pickering was just after the date for the assembling of Congress. Extracts only are here given :

NEW YORK, March 25th, 1789.

I am again returned to this place, in a situation which I did not calculate upon last year, when I left. [After stating that it was five weeks since he passed through Salem, on his way to his seat in Congress, he continues :] To our no small disappointment and mortification, we have not yet been able to make a quorum of either House, [they had been waiting since the 4th of March], but have reason to expect that, this day, there will be a sufficient number of the Representatives, four more only being now necessary. I wish

the prospect of the Senate was equally favorable. New York have not chosen their Senators. Several of those chosen are detained by sickness, and others by some unfortunate circumstances, so that our sole dependence for a quorum immediately is on a single gentleman from Delaware. He had not designed to come on until the 10th of April, but, in consequence of letters informing him of our situation, it is hoped that he will be here this week.

As we have not made a Congress, the votes for President and Vice President cannot be opened. However, it is well known that General Washington is unanimously chosen President, and Mr. Adams has thirty-three votes for Vice President, which is a clear plurality though not a majority. The others voted for are very scattering, and the number of votes for any is very inconsiderable. How the President and Vice President elect are to be notified is not yet determined. Many are applying for the honor of being the messengers. Considerable time must be taken up by those gentlemen in coming on, and no great business can well be completed until their arrival. Those delays are viewed by many as unfavorable to the introduction of the new government, and, at least for a while, will impede the revenue laws, which the United States are in distress for. But patience must have its perfect work. I cannot but hope and believe that our public affairs will bear a better aspect soon. The members which I have known yet appear to me to be worthy and good characters. I think the members of both houses will, almost unanimously, be firm friends to the government. Those who have heretofore had their objections will be so few that they will probably not think it expedient to raise difficulties. I am told that your old friend, Mr. Gerry, speaks very moderately upon the subject. Nobody thinks that a General Convention will be called. Possibly, in a convenient time, Congress may take up the consideration of amendments or alterations, and recommend some that may quiet the fears and jealousies of the well-designing, and not affect the essentials of the present system. I am rather inclined to suppose that this cannot be attended to immediately, but must be postponed for some important matters. I have some fears that a dispute may arise as to the place where Congress shall sit; but hope that an expedient plan will soon be adopted for fixing a permanent seat for Congress without affecting our revenue, and that this will preclude a disagreeable dispute on that head. New York have exerted themselves mightily, and, in my opinion, *excessively*, in fitting up the Federal hall. It is said they have expended fifty thousand dollars on the building. But there are some things which will make a continuance here long disagreeable; among others, the unreasonable expense of living is not inconsiderable. It is said by some to be one-third dearer than at Philadelphia. I believe it will be the disposition of the members in general to reduce their own pay, as well as that of the civil list, and the expense of living ought to be corres-

pondent. This reduction the finances of the United States seem to require. How this will suit the swarms of office seekers, I don't know; but it may at least rid us of some disagreeable importunities, and better reconcile the disappointed to their fate.

And while I am speaking of appointments I cannot forbear expressing my earnest wish that you might be placed in one, where the public would have a renewed experience of your integrity, ability, industry and economy. Whether any consideration would induce you to quit your present domestic and State employments, and whether it would be conducive to your interest or your happiness, I cannot tell; but I am sure it will be agreeable to many of your friends, and I think for the honor and interest of your country. I pretend not to know what the sentiments of the President will be towards you, who is well acquainted with you, nor what the dispositions of the Senators of Pennsylvania, who, I conclude, know you. Nor do I pretend to have any considerable share of influence in the Councils further than a single vote; but I am satisfied that your reputation is sufficiently established when partial considerations are out of view, which I hope will evidently be the case in matters of appointment. I will say no more on this head, only that I wish to have your sentiments on what I have now suggested as soon as you have an opportunity. I desire that you would give me your mind without reserve whether any thing, or what, would be agreeable to you. How long my continuance here will be is uncertain. The present session probably cannot be a short one, and the time for which I am elected will soon be decided by a lot.

Mr. Wingate, in a letter dated April 29, 1789, informs Col. Pickering of the speculations in which people indulged about appointments, the organization of the departments, and the policy of the administration generally.

Under date of July 11, 1789, he says:

I am sensible that there are crowds of seekers who want to quarter themselves on the country, and very likely in many instances will obtain, to the exclusion of others more deserving. I hope that this will not be universally the case. * * * * There has been a mighty struggle, and not a little heat, in the House of Representatives, respecting the permanent residence of Congress. They have, by a bare majority, ordered a bill to be brought in for fixing it on the Susquehanna, and to appropriate one hundred thousand dollars to provide the accommodations. After all, I think it doubtful whether it will pass that House, and it is more doubtful in the Senate. I begin to be of opinion that it will not be expedient to attempt a Federal town until the States are more united upon that

subject as well as upon some others. We seem disposed to contrive other ways enough for the public money, without applying any of it to that, or to paying the national debt.

Seven weeks later the following short note was penned to Mr. Lane:

NEW YORK, Aug. 29, 1789.

Dear Sir,

I have received your favour of the 14 instant, and thank you for your friendly mindfulness of me, & for the information you have given me. Those deaths you mention might naturally be expected from long indispositions & advanced age, & I think you have remarkably been favoured in Stratham with health & life for a long time. I am very sorry for the situation of M^r. Fogg, as well as of the people in that town. I think it not unlikely that M^r. Pickering may have the offer of being a federal judge for the district of New Hampshire, which according to the unbounded liberality of Congress, will probably be more lucrative tho' not more honorable than the place of Chief Justice in that State. I confess that I am far from being satisfyed with all our public affairs, especially with the appropriation of monies. However when I consider that a kind Providence has in a miraculous manner, & in many instances from the first settlement of the country saved us from destruction, so I hope that we shall be saved still & that we shall be a happy & a grateful people. I will not now give you any particular account of congressional matters but hope that within one month from this date to have the pleasure of seeing you, & communicating my sentiments in conversation. I am Sir with much esteem your affectionate

friend & humble Servant

Deacon Lane.   PAINE WINGATE.

Mr. Lane received from Mr. Wingate the following spring a long letter, under date of April 3, 1790, treating mostly upon religious subjects. The last part related to Congress and is here given, the remainder being presented in another part of this chapter:

* * * * You ask whether business goes on in Congress agreeably to my mind? I cannot say that it does. We have been a long time engaged on the subject of the national debt & have not yet come to any decisions that can be depended upon. The minds of Congress are much divided, but something must be done tho' it is yet uncertain what that will be. It gives me much uneasiness to find so many ways for our money to be applyed beside paying our creditors. We are told that the resources of our country are abundant without direct taxes, or oppressing any description of men. I

ardently wish it may prove so, but cannot rely on it, from what appears to me. I have not room in this letter to give you a more particular account of our doings but you will see by the newspapers generally what is doing & I hope to have the pleasure in two months more to communicate to you face to face & that the result of this session will be eventually for the peace & welfare of the country whose good I sincerely wish. My love to Mᵣˢ. Lane & all friends who am yʳ affectionate friend   PAINE WINGATE.

In a letter to Col. Pickering, August 2, 1790, Mr. Wingate says:

We have at last finished (I trust) two tedious subjects: those of residence and of the funding system; whether well done or not time must determine. There may perhaps yet be an attempt to keep Congress here two years longer, but I think with very little prospect of obtaining it. I expect, if nothing extraordinary should prevent, to be at Philadelphia next December, and should be very happy to have the opportunity of seeing you there, more especially if you had some agreeable appointment in the government and was removed there. It is said that Mr. Osgood will resign his place when Congress shall remove. If his place would be agreeable to you, it is my wish you might obtain it. As the Post-office bill is only continued until the next session of Congress, I suppose no new Postmaster-General will be now appointed; but if he should resign (which I hardly think likely) before the next meeting of Congress, the President would appoint one to succeed. I should think the business might not be disagreeable.

At the expiration of Mr. Wingate's term as Senator he was promptly elected Representative to the Third Congress as associate with Nicholas Gilman, J. S. Sherburne and Jeremiah Smith. We have no record of his course here except the bare fact that he voted against the non-intercourse act with England, of April 21, 1794, which however was passed by the House by a vote of 58 to 38.

From 1793 to 1795 Mr. Wingate was in the national House of Representatives and, having finished his term there in the latter year, was immediately sent, by the citizens of Stratham, to the State House of Representatives. In 1798 he was appointed a Judge of the Superior Court of New Hampshire and held that position until his seventieth year, 1809. During his residence in Stratham he was several times moderator, the last time being in 1811, and was also assessor and auditor. From the town records we find, under date of April 1, 1794, "Voted that the thanks of the town be presented to

the Hon. Paine Wingate for his service in procuring a bell for the town and that the town clerk be, and he is hereby, directed to transmit to Mr. Wingate a copy of the vote."

In 1822 an interesting personal letter came to Paine[4] Wingate from his brother Joseph[4]. It read as follows:

HALLOWELL, Jan. 1, 1822.

Dear brother:

I read your letter giving the account of the death of brother William. It was an unexpected death to me indeed. I had thought it very likely that he would have outlived the whole family. I hope he has left this for a better world. All his past errors we must forgive and forget. He is in the hands of a merciful God who can do no wrong. Our number grows small and will soon be extinct, and the places which now know us will soon know us no more for ever. It is this day twelve months that I was at your house. I then little expected that we should all live to this day. Sister Quimby was then the most infirm, and I then thought she would not live through the winter, but I hope she is yet living. I have once had a hope that I should have seen you once more, but as I can't see you this winter I now begin to think we did meet at your house for the last time. God only knows. It may be He will order it other ways. It would give me great pleasure to meet again and feel as well and as able to go another such journey as I did last winter. I now feel a greater desire to see you again than ever I had before, on account of the death of our two brothers, and if you and I can never meet here again I now bid you a last farewell, hoping we shall all meet again with all our friends in another world of spirits. My son Francis is on business and, if we could both have left home, I would gladly have gone with him. We should be exceeding glad to see any of your family here, and hope they will come.

From your affectionate brother,
Hon. Paine Wingate, Esq.   JOSEPH WINGATE.

N. B. My son Paine's wife is just gone with the consumption. He wanted very much to have gone up to see you. Neither Paine nor Francis have ever been up since I came from Amesbury, which is 23 years this month. My son will pay you the interest due on our note. I am sorry I can't sell my land in New Sharon so as to be able to pay you. I have two acres there and two lots in Solon, 50 miles from here. I hope Francis will stay with you one or two days, going or coming. I want him to see your son John and your daughter Wiggin before he leaves you. Be so kind as to write to me when you are able. I here send you a copy of a record as I find it in my father's old bible which I keep for his sake.*

*The record is then appended.

In 1827 Col. Pickering writing of Paine [4] Wingate says, "Mr. Wingate now 88 years old, enjoys excellent health, has strength to labor in the Summer, and his mental faculties, always respectable, remain unimpaired." The following letter was "written in his own clear and strong hand," when in his ninetieth year, on the occasion of the death of Col. Pickering's wife :

STRATHAM, August 22d, 1828.

On the 20th instant, I received your letter of the 15th, announcing the sorrowful tidings of the death of sister Pickering. I can very sincerely condole with you under the bereavement. Although her age was such that you could not expect to have enjoyed her society long; yet, even at this late period, you must feel the painful void occasioned by her death. Her amiable qualities of mind, and her very benevolent and affectionate treatment of her friends, had very greatly endeared her memory to us all. * *. * * We have no doubt that it is a happy change' to her ; and, considering how far we are advanced in the journey of life, you and I cannot be long before we shall follow her ; and I think we may innocently please ourselves with the hope and expectation of recognizing our Christian departed friends in a blessed hereafter. * * Desiring an affectionate remembrance to all friends, I am your mourning friend and brother,

PAINE WINGATE.

Col. Timothy Pickering.

Under date of Feb. 3, 1829, Paine [4] Wingate wrote the son of Col. Timothy Pickering, condoling with him for the death of his father, and saying : " I hope at a period not far distant to meet him in the world of spirits of just men made perfect, where we may spend an eternity in uninterrupted joy and felicity."

Mr. Wingate's ideas on certain religious topics are given by him in the letter to Mr. Lane from which an extract has already been made. The part which preceded that extract reads :

NEW YORK, April 3[d], '90.

Dear Sir,

I received your letter of March 17th by the last post. It gave me much satisfaction to hear from you, as it has a tendency to preserve the remembrance of that friendship & intimacy, which has subsisted between us, very agreeably to me, and I hope not wholly unprofitably to either of us, for several years. This acquaintance in the course of nature cannot continue a great many years ; for we are both advanced considerably toward the close of life, and the late

numerous instances of death, mentioned in your letter, must very sensibly admonish us of that approaching event. I had not heard of any of those deaths you mention, and do particularly sympathise with you on account of the death of M^r. Clarke whom I much respected as a worthy and sincerely good man. I am naturally lead to reflect what a breach those deaths have made in our church whose numbers before were very small. From a growing indifference to the profession of religion, and an attendance on the special ordinances of it, it seems as tho' in a few years we should scarce have in many places the remains of a Christian church. I wish some of the hindrances and discouragements to a standing in the ch^h could be removed, and that sober exemplary persons, who have a competent knowledge of religion, and who in a judgement of charity we ought to think are sincerely religious, tho' not without imperfections, which we all have, might be admitted to christian fellowship, if they desired it, without complying with some terms heretofore required. What I particularly refer to is the *relation* of their experiences & conversion. Good persons may be over backward in publishing to the world, what looks like boasting of experiences that are known only to God & their own souls. There is a natural diffidence in persons especially in those who are young to come before a whole congregation, consisting of their parents, of their companions, and of the irreligious as well as the religious and there laying open what they conceive to be the secret opperations of God upon their hearts. I believe that many good persons may from mere bashfulness be discouraged from it. And is it proper that we should lay those discouragements in their way? What can we derive from making this a term of communion? Can we know their hearts that they are sincere? May they not even be deceived themselves by the power of enthusiasm & much more others who can looke only to the outward appearance. And cannot we judge better by their lives than their words? Does Jesus Christ the head of the ch^h direct that such a relation should be a necessary term of discipleship? I think not. I believe that in the apostle's days, if a man owned that he believed in Jesus & was desireous to become his disciple, he was readily admitted to the privileges of a christian. And whence have we a right to make the gate of the Christian ch^h narrower? Why should we attempt to be wiser & stricter than the law-giver of his ch^h? I wish that we may not be found hurting the cause of religion instead of promoting of it; at a time when it seems almost ready to leave us. What with deism on one hand, prevailing among the fashionable world, and enthusiasm prevailing among the weak & ignorant, I think we are in danger of loosing the substantial form of godliness. I wish that we may not by any unscriptural & useless terms of communion be the means of promoting those evils. I do not doubt that the practice in our churches was introduced by our ancestors with a pious intention, & I am sensible that it is hard to overcome the

prejudices of long usuages but it is never amiss to endeavour to get righter and with a spirit of moderation & forbearance to reform past errors & promote as far as in us lies, the increase & prosperity of Christ's ch[h], & the mutual edification of each other. You will excuse my taking up so long a letter upon this subject, as it forcibly struck my mind on reflecting on the state of our ch[h] when I read your ac count of those deaths in it. (Note *q*.)

Judge Wingate lived indeed to a "good old age." It is related that when Judge Daniel[4] Gookin died Sept. 4, 1831, aged 75, Hon. Paine[4] Wingate, then upon his tenth decade of years, being told of the death, remarked, "The Gookins are a short-lived race. I always thought Daniel would die young." Paine[4] Wingate died March 7, 1838, in the 99th year of his age, having "out-lived all who were members of college while he was there, all who were members of the House of Representatives, and of the Senate in which he had first taken his seat; and all except one (Judge Timothy Farrar of New Ipswich) who were members of the court at the time of his appoint- ment to the bench." Says Blake's Biographical Dictionary regarding him : "He was highly esteemed by his contemporaries and was ven- erated by the new generation that had grown up around him." Allowing for the change of style his age was 98 years, 9 months, 13 days. His wife lived to be 100 years, 8 months, 8 days old. Their average age was 99 years, 5 months, 25 days. Such a joint longevity of husband and wife has, it is probable, rarely if ever oc- curred. (Note *r*.)

NOTE (*q*). The Lane letters have been set from the original manu- scripts, and are, therefore, exactly as they were written. The Pickering letters have been through the hands of copyists, and have been altered in spelling and punctuation.

NOTE (*r*). When Mrs. Wingate had attained one hundred years of age the venerable lady entertained her family and friends at a birthday party and on the occasion wore the same dress in which she had been married. Only the high heeled shoes of her apparel seemed much out of the prevailing fashion of the time (1842).

CHAPTER VII.

HISTORICAL AND BIOGRAPHICAL.

Included in this chapter are historical sketches of Hon. Moses [5] Wingate, and Mary [6] Ingalls, a description of the Wingate coat-of-arms, a list of relics in the possession of members of the Wingate family, and a short article regarding the Chase-Townley Legacy.

HON. MOSES [5] WINGATE.[*]

Hon. Moses [5] Wingate was born October 25, 1769, and was the son of William [4], and the grandson of the Rev. Paine [3] Wingate of Amesbury. His mother was Mehetable Bradley, a descendant of one of the earliest English settlers in Haverhill. He departed this life June 15, 1870 at the advanced age of 100 years, 7 months and 20 days, during all of which long life his place of residence was Haverhill. In his early manhood he kept a country store on Merrimack Street, and was postmaster for twenty years, commencing about 1793, when stage coaches first began to run to Boston. In 1816 he retired from active business, and purchased the present Wingate homestead in Haverhill, it being the place on which his maternal grandfather lived, and where his mother was born. It was known as the " Bradley estate."

Mr. Wingate was a member of the Massachusetts House of Representatives in 1820-21-22 and of the Senate in 1823-24-25, and was again elected to the House in 1826-27. He was also a delegate to the constitutional convention, which began its sessions November 15, 1820, and closed Jany. 9, 1821. Among his associates in this convention were Daniel Webster, John Adams, Chief Justice Parker, Robert Rantoul, Leverett Saltonstall, Samuel Hoar and Joseph Story.

---

[*] Sketch of Hon. Moses [5] Wingate, written by his son, Rev. Charles [6] Wingate.

He held the office of Justice of the Peace for nearly half a century, and at a time when a successful administration of that office was quite as difficult and delicate a matter, as is the office of Judge in the higher courts at this time. Indeed there were few severer tests of sound judgment, sterling integrity, ready tact, and freedom from prejudice than the exercise of the office in a rural population. A near relative as he was of the Hon. Timothy Pickering, Secretary of State, whose mother was a sister of the Rev. Paine[3] Wingate, like him he took a warm interest in the political life of the nation, and was earnest in the support of what he deemed to be right. He cast a vote at every Presidential election from Washington to Grant, and prepared himself to go and vote for our renowned hero and chieftain, but his family fearing the excitement and fatigue might be too great for him, he was persuaded to forego the pleasure.

A short time before his birthday some thoughtful citizens of Haverhill proposed to have Mr. Wingate's portrait painted, and a skillful artist was employed to do the work. The painting was finished in time to be presented on his one hundredth anniversary. James H. Carlton, Esq., in behalf of the donors, made a brief address, and Mr. Wingate responded in a few words expressive of his gratitude. The portrait has been permanently placed in the Public Library. The old gentleman was an honored member of the Masonic Fraternity. He was admitted into Merrimack Lodge in 1803, and afterwards served in all its offices. The anniversary was consequently a day of unusual interest for the members of the order. A special communication of the Lodge was arranged for the day, and, at the appointed hour, a procession was formed, and, with Masonic escort, he was conveyed from his residence to the hall. Business was suspended, and the schools closed for an hour, and, at one point, the street was lined with children, who stood with heads uncovered as the old gentleman passed by. Arriving at the hall and putting on the badge of a Past Master, he was seated "in the East," and, after the usual ceremonies, his son, the Rev. Charles[6] Wingate, fifty-four years old, was introduced, and in the presence of his father took his first degree of Masonry. The chimes of Trinity Church merrily rang out "Old Hundred" as the procession passed near the Church.

During no century since the creation had history been so full of wonders as during the life-time of this venerable man. He was born in the same year as three of the most remarkable of men, Napoleon,

Wellington and Humboldt. The first had closed his almost fabulous career nearly half a century before the death of Mr. Wingate. The "Iron Duke" was laid seventeen years before, beneath the dome of St. Paul's, and Humboldt died ten years before. Most of the prominent men of the Revolution were comparatively unknown at the time of his birth. Washington was quietly engaged on his farm at Mt. Vernon, and Franklin was almost the only American of English reputation. Webster, Clay and Calhoun were unborn. George III was King of England. The younger Pitt was a boy of ten, and Fox but just at his majority. Louis XV ruled in France. Frederick the Great was reposing in Prussia, after the Seven Years' War. Catherine the II, a wicked and licentious, but able woman was ruling Russia wisely, and Austria was governed by the celebrated Maria Theresa. In Europe occurred, in his life-time, the French Revolution, with its wonderful actors and important results, and in our own land a Republic was founded, whose history has been unparalleled; and railroads, telegraphs and steamships have opened the whole world to trade, civilization and Christianity.

In the last decade of his life Mr. Wingate had, as the oldest inhabitant, that respectful, reverent affection which men so gladly pay to extreme old age, when accompanied by a genial, gentle spirit, as from early manhood to its close he had commanded in full measure the confidence and good will of all who knew him. A life sufficiently employed in business cares, and in the various offices which his fellow citizens or the government confided to his administration, and yet eminently free from anxiety ripened into a calm and lovely old age. His closing years were especially marked by a quiet unobtrusive, but devout and reverent piety. A short time before his death he received the Holy Communion at the hands of his son, and with confiding trust and childlike faith, and mind unclouded he closed a life scarcely more ripe in years than in symmetry of character, and entered into the rest of Paradise.

"THE COUNTESS."

Mary[5] Ingalls, the daughter of Henry and Abigail[4] (Wingate) Ingalls, of Haverhill, Mass., and grand-daughter of Rev. Paine[3] Wingate, has been immortalized by the memorable verses of the poet, John G. Whittier. She married, in 1806, Count Francis de

Vepart, an exile from Guadaloupe in the time of the French Revolution, and their brief but happy married life is touchingly described in "The Countess." Five of the verses read :

> An exile from the Gascon land
>   Found refuge here and rest,
> And loved, of all the village band,
>   Its fairest and its best.
>
> For her his rank aside he laid;
>   He took the hue and tone
> Of lowly life and toil, and made
>   Her simple ways his own.
>
> Ah! life is brief, though love be long;
>   The altar and the bier,
> The burial hymn and bridal song,
>   Were both in one short year!
>
> Her rest is quiet on the hill,
>   Beneath the locust's bloom;
> Far off her lover sleeps as still
>   Within his scutcheoned tomb.
>
> The Gascon lord, the village maid,
>   In death still clasp their hands;
> The love that levels rank and grade
>   Unites their severed lands.

In response to a letter of inquiry written by Charles E. L.[7] Wingate to the poet he replied as follows :

AMESBURY, 4 mo., 15, 1886.

Dear friend,
    I think, from thy letter, that I have no facts in relation to Mary Ingalls and Count Vepart which are not already known to thee. My father, who knew them both, used to tell me of them. Mary Ingalls was a very lovely girl and Vepart was a gallant and light hearted young Frenchman. Louis Phillippe visited Vepart and his friend Poyen when he was in this country.

Thy friend,
JOHN G. WHITTIER.

THE COAT-OF-ARMS.

The coat-of-arms and the crest of the Wingate family of England as given in the "General Armory of England, Scotland, Ireland and Wales," by Sir Bernard Burke, Ulster King of Arms, are, for the

Harlinton and Sharpenhoe, County of Bedford, line : Coat-of-arms,—
"Sa. a bend erm. cotised or betw. six martlets of the last" ; Crest,—
"A gate or, motto over Win." Another crest,—"A hind's head
couped ppr." The Strandridge, County Surry, coat-of-arms differs
only in making the martlets argent instead of or.

On the old records of the family in England at the Manse
House there are the words "Vi Divina," around a drawing of the
crest. This would seem to uphold the legend of the tearing down of
the castle gate "by divine power," that is, with the help of God. An
antique certificate reads :

"This coate and creaste is peculiar to Roger Wyngate of Flam-
burghe in the County of Yorke, Esq., and to his family, they may
beare with this due differences in witness whereof I have set to my
hands. Vid. Sab. a bend ermyn between 2 bendletts & 6 martletts
or, upon a Force argent & sa. a hyndes head couped or with 2
collers sa.

4 July, 1609.

RI. S^t. GEORGE HORROY.

The definitions of the various heraldic terms used in these de-
scriptions are as follows :

Differences or *Marks of Cadency* are the distinctions used to indicate the various branches or Cadets of one family.

The *Martlet*, or merlion, is the distinctive mark of the fourth
son. It is a fabulous bird shaped like a martin or swallow and
always drawn without legs, but with short tufts of feathers instead,
divided into two parts somewhat like an erasure and forming as it
were thighs.

The *Bend* is formed by two lines drawn diagonally from the
dexter chief (right upper corner) to the sinister base (left lower corner), and comprises the third part of the shield. It represents a
shoulder belt or scarf.

Cotised is a diminutive of the bend, being one-fourth of its
breadth and one-half of the width of the bendlet. The cotises are
generally borne in couples with a bend or charge between them.

Couped is the term used when the head or limb of an animal is
cut off by an even line.

Ppr. is the abbreviation for proper, and means applicable to every
animal, tree, etc., when borne of their natural color.

Or is the tint of gold. *Ermine* is the tint of the fur of ermine. *Argent* is the white tint of silver.

The heraldic description of the coat-of-arms, with its abbreviations written out would be : Sable a bend ermine cotised or between six martlets of the last tint (i. e. or) ; and would mean, Sable, or black, in color, with an ermine colored belt extending diagonally across it and with narrower gold belts on either side of the ermine belt,—the belts lying between six golden martlets.

The crests fully described are : 1. A gate of gold with the motto "Win" over it. 2. A hind's head evenly cut off and colored the shade of the animal itself.

ANTIQUE RELICS.

A number of relics belonging to the Wingates of early date are in the possession of various members of the family.

Miss Eliza Gookin[7] Thornton, of Magnolia, Mass., has : 1. A china jar which belonged to Col. Joshua[2] Wingate. 2. A pair of smoking tongs which belonged to Col. Joshua[2]. 3. A mourning ring in memory of Hon. John Phillips ob., 1795, given to —— Wingate. 4. A "Tobacco boy that belonged to John W., of Hampton, N. H., H. U., 1744, brother of Love W., wife of Rev. Nath. Gookin, of North Hampton, N. H., H. U., 1731, my great grandparents. It was in possession of their son, Hon. Daniel Gookin, whose son John Wingate Gookin, Esq., my uncle, had it, and from him, after his decease, it came to me this Sept. 17, 1857, John Wingate Thornton." This inscription copied from the inner lid of the box.

Prof. Charles F[7]. Richardson, of Dartmouth College, has : 1. The desk of Joseph[4] Wingate (son of Rev. Paine[3]), marked "J. W., 1777". 2. Rev. Paine[3] Wingate's will, dated Jan. 1, 1777, and also the will of Richard Paine, 1708, whom he takes to have been Rev. Paine[3]'s maternal grandfather. 3. Rev. Paine[3]'s manuscript record of the doings of his church from 1726 to 1782.

Jeremiah Y[6]. Wingate, of Dover, has : 1. An old gun used in the Revolutionary war, and a side-board reconstructed from an old case of drawers, once the property of Captain Moses[4] Wingate, son of John[3]. 2. A cream brocade satin wedding dress, once worn by Joanna, the wife of Capt Moses[4].

Charles E. L.[7] Wingate, of Boston, has two books : 1. Ovid's Metamorphoses, pub. in London in 1779, on the cover of which is written "John Wingate's book, April 1, 1794." 2. Homer's Iliad, pub. in London in 1768, on the title page of which is written, "Paine Wingate, 1792, Ea Libris Gilberti Tenneret, A. D. 1772."

Rev. Daniel W.[7] Waldron, of Boston, has the family Bible of Frederick[5] (William[4], Paine[3]), and Hannah (Paige) Wingate.

Henry Lane, of Stratham, [not of the Wingate family] has the six letters written to Deacon Samuel Lane by Hon. Paine[4] Wingate. They are very well preserved and the writing is in a good, round hand, perfectly legible.

CHASE—TOWNLEY LEGACY.

Periodically during the past forty years a flurry of excitement has spread among the heirs of the reported "Lord Townley estate," of England, as the hopes of the distribution of vast property have arisen. The latest development was in 1885 when at a meeting of the Western heirs it was stated that the property then amounted to $800,000,000 besides 400,000 acres of land mostly in villages and cities, and that the English government had decided, by Act of Parliament, to pay over the sum. At this Western meeting a large number of Chases, Lawrences and Townleys gathered from nearly every State beyond the Mississippi, but as there was great uncertainty regarding the matter, no definite action was taken. Other meetings were afterwards called in other sections of the country, but these were all given up on account of the report of Minister Phelps of England, to the home government. He declared that the only "Townley estate" in England lay in York and Lancaster, and that that had been for a long time in possession of its lawful proprietors. The Act of Parliament in question, merely related to the settlement of an amicable suit between the possessors. Many heirs disputed Mr. Phelps's statements, but the whole matter was dropped for the time at least. It is claimed that there are two branches of the Wingate family who have heirship in this prospective wealth, the descendants of Rev. Stephen Chase who married Jane[3] Wingate, daughter of Col. Joshua[2] Wingate, and the descendants of Sarah Piper who married Deacon John[5] Wingate, the son of Hon. Paine[4], grandson of Rev. Paine[3], and great-grandson of Col. Joshua[2]

Wingate. The genealogy of Rev. Stephen Chase can be found in the "Genealogical Memoirs of the Chase family" by George B. Chase. A number of articles regarding the legacy were published in the Boston Daily *Journal*, during the month of December, 1885.

Although the stories of the legacy differ somewhat, and although many skeptics declare that the whole is a fabrication and that no "Lord Townley estate" ever existed, the following version is at least interesting: It is said that Sir Richard Townley had a daughter (or a sister) Mary who married a John Lawrence and emigrated to America. In this country she was lost sight of so that on the Knight's death, no trace of his relative could be obtained. Accordingly the vast wealth which he had inherited was taken under charge by the English government, in the absence of any heirs in England. While it is now claimed by many Lawrences that they are the rightful heirs, it is also claimed by the Chases that all rights in the property were transferred to Robert Chase who in turn left it to his four sons, Robert, William, Thomas and Aquila. The three latter sons came to this country and settled in New England as early as 1636, Thomas and Aquila being among the original settlers of Hampton, N. H. Aquila afterwards removed to Newbury, Mass.

CHAPTER VIII.

DESCENDANTS OF JOHN².

The genealogical tables in this chapter give the descendants, in both the male and female lines, of John² the oldest son of John¹, and in the next chapter of Joshua², the youngest son. The family ilnes of the other children of John¹ are not known, and in nearly every case have probably become extinct so far as the name of Wingate is concerned, for every Wingate yet heard from, except the Kentucky family, can be connected with the branches of John² or of Joshua².

The history of the first three generations having been fully given in the preceding chapters these tables begin with the fourth generation. But for the sake of convenient reference a diagram of the earlier branches is appended on page 100.

In the genealogical tables the descendants of each grand child of John² and of Joshua² are mentioned in due order so that all immediate relatives are practically together, being on immediately succeeding pages. Besides the use of small figures after the name, which denote the generation from John¹, the fourth generation is distinguished by names printed in capitals (JOHN⁴), the fifth generation by small capitals (JOHN⁵), the sixth generation by italics, indented (*John⁶*), the seventh, eighth and other generations by small letters, indented position. The method of finding one's connection with the line can be best illustrated by an example. Suppose Waldo H⁸. Wingate wishes to trace his descent. He looks in the Wingate index for Waldo H.⁸, and if there should be two or three of the same Christian name he would distingush his own by the date of birth, 1873. Then looking at the page given by the index he finds his name indented in the small letters. The first name above his marked by the preceding generation number (⁷) is Henry Clay⁷ and this he recognizes as his father's Christian name ; running his eye back he finds that the first name above marked by generation num-

TABLE IV.

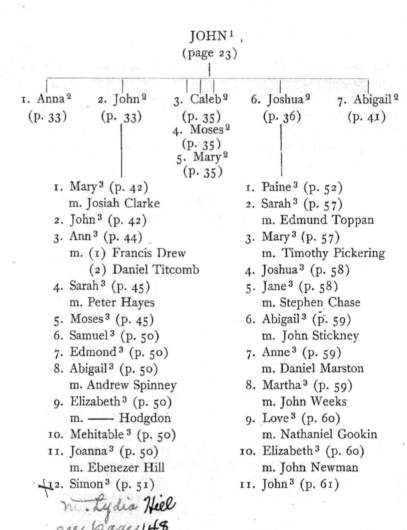

JOHN¹
(page 23)

1. Anna²   2. John²   3. Caleb²   6. Joshua²   7. Abigail²
(p. 33)   (p. 33)   (p. 35)   (p. 36)   (p. 41)
                            4. Moses²
                            (p. 35)
                            5. Mary²
                            (p. 35)

1. Mary³ (p. 42)   1. Paine³ (p. 52)
   m. Josiah Clarke   2. Sarah³ (p. 57)
2. John³ (p. 42)   m. Edmund Toppan
3. Ann³ (p. 44)   3. Mary³ (p. 57)
   m. (1) Francis Drew   m. Timothy Pickering
      (2) Daniel Titcomb   4. Joshua³ (p. 58)
4. Sarah³ (p. 45)   5. Jane³ (p. 58)
   m. Peter Hayes   m. Stephen Chase
5. Moses³ (p. 45)   6. Abigail³ (p. 59)
6. Samuel³ (p. 50)   m. John Stickney
7. Edmond³ (p. 50)   7. Anne³ (p. 59)
8. Abigail³ (p. 50)   m. Daniel Marston
   m. Andrew Spinney   8. Martha³ (p. 59)
9. Elizabeth³ (p. 50)   m. John Weeks
   m. —— Hodgdon   9. Love³ (p. 60)
10. Mehitable³ (p. 50)   m. Nathaniel Gookin
11. Joanna³ (p. 50)   10. Elizabeth³ (p. 60)
    m. Ebenezer Hill   m. John Newman
12. Simon³ (p. 51)   11. John³ (p. 61)

m. Lydia Hill
see page 148

ber (⁶) is the italicised *George Washington*⁶, his grandfather, and that the first name above that marked by the generation number (⁵) is the small cap CALEB ⁵, his great-grandfather. The first name above that marked by the generation number (⁴) is JOHN ⁴, his great-great-grandfather, and the three names above this show that JOHN⁴ was the son of John ³, and the grandson of John ². For the history of these earlier ancestors the searcher looks on appropriate pages, as denoted by the figures in the diagram on page 100. If the searcher should be a descendant through a daughter, he looks first at the index of surnames other than Wingate, and in that finds his starting place in the genealogical lists. In the tables, whenever a daughter marries, the name of her husband is given in italics, so that every change of name can be easily caught by the eye as it runs over the page.

Special Explanations :—b. means born ; d. means died ; m. means married ; unm. means unmarried ; dau. means daughter ; s. p. means sine prole (without issue) ; H. U. means Harvard University, D. C. Dartmouth College, Bowd. C. Bowdoin College. Most of the dates which pertain to the changing period in the calendar refer to the Old Style, and this fact may explain any deviation from dates given in other books in the New Style. All the towns and cities mentioned are in New Hampshire, unless it is specially stated otherwise,—except that the well-known cities are given without their State location.

JOHN¹.

JOHN².

MARY³.

m. Josiah *Clark*, of Kittery, Me., and had one child.

I. JOHN⁴ (Capt.) b. Febuary 16, 1718–19, d. January 7, 1800
    m. Sarah⁴ Pickering, (b. Jan. 28, 1730, d. Nov. 21, 1826)
    dau. of Deacon Timothy and Mary³ (Wingate) Pickering, of
    Salem. He was "master of a ship in yᵉ London trade."
    Lived in Salem, Mass., and had five children.
    [See Sarah⁴, Mary³, Joshua².]

JOHN¹.

JOHN².

JOHN³.

m. (1) Dorothy Tebbets, (2) Sarah Ricker, and had thirteen
children.

I. JOHN⁴, b. May 5, 1719, d. March 15, 1776.
    m. as early as 1748, Elizabeth Cushing, (b. Jan. 5, 1725, d.
    1811) daughter of Rev. Jonathan Cushing, of Dover. He
    moved to Madbury and lived next above Tobias Evans.
    John⁴ was a man of standing and property, "Squire John."
    His will, made March 14, 1776, gave to wife Elizabeth the
    one quarter part of produce of farm during her widowhood;
    also household furniture, two cows, nine sheep; also to wife
    and daughters Dorothy, Elizabeth, Deborah, Hannah, Mary
    and Abigail the northeasterly part of dwelling house; to
    daughters each £10; to son Jonathan seventy acres of land
    in Rochester; to son Aaron sixty acres of land in Barrington,
    on which Paul Hayes, Jr. was living; to son Ebenezer fifty-
    two acres in Rochester; to son Caleb, ninety-eight acres in
    Barrington, purchased by Joshua Foss, Jr.; to son John all
    other estate, also silver tankard and four leather chairs.
    John was executor. Proved May 8, 1776. John⁴ and Eliz-
    abeth had eleven children:

1. DOROTHY[5], b. Sept. 4, 1744, d. Aug. 1842 [? '22].

    m. as second wife, Moses *Hayes*, (b. June 15, 1750) far-mer, and lived at Farmington. They had five children :

    1. *Elizabeth*[6].

        m. James *Downes*, of Farmington, and had children :

        1. James[7].

        2. John[7].

        3. James[7].

        4. Mary[7].

            m. ——— *Pinkham*.

        5. Jeremiah[7].

        6. Dorothy Laura[7].

    2. *Mary*[6], b. June 2, 1782, d. s. p.

        m. Joseph *Buzzell*, of New Durham.

    3. *John*[6], twin to James[6], b. April 5, 1785.

        m. ———, lived in Farmington and had :

        1. Moses Wingate[7] (name changed to Wingate[7]). b. Aug. 4, 1823, d. Oct. 16, 1877.

            m. Aug. 22, 1849, Abby Maria Bowles.

            Lived in Providence, R. I., and had :

            (*a*) Charles Austin[8], b. Dec. 2, 1850, d. Aug. 15, '69.

            (*b*) Amy Lee[8], b. July 1, 1852.

            (*c*) Henry Wingate[8], b. July 5, 1855.

                m. Nancy Baker, of Bristol, R. I., and had :

                1. Francis Wingate[9].

                2. Arnold Lee[9].

            (*d*) Francis Harrison[8], b. Jly. 12,1858, d. Apr. 13,'81.

            (*e*) Frederic[8], b. April 1, 1860.

                Lived in Providence, R. I.

            (*f*) George Aborn[8], b. Nov. 23, 1862, d. Jly 23, '65.

            (*g*) Mary Manton[8], b. May 21, 1866.

            (*h*) Sarah Alice[8], b. May 11, 1871.

        2. Martha Jane[7], b. ———, d. young.

    4. *James*[6], twin to John[6], b. April 5, 1785.

    5. *Stephen*[6], b. Oct. 29, 1788, d. young.

2.   ELIZABETH[5], b. Aug. 16, 1746. d. s. p. April 20, 1837.
  m. 1796-97, as his second wife, Joseph *Hayes*, (b. May 1,
  1746, d. July 20, 1816.)   Lived in Strafford.

3.   DEBORAH[5], b. 1748-49, d. Sept. 18, 1838.
  m. July 18, 1776, Aaron *Hayes*, of Dover, farmer, (b. Sept.
  19, 1752, d. Feb. 14, 1816,) and had four children :

  1.   *John*[6], b. June 28, 1777.
    m. late in life ————.   Was a farmer in Dover, and "one
    of the pillars of the Congregational Church of that town
    for many years."   After marrying he sold his farm and
    moved to Boston where he lived the rest of his life.

  2.   *Jonathan*[6], b. Oct. 11, 1778, d. a young man.
    m. Sophia Wyatt.   Lived in Dover, and had :

    1.   Charles[7], b. ————, d. 1837-38.
      m. ————, and had three children.   Lived in
      Bangor, Me.
    2.   ———— [7].

  3.   *Paul*[6], b. Oct. 16, 1780.
    m. Mary[6] Wingate, (b. June 30, 1782,) his cousin,
    dau. of Jonathan[5] Wingate, of Durham.   Lived in Ports-
    mouth and had, besides four children who died young :

    1.   Deborah Wingate[7].
    2.   Jonathan Wingate[7].
    3.   Jacob Odell[7],
    4.   Mary Elizabeth[7].
    5.   John Paul[7].
    6.   Sarah Ann[7].
    7.   Lydia[7].

  4.   *Lydia*[6], b. March 25, 1784.
    m. late in life John *Nutter*, of Milton.

4.   HANNAH[5], b. August 25, 1751, d. unm., January 30, 1841.
  Lived in Weare.

5. JOHN[5], b. April 19, 1754, d. September 16, 1839.

m. Sarah Garland, daughter of Deacon John Garland, of Barrington. Lived in Madbury and Weare. He was delegate from Madbury at the Third Provincial Congress which met at Exeter, April 21, 1775, just after the Battle of Lexington, to consult on measures "most expedient to be taken at this alarming crisis." It was immediately voted to send troops to assist their Massachusetts brethren against the British. That John[5] Wingate took action favorable to the wishes of the people is testified by his return, May 17, 1775, to the Fourth Provincial Congress at Exeter. He was a Selectman in 1786. He had seven children:

1. *John[6]*, b. June 26, 1776, d. August 22, 1862.

m., 1800, Mary Cate, of Barrington. Lived in Farmington and Northwood [See History of Northwood], and had:

1. John Cate[7], b. October 15, 1802, d. Nov. 26, 1867.

m., June 21, 1832, Eliza Hayes (d. March 8, 1872), dau. of Ezekiel Hayes, of Milton. Lived in Farmington, Northwood, Tilton, Janesville, Wis., and had:

(*a*) Mary Jane[8], b. September 17, 1833.

Lived in Minneapolis, Minn.

(*b*) John Hayes[8], b. September 18, 1835.

m., October 12, 1858, Anna M. Knowles (b. Oct. 12, 1839), dau. of William Knowles, of Northwood, lived in Janesville, Wis., and Minneapolis, Minn., and had:

1. Charles Hayes[9], b. December 22, 1859.

m., Jan. 2, 1882, Ida Louise Bisbee, (b. Aug. 25, 1864,) dau. of John Bisbee of Minneapolis, Minn., and had:

Nellie Cora[10], b. August 15, 1883.

John Frank[10], b. February 8, 1885.

2. Nellie Jane[9], b. Apr. 24, 1861, d. Oct. 8, 1864.

3. Henry Knowles[9], b. May 23, 1865.

4. William Snell[9], b. March 28, 1868.

5. Fannie May[9], b. September 16, 1869.

(c)   Stephen[8], b. June 16, 1838, d. January 6, 1857.
(d)   Henry[8], b. June 29, 1842, d. July 4, 1863.
        Shot at the Siege of Vicksburg.
(e)   Anne Eliza[8], b. Dec. 13, 1844, d. Aug. 10, 1871.
(f)   Carrie[8], b. August 17, 1848.
(g)   Charles Elliot[8], b. Dec. 15, 1850, d. Oct. 16, 1856.

2.   Sarah[7], b. December 19, 1803, d. July, 1863.
        m., Jan., 1825, John *Hayes*, of Milton (d. 1847),
        lived in Rochester, and had :
    (a)   Mehitable[8], b. June, 1826.
            m. George W. *Whitehouse*, of Farmington, (d.
            1856,) and had :
        1.   Mary F.[9]. b. 1850, d. 1876.
    (b)   John Wingate[8], b. June, 1828, d. 1860.
            m. Sarah A. Currier, of Gonic, and had :
        1.   Annie E.[9].
                m. Alfred *Taft*, of Hopkinton, Mass., and
                had five children :
                    Fred[10].
                    Lillian A.[10].
                    Grace[10].
                    Florence[10].
                    Clarence[10].
    (c)   Henry[8], b. May, 1835.
    (d)   Mary F.[8], b. March, 1840.
            m. Franklin *McDuffie*, of Rochester, (d.
            1880), and had :
        1.   John Edgar[9].
        2.   Willis[9].

3.   Apphia[7], b. May 24, 1805.
        Lived in Portsmouth.

4.   Mary[7], b. March 28, 1807.
        m. Capt. Joseph *Grace*, and lived in Portsmouth.

5.   Caroline[7], b. January 18, 1810.
        m. Samuel *Wallace*, and lived in Concord.

6.   Charles[7], b. July 22, 1816.
        m. twice, and lived in Northwood.

2. *Stephen*[6], b. Aug. 24, 1778, d. April 15, 1784.

3. *Benjamin*[6], b. Nov. 27, 1781, d. Aug. 14, 1799.

4. *Stephen*[6], born November 5, 1784, died March 2, 1882.
    m. Abigail Cate, sister to Mary Cate who married his
    brother John, and after several changes settled in Laco-
    nia, where he lived about twenty years ; then moved to
    Plainfield and finally to Rockford, Ill.   He had :

    1. Benjamin[7], born 1808, died 1875.
        m. Mary Rogers, of Bangor, Me.   Went into mer-
        cantile business in Bangor in 1831–32 ; on account of
        ill health gave it up and went to California.   After-
        wards lived in Rockford, Ill.   He had :

        (*a*) Charles E.[8].
              m. ———, lived in Des Moines, Iowa, and
              had four children.

        (*b*) Walter[8].
              m. ——— and lived at Oak Park, Ill., near
              Chicago.

        (*c*) Emily[8].
              m. ——— *Blackmer*, of Oak Park, Ill., and
              had two sons.

        (*d*) ———[8].

        (*e*) ———[8].

    2. Charles[7], b. 1813.
        m. ———.   Settled in New York City, 1833.   In-
        surance broker since 1860.   Had children :

        (*a*) George[8].
              m. ———.   Lawyer.   Had two sons and a
              daughter.

        (*b*) J. Phelps[8].
              Clerk of Superior Court.

        (*c*) Charles F.[8].
              Journalist, and writer for "Independent,"
              Sanitary Engineer.

        (*d*) ———[8] (daughter).

        (*e*) ———[8] (daughter).

        (*f*) ———[8] (daughter).

5. *Sarah*[6], b. Nov. 21, 1786, d. Nov. 19, 1804.

6. *Moses*[6], b. July 7, 1789, d. 1861-62.
    m. four times (3) Abigail Adams, of Dover, (b. 1808-09, d. May 20, 1846). He had a son Benjamin, of Boston, and a daughter by his second wife, three sons and a daughter by his third wife, and a son, Charles H.[7], (d. aged 21,) by his fourth wife. Moses[6] lived in Troy, N. Y., and Bangor. Me.

7. *Aaron*[6], b. Dec. 21, 1796, d. Sept. 2, 1880.
    m. Aug. 31, 1826, Phœbe T. Lamos, of Dover. Lived in Weare, Me., and Worcester, Mass.   Had :

    1. Sarah[7], b. Nov. 27, 1827, d. Feb. 23, 1849.

    2. Ann Susan[7], b. Jan. 12, 1830.
        m. —— *Rice*, of Shrewsbury, Mass., a farmer.

    3. George[7], b. July 12, 1832.
        Lived in Worcester, Mass.

    4. Martha A.[7], b. Feb. 6, 1836, d. Feb. 13, 1837.

    5. Elizabeth C.[7], b. May 31, 1841.
        m. —— *Cook*, of Worcester, Mass.

    6. Emma Gertrude[7], b. Jan. 16, 1844.
        m. E. J. *Putnam*, of Worcester, Mass.

6. MARY[5], b. June 26, 1756.
    m. (1) Pierce *Powers*, an army officer who died s. p. soon after marriage, (2) Gen. Richard *Furber*, of Farmington. Gen. Furber lived to a great age ; his wife survived him one year. They had five children :

    1. *Richard*[6], b. June 11, 1787, d. young.

    2. *Pierce Powers*[6], (Major) b. Aug., 1788, d. —— 28, 1870.
        m. (1) Mehitable Winckley, of Barrington, (2) Mrs. Ford. He served under Capt. (afterwards Gen.) John A. Dix during the War of 1812, and shortly after was promoted to the command of a brigade stationed at Fort Constitution, Portsmouth. He was in the service some 15 months. Lived in Maine, in Minnesota, and in Wiscon-

sin. Soon after removing to St. Paul, Minn., 1853, he married as second wife a widow named Ford. In St. Paul he was Justice of the Peace, Overseer of the Poor, and Actuary at Oakland cemetery. He was at the time of his death, probably, the oldest member of the Masonic fraternity in the United States, having joined Humane Lodge, No. 21, of N. H., in 1811. "He was possessed of indomitable energy, great independence of character, a high sense of justice, and by those who knew him best of a warm and loving heart." He had :

1. Mary Wingate [7], b. —— ——, d. Jan. 1834.
    m. Allen *Munro*, of Milo, Me., and had :
    (a) ——[8] (son).
    (b) ——[8] (daughter).

2. Joseph Warren [7].

3. Theodore [7].

4. Samuel Wingate [7].
    Lived in Cottage Grove, Minn.

5. Richard [7], b. ——, d. very young.

6. Olive Wingate [7].

7. Mehitable [7].

8. John Pierce [7].

3. *Richard* [6], b. April 3, 1790.

4. *Elizabeth* [6], b. May 4, 1791, d. Dec. 20, 1831.
    m. March 15, 1826, Dr. *McCrillis*, and had five children.

5. *John Wingate* [6].
    m. ——, lived in Farmington and Rochester, and had :

1. Elizabeth Cushing [7], b. March 7, 1824.

2. Charles Henry [7], b. Sept. 12, 1825.

3. Edwin Pierce [7], b. Aug. 26, 1829.

4. Martha Nelson [7], b. Feb. 25, 1832.

7. JONATHAN ⁵, b. November 26, 1758, d. March 20, 1821.
  m. Sarah Drew (b. July 8, 1761), dau. of Silas Drew, of Barrington. Lived in Durham, N. H., and Parsonsfield, Me.,
  and had seven children :

  1. *Mary* ⁶, b. June 30, 1782.
    m. Paul ⁶ *Hayes* (b. Oct. 16, 1780), her cousin, of Ports-
    mouth, son of Deborah ⁵ Wingate Hayes, and had twelve
    children.

  2. *Elizabeth* ⁶, b. December 31, 1785, d. s. p.
    m., Oct. 13, 1816, Lot *Wedgewood*, of Parsonsfield, Me.

  3. *Simon* ⁶, b. March 18, 1788, d. September 5, 1830.
    m. ———, lived in Dover, and had, besides seven others :

    1. Anna Maria ⁷.

    2. Sarah Elizabeth ⁷.

    3. Dexter ⁷.

  4. *Jonathan* ⁶, b. June 29, 17—.
    m. ———, lived in Oxford, Mass., and had children.

  5. *Sarah* ⁶, b. July 5, 1797, d. April 7, 1830.

  6. *Hannah* ⁶, b. May 20, 1801.
    m., Jan. 29, 1828, Asa *Winckley*, of Barrington, and had :

    1. Jeremiah ⁷.

    2. Francis Stephen ⁷.

    3. Jonathan Wingate ⁷.

    4. William Wyman ⁷.

    5. ——— ⁷.

    6. ——— ⁷.

  7. *Lydia* ⁶, b. April 8, 1806, d. July 15, 1808.

8. ABIGAIL ⁵, b. November 6, 1761, d. April, 1848.
  m., April 11, 1728, Ephraim *Twombly* (d. March 15, 1818),
  of Sebec, Me., Dover and Milton, N. H., son of Ralph
  Twombly, of Dover. They had seven children :

1. *Susannah* [6].

   m. Jeremiah *Waterhouse*, of Barrington, farmer, and had :

   1. Maria [7], b. ——, d. young.
   2. Timothy [7].
   3. Alexander [7].

      m. Lucy Cate, and had :

      (*a*) Susan [8].
      (*b*) Mary [8].

         m. Alphonso B. *Locke*, and had :
         1. Edith [9].
         2. George [9].

      (*c*) George [8].
   4. William [7] (Dr.).

      m. Martha W. Buzzell, and lived in Barrington.
   5. Jeremiah [7].

      m. Martha Ann Winckley, and had :

      (*a*) William Edwin [8].

         m. Elizabeth S. Hale, and had :
         1. Jeremiah H. [9].

2. *Mary* [6], b. 1783–84, d. September, 1878.
   m. —— *Witham*, of Sebec, Me.

3. *Aaron* [6].

   Accidentally drowned in the Piscataqua river, aged 30.

4. *John* [6].

5. *Abigail* [6].

   m. William *Howard*, of Sebec, Me., and had children.

6. *Eliza* [6], b. August, 1805, d. January 30, 1885.

   m. George *Waterhouse*, of Durham, and had, besides four children who died in childhood :

   1. Eliza Ruth [7].

      m. —— *Heriman*, of Foxcroft, Me.

7. *James* [6].

   m. (1) Betsy Waterhouse, of Barrington, (2) Meribe Turner, of Foxcroft, Me., and lived in Foxcroft and South Dover, Me.

9.   AARON⁵ (Capt.), b. August 1, 1764.

m. Ruth Stackpole, of Somersworth, and lived in Portsmouth. August 12, 1796, he sailed on a voyage from Portsmouth, and was never heard of afterwards.   He had three children :

1.   *James*⁶ (Capt.), b. ————, d. s. p.

m. ————, and lived in Portsmouth.   Was a sea captain.

2.   *Aaron*⁶.

m. ————, lived in Boston, and had :

1.   Caroline⁷.

2.   Aaron⁷, b. ————, d. young.

3.   James⁷.

Lived in Lowell, Mass.

4.   Charles⁷.

5.   ————⁷, b.————, d. in childhood.

6.   ————⁷,   "   "

7.   ————⁷,   "   "

3.   *Charles*⁶, b. ————, d. an infant.

10.   EBENEZER⁵, b. January 16, 1767.

m. Hannah Edgerly, of Farmington, lived in Wolfboro, and had seven children :

1.   *John*⁶, b. ————, d. a young man.

Died at Franconia.

2.   *Jeremiah*⁶.

m. ———— and lived in Newburyport, Mass.

3.   *Elizabeth*⁶.

m. ————.

4.   *Mary*⁶.

m. ————.

5.   ————⁶, b. ——, d. in childhood.

6.   ————⁶,   "   "

7.   ————⁶,   "   "

11. CALEB[5], born April 3, 1769, died June 18, 1850.

m. Oct. 30, 1799, Elizabeth Palmer (b. Sept. 28, 1784, d. Aug. 13, 1857), dau. of William Palmer, of Milton. Lived in Sebec, Me., and had fourteen children:

1. *Susan Twombly*[6], b. April 24, 1802, d. Nov. 21, 1870.
   m. 1823, Samuel *Palmer* (b. ——— ——, d. Dec. 25, 1856,) of Dover, Me., and had:

   1. Nancy Wingate[7], b. May 24, 1824.
      Lived in Dover, Me.

   2. Caleb Orin[7].
      m. Amanda Thompson, of Dover, Me, and lived in Dover.

   3. Ira Franklin[7].
      m. Esther ———. Farmer in Dover, Me.

   4. Samuel Allen[7].
      Merchant of Dover, Me.

   5. Sarah Elizabeth[7].
      Lived in Dover, Me. Was a war nurse in the Washington Hospital under Miss Dix during the Rebellion.

   6. Charles Wingate[7].
      m. Nellie Newell. Farmer in Dover, Me. Had:
      (*a*) Susie[8].

   7. Augustus B.[7].

2. *Nancy Palmer*[6], born February 27, 1804.
   m. (1) June 26, 1834, Benjamin *Palmer* (b. 1806–07, d. Oct 16, 1838) of Lincoln, Me., (2) July 10, 1845, Frederick *Wingate*. By her first husband she had two children and by her second one child:

   1. Benjamin Wingate[7], b. Dec. 3, 1835, d. Oct. 31, 1841.

   2. Amos Tappan[7], b. Oct. 29, 1837, d. March 2, 1864.

   3. George Frederick[7], b. May 22, 1846.
      m. Dec. 4, 1865, Martha Jane Groesbeck. Farmer in Sidney, Neb.

3. *Caleb Cushing*⁶, b. Feb. 26, 1806, d. April 21, 1881.
    m. Sept. 18, 1832 Sarah Boardman Tappan (b. 1811–12,
    d. Dec. 9, 1833,) dau. of Amos Tappan, of Bangor, Me.
    Farmer of Sebec, Me., and had :

   1. Hannah Elizabeth⁷, b. Dec. 1, 1833.
    m. Feb. 28, 1860, Charles Edward *Paine.*   Lived
    in Sacramento, Cal., and had :
    (*a*) Sarah Wingate⁸, b. Nov. 19, 1861.
    (*b*) Charles Wilde⁸, b. March 22, 1863.
    (*c*) Robert Allen⁸, b. April 26, 1866.

4. *Eliza Cushing*⁶, b. Nov. 5, 1807.
    m. John Adam *Munsell*, lived in Scranton, Vt., and had :

   1. ——⁷, b. Dec. 31, 1840.

   2. Washington Wingate⁷ (Prof.), b. Feb. 19, 1842.
    m. Mrs. Martha Barney, widow of Col. E. I. Bar-
    ney.   Was a musician in the Civil War.

   3. William Henry⁷, b Dec. 9, 1843.
    m. June 14, 1870, Antha M. Warren, of St. Albans,
    Vt. Was in the Vt. Cavalry in the Civil War.
    Dentist.   Lived in Wells River, Vt., and had :
    (*a*) Ella E.⁸, b. May 17, 1872.
    (*b*) Lottie⁸, b. July 7, 1874.
    (*c*) Hattie⁸, b. Jan., 1877.
    (*d*) John Wingate⁸, b. June 27, 1878.
    (*e*) Willie Warren⁸, b. Jan., 1883, d. Sept. 18, 1885.
    (*f*) Antha⁸, b. July, 1884.

   4. Charlotte Elizabeth⁷, b. Oct. 19, 1845.
    m. Oct. 19, 1868, Eugene O. *Rousseau*, of High-
    gate, Vt., and had :
    (*a*) Arthur Munsell⁸, b. March 11, 1876.
    (*b*) Alta Mabel⁸, b. Oct. 12, 1881.

   5. John Edward⁷, b. Nov. 16, 1850, d. Jan. 3, 1854.

5. *William Palmer*[6], b. Oct. 30, 1809.

> m. Aug. 16, 1836, Phœbe Cook, of Newburyport, Mass.
> Lived in Bangor, Me. Was Custom House official 11
> or 12 years, Street Commissioner etc. Had :

> 1. ———[7] (son), b. ———, d. in infancy.

> 2. Helen Juliet[7].
>> m. William P. *Hubbard*, merchant of Bangor, Me.,
>> and had :
>> (*a*) Alice[8].
>> (*b*) William Wingate[8].
>> (*c*) Pierce[8].

> 3. Martha[7].
>> m. Frank W. *Cram*, of Bangor, Me., and had :
>> (*a*) Franklin[8].
>> (*b*) ———[8] (girl), b. ———, d. 1881.

> 4. Ada[7].
>> m. Charles B. *Wyman*, merchant of Bangor, Me.,
>> and had :
>> (*a*) ———[8] (girl), b. 1874-75, d. 1881.
>> (*b*) John[8], b. march 9, 1880, d. February 25, 1881.

> 5. Emma Florence[7].
>> m. Charles F. *Bragg*, of Bangor, Me., and had one
>> boy and three girls; one of the girls died young,
>> February, 1881.

> 6. Agnes[7].
>> m. Silas B. *Treat*, commercial agent at Brooklyn,
>> N. Y.

6. *Charles Dillimore*[6] (Col.), b. November 2, 1811.

> m., Jan. 1, 1841, Nancy Burns Greely, dau. of Daniel
> Greely, of Foxcroft, Me. Lived in Bangor, Sebec and
> Dover, Me., and in Sacramento, Cal. Had :

> 1. Anna[7], b. January 1, 1842, d. February 11, 1864.

> 2. Luella Isadore[7], b. January 7, 1844.
>> m., Dec. 3, 1867, Rev. Richard *Rosinthall*, of Berlin,

Germany, and settled in Orange, N. J. He was pastor of the First German Presbyterian Church. Had:

(*a*)   Anna Elenora⁸, b. November 29, 1868.

(*b*)   Morrits Greely⁸, b. February 1, 1870.

(*c*)   Edith Lancaster⁸, b. November 25, 1873.

(*d*)   Clarence Howard⁸, b. March 26, 1875, d. February 28, 1876.

7. *George Washington*⁶, b. Dec. 19, 1813, d. Sept. 15, 1878. m., Nov. 30, 1841, Catherine Knight. Farmer in Sebec, Me. Had:

1. George Evans⁷, b. Oct. 14, 1842, d. February, 1884.

2. Lizzie Catherine⁷, b. January 29, 1844.
       m., Dec. 8, 1867, Isaac W. *Hanscom*, and had:

       (*a*)   Henry W.⁸, b. April 11, 1874.

       (*b*)   ——⁸ (girl), b. 1878.

3. Henry Clay⁷, b. August 1, 1847.
       m., Nov. 15, 1872, Mary Morrison, and had:
       (*a*)   Waldo H.⁸, b. August 29, 1873.
       (*b*)   Caleb Cushing⁸, b. March 28, 1875.
       (*c*)   George Washington⁸, b. January 16, 1877.
       (*d*)   Nellie Mary⁸, b. August 14, 1878.

4. Harriet Louise⁷, b. September 29, 1849.
       m., January 1, 1876, John Quincy *Livermore*, farmer.

5. Charles E.⁷, b. October 20, 1855.
       m. —— Johnston, and had:
       (*a*)   ——⁸ (son).

8. *John Jay*⁶, b. December 18, 1815.
       m., Feb. 4, 1868, Anna Davis. Lived in Bangor and Portland, Me.

9. *Harriet Newell*[6], b. March 26, 1818.
   Lived in Carson City, Nev.

10. *Aaron M.*[6], b. March 14, 1820.
    Lived in Bangor until 1851, when he went to California.
    In 1862 helped found a mining town, and in 1863 a city
    government, and served as Selectman and Alderman;
    city was afterwards disincorporated, the mines having
    worked out.

11. *Daniel Palmer*[6], b. Sept. 2, 1822, d. Dec. 2, 1884.
    m. Feb. 15, 1859, Agnes Cargill, dau. of Henry
    Cargill. Lived in Bangor, Me.; was Street Commis-
    sioner. Had:

    1. Grace Agnes[7].

    2. Harry Cargill[7].

12. *Deborah Hayes*[6], b. Oct. 9, 1824.
    m. June 1, 1850, William A. B. *Cook*, of Bangor, Me.,
    California and Carson City, Nev. Had:

    1. William Henry McCrillis[7], b. July 2, 1852.
       m. Oct. 25, 1882, Emelyn Susan Walter. Lived in
       Dayton, Nev., and had:
       (*a*) William Walter[8], b. Ag. 30, 1883, d. Ag. 31, '83.
       (*b*) —— [8], (dau.) b. Oct. 15, 1884, d. Jan. 22, 1885.

    2. Harriet Wingate[7], b. Jan. 20, 1854.
       m. May 14, 1879, Franklin Jenkins *McCullough*.
       Lived in Glenbrook, Douglas Co., Nev., and had:
       (*a*) Franklin Jenkins[8], b. Aug. 21, 1882.

13. *Richard Pike*[6], b. June 16, 1827.
    Lived in Bangor, Me., and San Questin, Cal.

14. *Amos Tappan*[6], b. Dec. 21, 1829, d. Feb. 1, 1831.

II. SAMUEL [4], b. Feb. 19, 1721, d. ——.

m. Sarah Titcomb, daughter of Daniel Titcomb, of Dover, and lived in Rochester on the Rochester and Salmon Falls road. They had ten children, who all moved away:

1. SAMUEL [5].

m. ———, lived in Lebanon, Me., and had:

1. *Eunice* [6].

m. Stephen *Jones*, and had:

1. Samuel [7], (Dr.)

Lived in Wakefield, Me.

2. Cyrus [7].

Lived in Lebanon, Me.

3. Sophia [7].

m. —— *Furbish*.

4. —— [7] (daughter), unm.

2. ENOCH [5].

m. ———, lived in Milton, and had:

1. *Sarah* [6].

3. JOSEPH [5].

m. ———, and had:

1. —— [6] (daughter), who lived in New York.

4. BENJAMIN [5].

Lived in Rochester.

5. MOSES [5].

6. ELIZABETH [5].

m. Capt. Moses *Roberts*, of Rochester.

7. SARAH [5].

m. Nathan *Lord*, of Lebanon.

8. JOSEPH [5].

Died suddenly in New York, of small pox during the Revolutionary War.

9. ANNA [5].

m. David *Farnham*, of Lebanon.

10. DOROTHY [5], b. ——, d. young, unm.

III. DANIEL[4], b. Jan. 23, 1722-23, d. 1793.

    m. Mary Frost, daughter of William Frost, of Dover. Lived in Rochester. Daniel[4] made his will Feb. 9, 1793, giving to wife Mary one-third of produce of the estate, two rooms, etc., during widowhood, also two cows, two sheep ; to son Daniel £2 ; to daughter Mary Horne, bed, furniture and £5 ; to son David, the homestead, stock, etc. ; to grand-daughter Sarah Wingate, bed and furniture when she is 18 years old. David was executor. Will proved April 19, 1793. Daniel[4] and Mary had six children :

1. WILLIAM[5], b. Nov. 8, 1750 (prob.).

    m. Deborah Buzzell, of Farmington. Moved to Farmington several years before 1800. They had twelve children :

    1. *Daniel*,[6] b. Feb. 22, 1780.

        m. Dolly Walker. Moved to Canada. Had :

        1. Joseph[7].

        2. Lucy[7].

        3. Deborah[7].

        4. Mary[7].

    2. *Sally*[6], b. Jan. 9, 1781.

        m. Nicholas *Tebbetts*, and had two children.

    3. *Deborah*[6], b. Jan 6, 1782.

        m. Ezra *Corson*, and had :

        1. Ezra[7].

        2. William[7].

        3. Emily[7].

            m. —— *Slocum*, and lived in Sutton, Mass.

    4. *William*[6], b. June 21, 1783, d. unm.

    5. *Mary*[6], b. Aug. 5, 1785, d. s. p.
        m. Durrell *Stevens*.

    6. *Lydia*[6], b. Sept. 19, 1786, d. young.

    7. *Joseph*[6], b. July 26, 1789, d. young.

8. *Abigail*[6], b. Aug. 19, 1791.
     m. John *Roberts*, and had :
     1. William[7].
     2. Horatio[7].
     3. Bartlet[7].
     4. Frank[7].
     5. Joseph A.[7].
          Lived in Farmington.
     6. Edwin[7].
     7. Henry L.[7].

9. *Jonathan*[6], b. Sept. 18, 1794, d. Nov. 10, 1871.
     m. (1) Jan. 4, 1821, Eunice Roberts, of Farmington, a
     Quaker lady (b. Aug. 8, 1799, d. July 9, 1839) ; (2)
     Betsy H. Cook, of Sandwich, (d. May 1883). He had
     six children, all by his first wife :
     1. Lydia[7], b. Dec. 29, 1821.
          m. April 30, 1848, Hiram R. *Flanaers*, (d. Sept.
          16, 1862). They lived in Schaller, Iowa, and had :
          (*a*) Mary E.[8], b. March 5, 1849.
               m. Lowell M. *Woodward*, lived in Parker,
               Dakota, and had :
               1. Earl L.[9].
          (*b*) Eliza Ann[8], b. Aug. 25, 1850, d. Aug. 11, 1878.
               m. James *Caurtright*, of Mechanicsville,
               Iowa, and had five children, of whom two
               were alive in 1885.
          (*c*) Frank H.[8], b. Jan. 29, 1854.
               m. Agnes Speaker. Farmer in Schaller,
               Iowa, and had :
               1. Edith May[9].
          (*d*) Martha B.[8], b. May 15, 1858.
               m. Rev. George W. *Sauttwell*, Methodist
               minister, and lived in Nebraska.
          (*e*) Clara E.[8], b. Sept. 16, 1861.
               m. Charles H. *Fox*, farmer in Silver Creek,
               Iowa, and had :
               1. Ethel Viola[9].

2. William[7], b. Dec. 8, 1825.

    m. Eliza[7] Wingate (b. July 2, 1830) his cousin, dau. of Benjamin[6] Wingate, and lived in Farmington

3. Moses[7], b. March 6, 1828.

    m. twice. Lived in San Jose, Cal.

4. George H.[7], b. April 25, 1830.

    Lived in Dover.

5. Hiram[7], b. Aug. 23, 1832, d. unm. 1854,

6. James Roberts[7], b. Nov. 18, 1834.

    m. (1) Oct. 16, 1856, Lucina Averry, of Pershia Pt. (d. May 14, 1862); (2) Oct. 13, 1872, Ellen H. Torr. Lived in Peabody, Mass., and had one child by first wife and one by second:

    (*a*) Herbert M.[8], b. Mar. 24, 1859, d. July 11, '79.

    (*b*) Frank Torr[8], b. Dec. 12, 1873.

7. Martha Ann[7], b. Oct. 11, 1836, d. Oct. 13, 1880.

    m. (1) True E. *Dudley;* (2) June, 1875, Jacob *Mooar* of Manchester.

8. Eunice[7], b. April 10, 1839, d. Sept. 10, 1839.

10. *Benjamin*[6], b. Jan. 6, 1797.

    m. Lavina Davis (b. Sept. 4, 1811, d. March 30, 1830). Lived in Farmingon, and had:

1. Eliza[7], b. July 2, 1830.

    m. William[7] *Wingate* (b. Dec. 8, 1825), her cousin, son of Jonathan[6] Wingate, and had:

    (*a*) Charles B.[8], b. August 20, 1850.

        m. Ida Hartshorne, lived in Manchester, and had:

        1. Maud[9], b. August 4, 1878.

    (*b*) Emma J.[8], b. August 12, 1853.

        m. Hervey B. *White*, and had:

        1. Leon E.[9], b. October 11, 1878, d. aged abt. 5.

        2. Carl P.[9], b. October 25, 1883.

    (*c*) Lillian M.[8], b. April 11, 1865.

2. Lydia[7], b. October 16, 1832.

    m. Edwin P. *Longley*. Lived in Boston.

3. Emily[7], b. July 20, 1835, d. August 7, 1838.

4. Mary[7], b. June 5, 1838.
    m. Daniel W. *Kimball*, and had :
    (*a*)   Clara[8], b. June 17, 1858.
    (*b*)   Annie[8], b. August 3, 1860.
    (*c*)   Benjamin F.[8], b. July 7, 1863.
    (*d*)   Mary[8], b. November 11, 1876.
    (*e*)   Ernest[8], b. December 27, 1879.

5. Caroline V.[7], b. September 7, 1840.
    m. Lewis C. *Fernald*, of Melrose, Mass., and had :
    (*a*)   Edmund[8], b. August 11, 1868.

6. Clara[7], b. February 10, 1843, d. January 29, 1858.

7. Ellen[7], b. November 21, 1845, d. January 29, 1858.

8. Harriet L.[7], b. February 27, 1848.

9. Abbie E.[7], b. July 18, 1851.
    m. Albert E. *Putnam*, lived in Farmington, and had :
    (*a*)   ———[8] (son), b. Aug. 5, 1879, d. Oct. 12, 1879.

11. *Betsey*[6], b. April 3, 1798.
     m. Joseph *Kelley*, and had :
     1. Francis[7].
     2. Austress[7].
     3. Sophia[7].
     4. William[7].
     5. Emma[7].

12. *Sophia*[6], b. January 23, 1800.
     m. William *Mason*, and had :
     1. Wingate[7].
         Lived in Sandwich.
     2. Matilda[7].

2. JOHN[5], b. Aug. 11, 1753, d. Nov. 25, 1827.
   m. Mar. 1, 1784, Susan Canney, of Dover, (d. Feb. 11, 1835),
   lived in Farmington, and had six children :

   1. *John*[6], b. July 28, 1785, d. May 27, 1868.
      m. ————, lived in Wakefield, and had, besides several daughters :

      1. John[7], b. 1831, d. s. p. Oct. 10, 1881.
         m. ——— Nudd, of Wolfboro. Bowd. Col. Lived in
         St. Louis. ,

   2. *Joseph*[6], b. Jan. 10, 1788, d. Aug. 28, 1790.

   3. *Daniel*[6], b. March 20, 1791, d. Jan. 17, 1872.
      m. Sally Wiggin, of Wolfboro, (b. Jan. 31, 1798, d. Mar.
      31, 1867), lived on his father's homestead in Farmington, and had :

      1. Joseph[7], b. Oct. 22, 1822, d. Sept. 22, 1841.

      2. Charles W.[7], b. May 18, 1824.
         m. Sept. 17, 1856, Mary E. Clough, of Laconia,
         lived in Farmington, and had :
         (*a*) Charlotte R.[8], b. Jan. 2, 1859.
             m. Mar. 15, 1883, Charles A. *Duntley*, of
             Farmington.
         (*b*) Charles Albert[8], b. ———, d. in infancy.
         (*c*) John C.[8], b. Dec. 23, 1867.
         (*d*) Arthur R.[8], b. Sept. 2, 1875.

      3. Sarah J.[7], b. July 28, 1828.
         m. George L. *Wiggin*, and had two children.

   4. *Jonathan*[6], b. Feb. 2, 1793, d. Nov. 6, 1855.
      Lived in Maine.

   5. *Mary*[6], b. July 16, 1796, d. Oct. 29, 1881.
      Lived in Farmington.

   6. *Lovey*[6], b. July 16, 1800, d. 1867.
      Lived in Iowa.

3. DANIEL.⁵.

>m. Lydia White, of Dover. He was a soldier from May 23, 1777 for three years; he was probably one of the first census takers of the nation, as we find him, June 5, 1786, one of three appointed to "number the inhabitants of the town of Rochester." He had:

1. *Jeremiah*⁶.
    Lived in Alton.

4. DAVID⁵.

>m. Eunice Tebbetts, a Quakeress. He was in the militia in 1780. Had three sons and one daughter:

1. *Stephen*⁶, (Dr.) b. Sept. 29, 1787, d. Dec. 30, 1875.
    m. Jan. 28, 1813, Hannah Hanson, (b. Nov. 1, 1793, d. Mar. 7, 1881,) of Dover. Was in the N. E. Conference of the M. E. Church; afterwards physician; practiced his profession in Great Falls, N. H., and in Decatur, Ill., for more than fifty years. Had ten children, the following four surviving him:

— Thomas H.⁷.
   Lived in Decatur, Ill.

— ————⁷ (dau.)
   m. Rev. Dr. *Dimond*, of Brighton, Ill.

— Eliza⁷.
   m. Rev. Lyman *Marshall*, of Lebanon, Ill.

— Charles H.⁷.
   Lived in Ishpeming, Mich.

2. *David*⁶, b. Nov. 22, 1789, d. Nov. 16, 1881.
    m. May, 1817, Lucy Tebbetts, (d. 1870). David⁶ Wingate was one of the famous Dartmoor prisoners. He sailed from Dover in the good ship Horace, Capt. William Appleton, bound for Chatham and Falmouth, England. While furling sails in the latter port on the last day of the year 1811 a press gang came on board from the guard-ship Experiment and took him off under the pretext that the Horace had an excess of men. He was then sent to

the Mediterranean on an English merchantman, and on his return, on the last day of the year 1812, he was made prisoner and confined on the prison-ship Crown Prince. He remained about a year on the ship, when he and others were taken to Plymouth Sound. There he jumped overboard and swam away but was soon recaptured. As he was not willing to serve the English against his own country, he and many other prisoners were marched eighteen miles overland to Dartmoor Prison where they arrived at night cold and hungry. He remembered till his death the iron gates as he passed them, and which were to close upon him for the next eighteen months. Finally, peace having been declared, he and about two hundred others were released on the 26th of April, 1815, and sent home. After that Mr. Wingate lived quietly on his farm at Rochester until his death. He had eleven children :

1. Asa[7], b. March, 1818, d. s. p.

2. Lewis[7], b. Sept. 1819.
   m. ———— and had :
   (*a*) Abbie A.[8]

3. David[7], b. Sept. 1821, d. March 26, 1857–58.
   m., 1846, Lydia T. Wentworth (b. Feb. 17, 1824). She married (2) Sewell Gowell of Lebanon, Me. David[7] had :
   (*a*) Uranus O. B.[8] (Dr.) b. Sept. 14, 1848.
       m. ————, lived in Wellesley, Mass., and had :
       1. Lily M.[9], b. Feb., 1878.
       2. Newell A. T.[9], b. Oct., 1880.
   (*b*) Isabella[8], b. ————, d. an infant.
   (*c*) Lucy J.[8], b. Dec. 7, 1854, d. Dec. 14, 1865.

4. Mary[7], b. May, 1823.
   m. James H. *Corson*, of Rochester, and had three children, among whom was :
   (*a*) J. Edwin[8].
       Lived in Allston, Mass.

5. William[7], b. April, 1825.

6. James F.[7], b. May, 1827, d. unm. ———

7. Samuel N.[7], b. June, 1829.
     m. ——— Tibbits, lived in Rochester, and had several children:

8 Lucy[7], b. Aug., 1831.
     m. Charles C. *Chisholm*, lived in East Rochester, and had several children.

9. Clara[7], b. Dec., 1833, d. unm.———.

10. Amasa[7], b. Jan., 1836.

11. Martha[7], b. May, 1839, d. young.

3. *Jonathan*[6], b. July 20, 1792, d. April, 1882.
     m. (1) Patience Tebbetts; (2) Mehitable Tebbetts, lived in Rochester and Great Falls, and had by first wife three children, by second wife four:

1. Lydia[7].
     m. ——— *Corson*, and had:
     (*a*) Frank W.[8]

2. Charles[7].

3. Joseph[7].

4. Mary Ann[7].

5. Patience[7].

6. Louise[7].

7. Susan[7].

4. *Daniel*[6], b. May 29, 1795, d. Nov., 1864.
     m. Sabina Tebbetts, and had:

1. Harriett[7].

2. Daniel[7].

3. David[7].

4. Sabina[7].

5. *Mary*[6], b. June 15, 1801.
     m. Asa *Tebbetts*, (d. s. p., Jan. 25, 1880).

IV. JOSHUA[4] (Col), b. July 28, 1725, d. February 9, 1796.
m., near 1757, Abigail Roberts (b. Feb. 18, 1736, d. Aug.
22, 1813). Lived on the "Blake farm" at "Littleworth," in
Dover. He was appointed, on Aug. 24, 1775, First Major
of the Second Regiment. On Sept. 1 of the same year the
twelve regiments of the colony were consolidated into four,
and Joshua[4] was made First Colonel of the First Regiment.
Nov. 2, 1775, we find him at Fort Sullivan, Seavey's Island,
and Nov. 8, he is appointed to command 500 men raised
for the defence of the forts in Piscataqua river. That same
month, Gen. Jno. Sullivan wrote the Honorable Committee
of Safety, "I should have rejoiced to have had Col. Wingate,
Burnum and Hackett at their head [i. e., his troops] as Field
Officers, but the Committee from the Massachusetts General
Court, and the Council of General Officers have determined
the contrary." In the year 1776 Col. Wingate was appointed First Colonel of the Second Regiment, then being
raised in the colony for a reinforcement to Gen. Sullivan
who was to repel the enemy coming from Canada. Col.
Wingate marched to Ticonderoga, and was stationed at Mt.
Independence in the Summer of this year. In the Summer
of 1778, the French fleet, France having become our ally,
was to attack, in concert with Gen. Sullivan, the British
forces at Newport, R. I. A call upon the militia of New
England to take part in the "Rhode Island Expedition"
brought to the standard of Sullivan an army of 10,000 men.
Col. Wingate led a regiment, partly of Madbury men, to the
expedition, they going as Volunteers. A storm dispersed
the fleets, both of British and of French, and Gen. Sullivan,
thus left alone and finding it unsafe to remain longer, re-
treated, was pursued and attacked, but, gallantly resisting,
repulsed the British. Then with face to the foe he beat a
safe and discreet retreat. Col. Joshua[4], in his civil career,
served as Selectman of Dover in 1773 and 1779, and as Representative from Dover, in 1781, to the Second Constitutional Convention. On the day preceding his death he
made a will, giving to son Edmund a life estate in 130 acres of
land in Rochester, "where he now lives," which should afterwards descend to Edmund's son Joshua, and also gave cattle ;

to son Stephen 100 acres in Rochester, "provided he returns
within fourteen years, it being uncertain whether he is living," " he having been absent a number of years," until his
return Edmund to use it, and if not claimed by Stephen,
then to go to Edmund's son Stephen; to grand-daughters
Lydia and Mary the reversion of 84 acres in Rochester; to
daughters Elizabeth and Mary $100 each; to wife Abigail
the homestead for life, after which it was to go to his two
daughters. Proved Feb. 17, 1796. On Nov. 26, 1813, the
homestead was divided, Mary Wingate Gage, daughter of
Joseph Gage, of Dover, and Elizabeth, Abigail, and Lydia
Ham Blake, children of William Blake, Jr., of Dover, being
the heirs. The six children of Joshua[4] and Abigail were:

1. EDMUND[5].
>   m. ———, *LOIS BERRY* lived in Farmington, and had five children:

>   1. *Lydia*[6].
>   m. John *Foss*, of Milton.

>   2. *Stephen*[6].
>   m. Susan Calef, dau. of Daniel Calef, of Rochester, lived
>   in Farmington, and had eight children:

>   >   1. John[7].
>   >   m. Nabby Berry.

>   >   2. Daniel[7].

>   >   3. Louisa[7].
>   >   m. —— *Wyatt*.

>   >   4. Mary[7].
>   >   m. Asa *Littlefield*.

>   >   5. Stephen[7].
>   >   m. Mary Parker, and lived in Chelsea, Mass.

>   >   6. Abby[7].
>   >   m. Joseph T. S. *Libbey*.

>   >   7. William[7].
>   >   m. (1) Nancy Morrison; (2) Lydia S. Preston, and
>   >   had a child by each wife:
>   >   (a) Emma[8].

(*b*) Woodbury H.[8], b. September, 1858.

    m., September, 1883, Sadie M. Mack, of Boston, and lived in Portsmouth.

8. Lyman[7].

3. Mary[6].

    m. Richard *Davis*, of Exeter.

4. Joshua[6].

    m. Miss McNeale, dau. of Daniel McNeale, and lived in Strafford.

5. Abigail[6].

    m. Jan. 14, 1819, Capt. John *Wentworth*, of Milton, and Great Falls, (b. Oct. 21, 1795, d. Sept. 9, 1836), son of John and Rebecca (Horne) Wentworth. They had :

  1. Louisa Maria[7], b. March 10, 1820.

    m. May 2, 1848, John P. *Jones*, lived in Milton, and had :

    (*a*) Susan Abby[8], b. March 3, 1849.

    (*b*) Mary Jane[8], b. June 28, 1853.

    (*c*) Joshua R.[8], b. April 16, 1859.

    (*d*) Lydia Eggleston[8], b. Jan. 29, 1864.

  2. Roxanna[7], b. June 7, 1822.

    m. Dec. 13, 1842, Rufus *Colcord*, lived in Parsonsfield, Me., and had :

    (*a*) Henry A.[8], b. Nov. 23, 1844.

    m. Nov. 16, 1873, Eva A. Moulton, dau. of William E. and Priscilla Moulton, of Parsonsfield, Me.

    (*b*) Edward John[8], b. July 28, 1849.

    (*c*) Rufus Judson[8], b. Oct. 4, 1851.

  3. Delana[7], b. Jan., 1825, d. Feb., 1833.

  4. Abigail Frances[7], b. July, 1827, d. July, 1832.

  5. Lydia Matilda[7], b. Oct. 27, 1829, d. Aug. 28, 1863.

    m. April 25, 1850, Harvey John *Eggleston*, of Flatbush, N.Y. Lived in Brooklyn, N.Y., and had :

    (*a*) Abby Harding[8], b. Jan. 5, 1854.

6. Frances Delana [7], b. Nov. 2, 1833.

> m. (1) Aug. 3, 1850, David R. *Jones*, of Milton ;
> (2) C. A. *Dodge*. Lived in Haverhill, Mass., with
> her first husband and at South Dedham, Mass., with
> her second. Had by her first husband, (beside
> two who died young) :
>
> (*a*)   Frank Everett [8], b. Oct. 19, 1852, d. Oct. 29, '70.
>
> (*b*)   David Herbert [8], b. May 23, 1860.

7. John Wingate [7], b. Aug. 27, 1836.

> m. (1) May 29, 1860, Ellen E. Canney, of Lebanon,
> Me., (d. July 23, 1861) ; (2) Dec. 16, 1865, Susan
> M. Symonds. Lived in Williamsburg, N. Y., and
> had by first wife one child who died in infancy, and
> by second wife :
>
> (*a*)   Mabel [8], b. July 16, 1871.

2. STEPHEN [5].

> Lived in Dover.

3. ELIZABETH [5], b. 1762, d. Jan. 16, 1809.

> m. 1800, Major William *Blake*, of Dover, (b. 1777, d. April
> 10, 1823,) and had three children :

1.   *Elizabeth* [6].

> m. Joseph *Nason* of Dover, and had :
>
> 1.   Elizabeth [7].
>
> 2.   Wingate [7].
>
> 3.   John [7], b. ———, d. an infant.

2.   *Abigail* [6].

> m. Daniel *Hussey*, of Dover, and had :
>
> 1.   Sophia [7].
>
> 2.   Clarissa [7].
>
> 3.   Eliza Jane [7].
>
> 4.   Lydia [7].
>
> 5.   Mary Frances [7].
>
> 6.   Charles William [7].
>
> 7.   Abigail [7].

3. Lydia [6].

> m. Samuel *Horne,* of Dover, and had :

> 1. Leonard [7].

> 2. Mary [7].

> 3. Daniel [7].

> 4. Harriett Newell [7].

> 5. George William [7].

> 6. Susan Porter [7].

> 7. Lydia Susan [7].

> 8. John [7].

4. MARY [5], b. 1767-8, d. May 26, 1799.

> m., near 1798, Joseph *Gage,* of Dover, and had :

> *1. Mary* [6].
> > m. Charles *Woodman,* of Dover.

5. JOSHUA [5].

6. ——— [5].

V. JONATHAN [4], bapt. October 22, 1727.

> m. ——— Bampton. Lived in Scarboro, and had one child :

1. JONATHAN [5], b. ———, d. s. p. ———.

> m. ——— Moulton, and lived in Scarboro.

VI. DOROTHY [4], bapt. September 23, 1733, d. young.

VII. NOAH [4], bapt. September 27, 1735, d. young.

VIII. AARON [4], bapt. February 6, 1737, d. young.

[NOTE : Regarding the births of John[3]'s children between Jonathan and Sarah recorders differ, some giving, instead of the above three, VI. Moses (twin), VII. Betty (twin), VIII. Noah, IX. Betty, X. ———, all dying young. In this case, as in others similar, I have taken the best authenticated.—C. E. L. W.]

IX.   SARAH[4], bapt. August 20, 1738.

m., 1760, Samuel *Ham*, of Dover (b. near 1736, d. 1788). (He m. a second wife, by whom he had sons Samuel, Jeremiah and William).   Sarah[4] and Samuel had three children :

1.   SARAH[5], b. ――――, d. young.

2.   LYDIA[5],

m. Amos *Peaslee*, of Dover.   After his death she moved to Burlington, Vt.   They had five children :

   1.   John[6].

m. Mrs. Richardson, of Gilmanton.

   2.   Samuel[6].

   3.   Lydia[6].

   4.   Amos[6].

   5.   Sylvester[6].

3.   SARAH[5].

m. John[5] *Titcomb*, son of· Major John[4], and grandson of Daniel and Ann[3] (Wingate) Titcomb.   They had :

   1.   Elizabeth[6].

m. John *Foss*, of Portsmouth.

   2.   Abigail[6].

m. George *Pendexter*, of Dover.

   3.   John[6].

m. Sarah C. Swett, and lived in Portsmouth.

   4.   Samuel[6], b. ――――, d. at sea.

   5.   Mary[6], b. July, 1795, d. April, 1822.

m. May 25, 1818, Jeremiah[5] *Wingate*, of Farmington, (b. June 7, 1785, d. s. p.) son of Judge Aaron[4] Wingate, who was brother of Sarah[4].

   6.   Lydia[6].

m. Isaac *Folsom*, of Boston.

   7.   Martha[6].

m. James C. *Small*, of New York.

   8.   Jeremiah[6].

m. Joanna Rollins, and lived in Great Falls.

   9.   George[6], b. ――――, d. an infant.

   10.   Sally[6], b. ――――, d. an infant.

   11.   Sally[6], b. ――――, d. an infant.

X. ANN[4], bapt. Mar. 14, 1742, d. Mar. 25, 1826.

m. near 1765, Capt. Shadrach[4] *Hodgdon*, Jr., her cousin, (page 33) of Dover, (b. Feb. 4, 1742, d. May 3, 1776). Had five children :

1. SHADRACH[5];

m. Elizabeth Gage, dau. of Jonathan Gage, of Dover, and had four children :

  1. Elizabeth[6].

  m. John *Mann*, of Dover.

  2. Rebecca[6].

  m. Jonathan *Rawson*, Jr.

  3. Mary[6].

  m. Eri *Perkins*, of Dover.

  4. Susan[6].

  m. Capt. Moses *Paul*, of Dover.

2. JOHN[5].

unm. Shipmaster.

3. ANNA[5].

m. Col. Edward *Sise*, of Dover, and had seven children :

  1. Shadrach[6].

  m. Jane Neale, dau. of Thomas Neale, and lived in Portsmouth.

  2. Maria[6].

  3. John[6].

  4. Anna[6].

  5. Edward F.[6].

  m. Ann Sims, and lived in Portsmouth.

  6. William[6].

  7. Joseph Gage[6].

  m. Abigail Lyman, of Portsmouth, and lived in Portsmouth.

4. MOSES[5].
    Counsellor at law in Dover.

5. MARY[5].
    m. (1) Daniel *Libbey*, of Dover; (2) Benjamin *Brown*, of
    Moultonboro. By first husband had five children, by second,
    three :

    1. Charlotte[6].

    2. Charles[6].

    3. Charles[6].

    4. Rebecca Gage[6].

    5. Daniel[6] (Capt.).

    6. Mary Ann[6].

    7. Moses Hodgdon[6]

    8. Shadrach Hodgdon[6].

XI. AARON[4], (Jd.) (twin to Moses) b. Nov. 23, 1744, d. Feb, 1822.
     m. Dec. 25, 1770, Elizabeth[5] Plummer, (b. Feb 22, 1750,
     d. May, 1841) dau. of Judge John Plummer, of Rochester,
     who married Elizabeth[4] Titcomb, dau. of Daniel Titcomb,
     who married Ann[3] Wingate. They removed to Farmington
     about 1779, living near Chestnut Hills. He was a well
     known citizen and much respected. Was Representative
     from Rochester for several years, (Rochester then including
     Farmington), was councillor for Strafford County from 1797
     to 1803, Justice of the Peace and Quorum throughout the
     State, and from 1803 to 1813 was Judge of the Court of
     Common Pleas. Had eight children :

1. ELIZABETH[5], b. Jan. 18, 1772, d. unm. July 29, 1797.

2. JOHN[5], b. July 13, 1773, d. Jan. 26, 1852.
 m. Mrs. Esther Varney, of Rochester, (d. 1841,) widow of Silas Varney.

3. SARAH[5], b. Jan. 26, 1775, d. Feb. 3, 1811.
 m. Hon. Jonas C. *March*, of Rochester, [after her death he married Lydia[5], her sister.] Sarah[5] had eight children:

 1. Eliza[6].
  m. Benjamin *Barker*, of Rochester, and had three children.

 2. Hannah[6].
  m., as second wife, Joseph *Hanson*, of Dover, and had:
  1. Caroline[7].
  2. Sarah Wingate[7].
  3. Jonas March[7].
  4. Lucy Howe[7].

 3. Jonas C.[6].
  m. Sarah Ann Shannon, dau. of William Shannon, of Dover.

 4. Caroline[6].

 5. Sarah Ann[6].
  m. Jonathan *Freeman*, of New York.

 6. Aaron Wingate[6].
  m. Ann ———.

 7. Emily[6].
  m. George *Barker*, of Rochester.

 8. John Plummer[6].

4. LYDIA[5], b. Aug. 9, 1777.
 m., after 1811, Hon. Jonas C *March*, after the death of his first wife, her sister Sarah[5].

5. SHADRACH[5], b. Aug. 12, 1780, d. Feb., 1853.
    m. Feb. 27, 1815, Sarah Patten, dau. of Stephen Patten, of Dover. Lived in Rochester and had three children :

    1. Aaron P.[6], b. 1824.
        m. (1) Jan., 1849, Eliza C.[6] Wingate, (b. Aug. 4. 1824, d. July, 1855,) dau. of William P. M.[5] Wingate ; (2) Elizabeth Goodwin, of Lebanon, Me. Lived in Exeter, N. H., and Walpole, Mass., and had :

        1. Homer S.[7], b. Jan., 1853, d. June, 1855.

        2. Sarah E.[7], b. 1857.
            m. J. E. *Dennison*, of Lawrence, Mass., and had :
               (*a*) Alice[8].
               (*b*) Walter[8].
               (*c*) Edith[8], b. ———, d. an infant.

        3. Frank E.[7], b. 1859.
            m. Sadie Waldron, of Boston, and lived in Boston.

        4. Arthur Roscoe[7], b. 1860.
            m. Fannie Mellen, of Fall River, Mass., and lived in Fall River.

        5. Mattie A.[7].

    2. Hannah Elizabeth[6].
        Lived in Rochester.

6. MOSES[5], b. Aug. 4, 1782, d. May, 1783.

7. JEREMIAH[5], b. June 7, 1785, d. s. p. ———.
    m. May 25, 1818, Mary[6] Titcomb, (b. July, 1795, d. April, 1822), dau. of John[5] Titcomb, of Dover. Lived in Farmington.

8. NANCY[5], b. Oct. 18, 1791.
    Lived in Rochester.

XII. MOSES[4] (Capt.), (twin with Aaron), b. Nov. 23, 1744, d. April 29, 1829.

> m. 1780 Joanna Gilman Wentworth, (b. June 21, 1755, d. Dec. 24, 1806), dau. of Col. John and Abigail (Millet) Wentworth. He was a Farmer and with Aaron[4], his twin brother, *inherited the old homestead.* He was Representative in 1798; was Captain, etc. Had four children:

1. JOHN[5], b. May 7, 1782, d. Sept. 5, 1827.

> m. Sept 15, 1803, Mary Torr, (b. 1783-4, d. April 8, 1831), dau. of Andrew Torr, of Dover. (After his death she married William Drew.) Lived in Dover and had eleven children:

> *1. Mary[6]*, b. ——, d. an infant.

> *2. Mary[6]*, b. Feb. 13, 1806, d. Sept 27, 1883.
> > m. (1) Jan. 1, 1832, George *Williams*, (d. about 1836); (2) Aug 13, 1839, Joshua *Parker.* Lived in Dover. Had one child by each husband but both children died in infancy.

> *3. Joanna[6]*, b. March 10, 1808.
> > Lived in Concord.

> *4. Susan[6]*, b. May 5, 1810.
> > m. Ebenezer *Swain*, of Strafford, (d. 1868.) Lived in Dover, and had:
> > 1. Sarah[7].
> > > m. ————.

> *5. John[6]*, b. Aug. 12, 1812.
> > Lived in Council Bluffs and Farragut, Iowa.

> *6. George[6]*, b. April, 1814, d. April 11, 1850.

> *7. Eliza[6]*, b. Sept., 1816, d. Oct. 27, 1837.

> *8. Moses[6]*, b. March, 1820.
> > m. 1842, Martha D. Walker, (b. 1822, d. June 19, 1879), dau. of William and Elizabeth (Dunham) Walker. Lived in Rome, N. Y., and had:
> > 1. Mary Elizabeth[7], b. March 4, 1843, d. Sept. 18, 1857.

2.   John W.[7], b. July 16, 1845.
     m. Jan. 8, 1885, Julietta A. Congar, dau. of Hanford
     A. and Lorancy De Mary Congar, of Attica, N. Y.
     Lived in Silverton, Cal.

3.   Angeletta M.[7], b. Feb. 13, 1851, d. May 9, 1851.

4.   Franklin D.[7], b. April 27, 1854, d. April 28, 1859.

5.   Martha Elizabeth[7], b. Nov. 12, 1857.
     m. 1876, Henry V. *Adams*, of Rome, N. Y., son of
     Sanford and Martha Lamphier Adams.   Lived in
     Rome, N. Y., and had :
          (*a*)   Edith May[8], b. May 26, 1877.
          (*b*)   Martha Irene[8], b. June 30, 1882.

6.   Frank A.[7], b. May 1, 1860.

9.   *Andrew*[6], b. 1821–22.
     m. Oct. 3, 1845, Sarah Hamlin, of Hampden, Me.
     Lived in Boston, and had two daughters.

10.   *Aaron*[6], b. ———, d. an infant.

11.   *Sallie*[6], b. ———, d. an infant.

2.   SARAH[5], b. Aug., 1784, d. April 19, 1827.
     m., as second wife, Oct. 24, 1819, James *Rollins*, of Somers-
     worth and Rollinsford, (b. July 4, 1776, d. 1854).   His first
     wife was Dolly Folsom, his third Abigail[5] Wingate, sister of
     Sarah[5].   He was a grandson of Judge Ichabod Rollins.
     Sarah[5] had one child :

1.   *James Wingate*[6], b. April 19, 1827.
     m. Nov. 22, 1855, Mrs. Sophia W., dau. of Soloman
     Hutchins and widow of James W. Atwill, of Boston.
     D. C. 1845.   Was lawyer in Boston.   Had, besides one
     child who died in infancy :

     1.   Mary H.[7], b. Nov. 15, 1856.

     2.   James W.[7], b. Oct. 17, 1858.

     3.   Alice S.[7], b. May 8, 1861.

     4.   Edward Albert[7], b. Oct. 8, 1865.

3. ABIGAIL[5], b. Mar., 1787, d. s. p. Oct. 18, 1858.

   m., as third wife, Sept. 7, 1828, James *Rollins*, her sister Sarah[5] having deceased.

4. WILLIAM PITT MOULTON[5], b. July 7, 1789.

   m. (1) Jan. 24, 1822, Eliza Chandler, (b. 1796–97, d. July 15, 1825) ; (2) Lydia Gray Chandler, (b. June 20, 1801, d. Jan. 1, 1871), both daughters of Philemon and Abigail (Torr) Chandler, of Dover. William Pitt Moulton[5] *inherited the old homestead.* By first wife had two children ; by second, seven :

   1. Moses[6], b. Mar. 13, 1823.

   m. Dec. 22, 1847, Lydia Snell, dau. of Col. Samuel and Sally (Horne) Snell, of Dover, and had :

   1. Ellen Augusta[7], b. Feb. 19, 1849.

      m., June 6, 1867, Henry *Vatter*, (b. 1846), of New Orleans. Lived in Haverhill and Lawrence, Mass., and had :

      (*a*) Alice Maud[8], b. Oct. 20, 1868.

      (*b*) George Henry[8], b. Mar. 1, 1870.

      (*c*) Wilber Lewis[8], b. Dec. 19, 1878.

   2. Charles Edwin[7], b. April 26, 1851.

      m. (1) Sept. 18, 1872, Mrs. Mary E. Carter, of Lawrence, Mass., (b. 1846, d. July 1, 1874) ; (2) Adna R. Pitman, (b. 1851), dau. of Judge Pitman, of Bartlett. Lived in Lawrence, Mass. By first wife had one child, by second five :

      (*a*) Charles Edwin[8], b. Aug. 3, 1873.

      (*b*) Winifred Eva[8], b. June 11, 1877.

      (*c*) Blanche Pitman[8], b. Jan. 3, 1879.

      (*d*) Addie[8], b. April 14, 1880.

      (*e*) Tom Chubbuck Moses[8], b. Sept. 24, 1883.

      (*f*) Roy[8], b. Aug. 2, 1885.

3. Harriet Frances[7], b. April 1, 1856.
        m. June 24, 1880, Benjamin *Rogers*, (b. 1851).
        Lived in Lawrence, Mass., and had :
        (*a*)   Frances[8], b. May 11, 1881.
        (*b*)   Leslie[8], b. Mar. 5, 1883.
        (*c*)   Harold W.[8], b. Sept. 28, 1885.

4. Mary Emma[7], b. July 7, 1859.
        m. June 11, 1879, Horace S. *Fowle*, of Boston, (b. 1848,) and had :
        (*a*)   Horace Wingate[8], b. March 1, 1881.
        (*b*)   Mildred Endicot[8], b. Feb. 17, 1883,

2. *Eliza C.*[6], b. Aug. 4, 1824, d. July, 1855.
        m. Jan., 1849, Aaron P.[6] *Wingate* of Rochester, (b. 1824), son of Shadrach[5] Wingate. [For children see Aaron P.[6] Wingate.]

3. · Joseph William[6], b. July 5, 1827.
        Lived at the old Wingate homestead.

4. Sarah A.[6], b. Oct. 17, 1829.
        Lived in Dover.

5. *Mary F.*[6], b. Jan. 27, 1835, d. Sept. 21, 1855.

6. *Lydia A.*[6], b. March 13, 1837, d. May 5, 1841.

7. *Jeremiah Y.*[6], b. June 15, 1842.
        m. Nov. 22, 1870, Arvilla S. Clements, dau. of John Clements, of Dover, lived in Dover, and had :
        1. Florence Lydia[7], b. Sept. 2, 1872.
        2. Alice M.[7], b. June 17, 1876.
        3. Mattie C.[7], b. March 20, 1880.
        4. William H.[7], b. June 29, 1885.

8. *Henry M.*[6], b. Mar. 27, 1845, d. Aug. 9, 1863.

9. *Helen Cecilia*[6], b. June 20, 1851.
Lived at Dover.

XIII. MEHITABLE[4], bapt. February 22, 1747, d. 1842-43.
m., (1) Feb. 2, 1769, William *Hanson*, Jr. (b. Dec. 19, 1732) ; (2) James *Libby*, both of Dover. Lived on the "Mast road" in Madbury, at Enoch Drew's. Had four children :

1. WILLIAM[5].
Went to sea and never returned.

2. SARAH[5], b. 1770-71, d. unm., 1834.

3. BETSY[5].
m. Enoch *Drew*, of Dover.

4. MEHITABLE[5].
m. (1) Moses *Ham*, Jr., of Dover, then of Danville, Vt.; (2) James *Libby*, of Dover, and had :

1. *Amoret*[6].

2. *Sophronia*[6].

3. *Joshua*[6].

4. *William Hanson*[6].

5. *Sarah Jane*[6].

JOHN[1].

JOHN[2].

ANN[3].

m. (1) Joseph *Drew*, by whom she had one child, and (2) Daniel *Titcomb*, by whom she had seven children :

I.   JOSEPH[4], b. April 8, 1717.

    m. Tamson Drew, dau. of Thomas Drew, of Dover, and had five children :

    1.   FRANCIS[5].

        Lived in Dover.

    2.   JOSEPH[5].

        m. (1) Sarah Nute, dau. of Joseph Nute, and granddaughter of Samuel Hayes, of Portsmouth ; (2) Betsy Libby. Lived in Dover.

    3.   ELIJAH[5].

        m. Abigail Thomas, dau. of the third wife of Samuel Hayes by a former husband.

    4.   TAMSON[5].

        m. John *Drew*, of Barnstead.

    5.   ABIGAIL[5].

        m. Paul *Hayes*, of Acton, Me.

II.   ENOCH[4], b. ———, d. young.

III. JOHN⁴ (Major).

> m. Sarah Waterhouse, of Portsmouth, lived in Portsmouth, and had three children :

1. JOHN⁵.

> m. Sarah⁵ Ham, dau. of Samuel Ham, of Dover, who m. Sarah⁴ Wingate (b. 1738), dau. of John³ Wingate. They lived in Dover. [For children, see Sarah⁵ Ham].

2. SARAH⁵.

> m. Richard *Waldron*, son of Capt. Thomas W. Waldron, of Dover.

3. MARTHA⁵.

> m. —— ——, of Andover, Mass.

IV. ABIGAIL⁴.

> m. Benjamin *Libby*, of Dover, and had eight children :

1. SARAH⁵.

> m. Francis *Winkly*, of Canterbury.

2. ANN⁵.

> m. D. *Wentworth*.

3. ABIGAIL⁵.

> m. Major William *Blake*, of Dover.

4. DANIEL⁵.

> m. Mary Hodgdon, dau. of Shadrach Hodgdon, and lived in Dover.

5. ENOCH⁵.

> m. Martha Parshley, and lived in Strafford.

6. LYDIA,⁵ (twin to Betsy), b. ——, d. unm.

7. BETSY,⁵ (twin to Lydia).

> m. (1) Joseph *Drew*, of Dover; (2) William Plaisted *Drew*.

8. MARY⁵.

> m. William *Leighton*, son of Tobias Leighton, of Madbury.

V. BENJAMIN[4] (Col.).

m. Hannah Hanson, and lived in Dover. He was a Colonel in the Revolutionary War, and received wounds that troubled him through life. Had ten children :

1. DANIEL[5], b. ———, d. unm.

2. BENJAMIN[5].
    m. Mary Whitehouse, of Somersworth, and lived in Acton, Me.

3. JOSEPH[5].

4. NANCY[5].
    m. Ephraim *Wentworth*, of Newfield.

5. ISAAC[5], b. ———, d. unm.

6. SUSAN[5] (twin to William).
    m. Capt. James *Whitehouse*, of Dover.

7. WILLIAM[5] (twin to Susan).
    m. Eunice Whitehouse, and lived in Lebanon.

8. HANNAH[5].
    m. Nicholas *Peaslee*, of Dover.

9. SARAH[5], b. ———, d. young.

10. BETSY[5], b. ———, d. unm.

VI. ELIZABETH[4].

    m. Judge John *Plummer*, of Rochester, and had four children :

1. JOSEPH[5].

    m. Hannah Bickford, and lived in Milton.

2. ELIZABETH[5], b. February 22, 1750, d. May, 1841.

    m., Dec. 25, 1770, Hon. Aaron[4] *Wingate*, of Milton (b. Nov. 23, 1744, d. Feb. 1822). [For descendants, see Aaron[4], son of John[3]].

3. BEARD[5] (Hon.).

    m. Susan Ham, dau. of Capt. Jonathan Ham, of Rochester.

4. JOHN[5], b. ———, d. unm.

VII. SARAH[4].

    m. Samuel *Wingate*, of Rochester, her cousin.

VIII. MARY[4].

    m. ——— *Woodman*, of Lee, and had :

1. EBENEZER[5], b. ———, d. unm.

JOHN[1].

JOHN[2].

SARAH[3].

    m. Peter *Hayes*, and had eight children :

I. BENJAMIN[4].

    Lived in Harrington.

II. REUBEN[4].

    Lived in Dover.

III. JOHN[4].

    Lived in North Yarmouth, (Mass.) ?

IV. JOSEPH[4].

V. ICHABOD[4].

    Lived in Berwick, Me.

VI. ELIJAH[4].

VII. ANNA[4].

VIII. MEHITABLE[4].

JOHN 1.

JOHN 2.

MOSES 3.

m. (1) Abigail Church ; (2) Deborah (Cushing) Watson, and had eight children :

I. EDMOND 4, bapt. Sept. 14, 1729
m. ———, and had (probably) :

1. ANNA 5, bapt. Oct. 6, 1751.

— 2. JOHN 5, bapt. Sept. 23, 1753.

II. ABIGAIL 4, bapt. Sept. 14, 1729.
m. ——— *Tebbets*.

III. DEBORAH 4, bapt. Aug. 2, 1730.

IV. EBENEZER 4, bapt. Mar. 18, 1733.

V. ANN 4, bapt. Oct. 3, 1736.

VI. MOSES 4 (Capt.), bapt. Aug. 20, 1738, d. before June 27, '69.
m. Elizabeth Bennett, dau. of George and Elizabeth Bennett (the latter being dau. of George Vaughan, Lieut Gov. of N. H.).   Was shipmaster, of Portsmouth.   Had :

1. ELIZABETH B. 5.
m. John *Parker*, son of Rev. Noah Parker, and had one child :

   1. *William Bennett* 6.
   m. Elizabeth Marshall, dau. of Deacon Marshall, of Portsmouth, lived in Portsmouth, and had :
      1. John 7.
      Lived in Boston.   U. S. N.
      2. George 7.
      Lived in Great Falls [Somersworth].
      3. William 7
      U. S. N.
      4. Hannah 7.
      5. Charles 7.
      6. Daniel Ham 7.

VII. BENJAMIN 4, bapt. Sept. 28, 1740.

VIII. EBENEZER 4, bapt. May 23, 1742.

JOHN[1].
JOHN[2].
SAMUEL[3].

m. Mary (Roberts) Hurd, and had one child :

I. MARY[4].

m. near 1760, Lieut. Jonathan *Hayes*, of Dover, (b. Apr. 17, 1732, d. Apr. 15, 1787), youngest son of Deacon John Hayes [who when a widower married Mary[4]'s mother, when a widow], by his first marriage. Name extinct in this branch. Mary had eight children :

1. POLLY[5], b. ————, d. unm.

2. TAMSON[5].

m. Daniel *Cushing*, of Dover, and had seven children :

 1. Jonathan Hayes[6].
 2. Mary Hayes[6].
 3. Lydia Wingate[6].
 m. David *Sargent*, of Dover.
 4. Peter[6] (Deacon).
 5. Robert Hayes[6].
 6. Clarissa Ann[6].
 7. Samuel Wingate[6].
 Lived in Dover.

3. ROBERT[5], b. ————, d. an infant.

4. JONATHAN[5], b. ————, d. an infant.

5. ROBERT[5].

Lived in Vermont.

6. SARAH[5].

m. Samuel *Jackson*, of Rochester.

7. NANCY[5].

m. William *Cushing*, of Dover, and had four children.

 1. Thomas[6].
 2. Augustus[6].
 m. Rachel Parker, and lived in Somersworth.
 3. Jarvis[6].
 4. Nathan[6].

8. ELIZABETH[5].

m. ———— *Jackson*, of Rochester.

JOHN¹.

JOHN².

SIMON³.

m. Lydia Hill and had twelve children :

I.   ANNA⁴.

Admitted to First church, Biddeford, Me., May 9, 1762.

II. ELIZABETH⁴.

m. Dec. 24, 1761, Joshua *Haley*, of Biddeford, Me..

III. HANNAH⁴.

m. May 10, 1761, Samuel *Chase*, of Pepperelboro, Me.

IV. SNELL⁴, bapt. Feb. 3, 1744.

m. (1) Dec. 1, 1768, Margaret Emery, of Biddeford, Me.,
(d. Nov. 29, 1783) ; (2) June, 1788, Mehitable Crocker, of
Dunstable, Mass., widow of Elijah Crocker, a sea captain, and
sister of Solicitor-General Daniel Davis. (Mehitable Crocker
had by her first husband a daughter who married, Oct. 30,
1796, Edward Woodman, of Searsmont, Me. ; descendants
now living in Cambridge, Mass). Snell settled in Buxton,
Me., in that part of the town now known as Buxton Centre.
He lived and died in a house now [1885] standing, which
he probably built, the house standing on Lot 12, Range D.
of 3rd Div. He was Selectman for eleven years. Snell had
five children by his first wife and six by his second :

1.   MOLLY⁵, bapt. April 3, 1770.

m. Dec. 27, 1788, Daniel *Bradbury*, of Athens, Me.

2.   SAMUEL⁵, bapt. Aug. 26, 1772.

m. Oct. 7, 1796, Molly Woodman, of Buxton, Me., and had
five children :

1.   *William*⁶.

Lived in Standish, and Limerick, Me.

2.   *Edmund*⁶.

Lived and died in Saco, Me., leaving a son who lived in
Boston.

3. *Margaret* [6].

4. *" Nabby "* [6].
> m. —— *Scribner,* and had three sons.
> Lived in Buxton, Me.

5. *Harriet* [6].

3. DANIEL [5], bapt. Aug. 27, (prob. 1775-76), d. Feb. 5, 1832.
m., 1802, Sarah Whittier. Settled near his father and lived
there until his death. Had numerous daughters and one son,
John [6], who left town young and was never heard from afterwards. The daughters also left Buxton.

4. ABIGAIL [5], bapt. Aug. 3, 1777.
[Authorities differ: Some have, instead of Abigail [5], Snell [5],
b. Aug. 17, 177-, d. Aug. 22, 1779].

5. SIMON [5], b. Aug. 27, 1780.
[Or, "bapt. Sept. 1, 1771," authorities differing].

6. ROBERT DAVIS [5], b. Aug. 8, 1789, d. April 23, 1806.

7. ELIJAH CROCKER [5], b. Dec. 17, 1790, d. s. p.
m. Mary Lombard, of Gorham, Me.

8. SNELL [5], b. Aug. 7, 1792, d. 1814.

9. ANSEL [5], b. March 16, 1794, d. 1814.
Died in the War of 1812.

10. MARGARET EMERY [5], b. Jan. 3, 1797.

11. JOHN [5], b. April 28, 1799, d. 1859.
m. Jan. 22, 1821, Salome Small, of Buxton, Me., (b. Dec. 10,
1802); (2) Sept. 22, 1829, Mrs. Sophronia Frost, widow,
(b. Sept. 5, 1799). Lived in Gorham, Me., and had, by
first wife, three children, by second, eight:

1. *Ansel D.* [6], b. May 31, 1822.
· m. Sept. 1, 1848, Almira Scamman, and had:
1. Martha S. [7], b. July, 1849.
m. Calvin J. *Rothe,* and had:
(*a*) Lewis C. [8].
(*b*) Eugenia [8].
2. Maria [7].

2. *Sarah P.*[6], b. November 22, 1823.
    m. Oct. 8, 1847, Edward A. *Scamman,* and had :

1. Elizabeth[7], b. September 3, 1848.
    m. June, 1881, Henry C. *Hallowell,* and had :
    (*a*)   Susan E.[8], b. April 16, 1885.

2. Anna M.[7], b. October 6, 1851.

3. Edward A.[7], b. March 13, 1858.

3. *Maria J. H.*[6], b. November 7, 1825.
    m. Nov. 3, 1848, Leander *Stevens,* and had :

1. Leander L.[7], b. November 20, 1849.
    m. Dec. 16, 1874, Mrs. Lucy Blanchard, and had :
    (*a*)   L. Elwood[8], b. September 6, 1877.
    (*b*)   Alice G.[8], b. March 3, 1879.

2. John C.[7], b. October 8, 1855.
    m. December 25, 1876, Louisa Waldron, and had :
    (*a*)   John H.[8], b. February 23, 1879.
    (*b*)   Caroline M.[8], b. September 2, 1880.
    (*c*)   Margaret L.[8], b. October 8, 1884.

3. Lydia M.[7], b. August 10, 1859.

4. Harry W.[7], b. January 8, 1869.

4. *Rebecca I.*[6], b. October 30, 1830.

5. *Salome S.*[6], b. March 4, 1833.
    m. (1) July 1, 1852, George J. *Prentiss;* (2) Jan. 6, 1877, George W. *Newbegin.*

6. *Henry F.*[6], (twin), b. February 28, 1835.

7. *James I.*[6], (twin), b. February 28, 1835.

8. *James I.*[6], b. June 4, 1837.
    m. May 18, 1870, Helen Frances Edgecomb, and had :

1. Frank Elmer[7], b. January 3, 1872.

9. *Mary G.*[6], b. March 13, 1840.

10. *Ellen L.*[6], b. April 2, 1843.

11. *John P.*[6], b. March 7, 1846.

V. SIMON[4], bapt. June 21, 1747, d. unm.
Went to sea with his uncle, Capt. John[4] Clark, of Portsmouth, and d. in London, Eng.

VI. JOHN[4], bapt. April 8, 1750.
m. Aug. 26, 1773, Lydia Hill, dau. of Jeremiah Hill, of . Biddeford, Me.   Had nine children:

1. JEREMIAH[5], b. February 23, 1775.

2. MOLLY[5], b. April 20, 1777.

3. EDMUND[5], b. June 15, 1779.

4. JOHN HILL[5], b. May 5, 1781.

5. REBECCA[5], b. April 17, 1784.

6. SARAH[5], b. May 21, 1785, d. April, 1806.
m. William *Perry*, and had one child:

   1. Samuel Hill[6], b. February 25, 1806.

7. HANNAH[5], b. August 2, 1788.

8. EBENEZER[5], b. January 7, 1791.

9. LYDIA[5], b. July 16, 1793.

VII. LYDIA[4], bapt. April 26, 1752.
Admitted to First Church, Biddeford, Me., July 20, 1777.

VIII. EDMUND[4], bapt. January 5, 1755.
Lived in Newburyport, Mass.

IX. ———[4].

X. LUCY[4], bapt. December 25, 1757.

XI. SARAH[4], bapt. March 22, 1761.

XII. SUSANNA[4].

CHAPTER IX.

DESCENDANTS OF JOSHUA[2].

The genealogical tables in this chapter give the descendants of Joshua[2], youngest son of John[1] Wingate.

JOHN[1].
JOSHUA[2] (Col.).
PAINE[3] (Rev.).
m. Mary Balch, and had twelve children:

I. MARY[4], b. December 28, 1728, d. March 16, 1800.
    m. January 20, 1752, Ephraim *Elliott.*

II. ELIZABETH[4], b. September 17, 1730, d., s. p., Nov. 5, 1815.
    m. June 4, 1735, Dr. Gershom *Bartlett.*

III. PAINE[4], b. August 10, 1732, d. October 10, 1736, "with ye canker."

IV. SARAH[4], b. November 23, 1734, d. November 6, 1736, "with ye canker."

V. SARAH[4], b. April 27, 1737 (O. S.), d. August 28, 1824.
    m. (1) Dec. 18, 1760, Samuel *Bradley* (b. 1731), son of Daniel and Elizabeth (Ayer) Bradley, and grandson of Joseph and Hannah (Heath) Bradley; (2) Daniel *Quimby.*

(VI.) PAINE[4] (Rev. and Hon.), b. May 14, 1739, d. March 7, 1838, m. May 23, 1765, Eunice[4] Pickering, his cousin (b. April. 19, 1742, d. Jan. 7, 1843). Paine[4] lived in Hampton Falls and Stratham ; was clergyman, Representative in Legislature, Representative in Congress, United States Senator and Judge. [See Chapter VI for full sketch.] They had five children :

1. MARY[5], b. July 12, 1766, d. October 6, 1840.
   m. Jan. 6, 1788, as second wife, Major Andrew *Wiggin*, of Stratham (b. July 14, 1752, d. Jan. 22, 1836). They had seven children :

   1. *Harriet*[6], b. October 27, 1788, d. April 6, 1836.

   2. *Caroline*[6], b. April 20, 1790, d. June 19, 1817. ·

   3. *Andrew Paine*[6], b. Sept. 1, 1791, d. s. p. May 20, 1846.
      m. Jan. 23, 1821, as second husband, Olive Gilbert, (d. Dec. 31, 1822).

   4. *Eliza*[6], b. February 23, 1794, d. December 9, 1872.
      m. April 23, 1820, Andrew *Taylor*, (b. Sept. 12, 1789, d. Dec. 27, 1862), and had :

      1. Andrew Bartlett[7], b. February 14, 1821.
         m. Jan. 28, 1847, Hedassah E. Harriman, (b. July 8, 1827), and had :
         (*a*) Charles Green[8], b. Oct. 15, 1848, d. Aug. 23, 1867.
         (*b*) Flora Maria[8], b. August 9, 1851.
            m. George Daniel Sawyer *Noyes*, (b. Aug. 18, 1847), son of George and Mary E. (Sawyer) Noyes, of Concord. Lived in Pittsfield.

      2. Charles Green[7], b. August 8, 1823, d. June 14, 1842.

      3. George Osgood[7], b. Feb. 19, 1826, d. Dec. 27, 1851.

   5. *Caleb*[6], b. January 8, 1796.
      m. (1) Oct. 23, 1839, Eliza Adams, (b. Aug. 8, 1806, d. Feb. 27, 1847) ; (2) June 13, 1848, Amelia Robinson, and had :

      1. Mary C.[7], b. April 11, 1841.

      2. Annie E.[7], b. October 31, 1843.

      3. Caleb Miltimore[7], b. June 28, 1846, d. Nov. 25, 1846.

6. *Josiah Bartlett*⁶, b. February 10, 1801, d. August, 1811.

7. *Sarah Bartlett*⁶, b. August 19, 1803.
    m. May 13, 1827, Andrew W. *Miltimore*.

2. SARAH⁵, b. November 7, 1769, d. s. p., December 27, 1808.
    m. Hon. Dr. Josiah *Bartlett*, of Stratham, (b. Aug. 29, 1768,
    d. s. p. April 16, 1838). (He married a second time).

3. GEORGE⁵, b. May 14, 1778, d. September 12, 1852.

4. JOHN⁵ (Deacon), b. October 12, 1781, d. January 28, 1831.
    m., May 5, 1808, Sally Piper, (b. Jan. 25, 1788, d. March 21,
    1872), dau. of Samuel Piper, of Stratham, and his wife, Mary
    (Robinson) Piper, whose mother was Mercy Chase. [See
    "Chase-Townley Legacy," chapter VII]. John⁵ and Sarah
    lived in Stratham, and had ten children :

    1 *Sarah*⁶, b. March 14, 1809.
         m. May 12, 1832, Asa Pratt *Parkman*, of Palmyra, Me.,
         (b. Oct. 18, 1810), and had :
         1. Caroline Anna⁷, b. July 15, 1833, d. June 8, 1882.
             m. April 17, 1853, Daniel F. *Cook* (b. Sept. 3,
             1827), and had :
             (*a*) Francis Asa⁸, b. Aug. 18, 1855, d. Aug., 1867.
             (*b*) Maurice Benjamin⁸, b. March 31, 1858.
             (*c*) Abbie L.⁸, b. October 12, 1860.
                    m. Dec. 23, 1880, Cyrus L. *Hamilton*, of
                    Albion, Me.
             (*d*) Carrie Mabel⁸, b. March 13, 1865.
             (*e*) Frank Leslie⁸, b. Feb. 12, 1867, d. May, 1873.
             (*f*) Clarence D.⁸, b. October 30, 1870.
         2. John Letburn⁷, b. May 11, 1835.
         3. Sarah Elizabeth⁷, b. Jan. 24, 1837, d. Sept. 12, 1873.
             m. Sept. 17, 1854, Erasmus *Littlefield*, and had :
             (*a*) Edgar E.⁸, b. December 25, 1855.
                    m. May 6, 1883, Cora Foster, of Winthrop.
             (*b*) Oscar Leslie⁸, b. December 16, 1860.
             (*c*) Orietta M.⁸, b. May 23, 1863.
         4. Mary Helen⁷, b. March 12, 1840, d. July 31, 1863.

5. George Wingate[7], b. January 16, 1841.
    m. 1866, Melissa F. Robinson, and had :
    (*a*) George Willard[8], b. May 7, 1868.
    (*b*) Charles E.[8], b. March 13, 1870.
    (*c*) Annie Helen[8], b. February 25, 1872.
    (*d*) Nellie Emma[8], b. June 16, 1876.
    (*e*) Amy G.[8], b. Oct. 25, 1878, d. Jan. 23, 1881.
    (*f*) Albert Russell[8], b. April 2, 1881.
    (*g*) Ralph[8], b. 1884.
6. Loretta Eldora[7], b. 1843, d. 1846.
7. Augustine Henry[7], b. August 3, 1846.
8. Sylvester Dana[7], b. January 5, 1849.
9. Charles Frederic[7], b. September 8, 1852.
10. Laura J. Bartlett[7], b. February 15, 1855.
    m. March, 1876, Frederick E. *Flanders*, (b. April
    7, 1855).

2. *Mary*[6], b. November 2, 1810.
    m. April 18, 1833, Rev. George William *Thompson*, of
    Stratham, (b. March 29, 1807).

3. *Elizabeth*[6], b. August 25, 1812.
    m. March 17, 1831, Benjamin Franklin *Clark*, son of
    Benjamin and Elizabeth (Wiggin) Clark. Lived in
    Stratham and Exeter, and had :
    1. John Wingate[7], b. April 16, 1832.
        m. Martha Ellen Sarah Philbrick, and had :
        (*a*) Lizzie Ellen Sarah[8], b. March 25, 1854.
            m. August, 1876, William H. *Blodgett*, and
            had :
            1. Frankie Elizabeth[9], b. March, 1878.
            2. Alice Agnes[9], b. December, 1879.
            3. Clara Belle[9], b. December, 1881.
            4. Mary Clark[9], b. 1884.
        (*b*) Jessie Hannah Perry[8], b. June 24, 1856.
            m. January, 1879, Edgar T. *Humphrey*, and
            had :
            1. Nellie E.[9], b. August, 1880.
        (*c*) John Franklin[8], b. September 2, 1861.
        (*d*) Daniel[8], b. January 20, 1866.

2.   George Franklin[7], b. August, 1834, d. 1845.

3.   Mary Elizabeth[7], b. February 15, 1841, d. April 6, 1883.

4.   Sarah Caroline[7], b. August 10, 1843.

5.   Anna Robbins[7], b. Nov. 26, 1850, d. Aug. 20, 1870.

6.   Benjamin Franklin[7], b. Dec. 4, 1852, d. April 13, 1873.

4.   *John Paine[6]*, b. June 10, 1814, d. April 9, 1841.
     m. Mary O. Folsom, and had :

     1.   Elias Paine[7], b. April, 1840, d. November 12, 1840.

5.   *Anna Homer[6]*, b. December 1, 1816.
     m. Feb. 5, 1845, John H. *Gilbert*, (b. Jan. 8, 1816).
     Lived in Stratham and in Ipswich, Mass., and had :

     1.   John Ransom[7], b. October 22, 1848, d. April 6, 1869.

     2.   Anna Olive[7], b. September 17, 1850.
          m. Dec. 31, 1869, Clarence A. *Wonson*, and had :
          (*a*)   Gertrude Homer[8], b. March 14, 1872.
          (*b*)   Marion Stuart[8], b. December 27, 1878.

     3.   Andrew Paine Wingate[7], b. August 28, 1855.

     4.   William Murray[7], b. April 10, 1860, d. May 5, 1860.

     5.   Sarah Miltimore[7], b. February 20, 1862.

6.   *Caroline Wiggin[6]*, b. January 31, 1819.
     m. May 31, 1851, Samuel *Baker*, (b. Oct. 26, 1809).
     Lived in Portsmouth, Stratham and Exeter, and had :

     1.   Mary Thompson[7], b. February 3, 1853, d. May 1, 1867.

     2.   Caroline Wingate[7], b. April 4, 1857, d. August 9, 1857.

     3.   Florence Ella[7], b. June 8, 1859, d. July 15, 1883.

     4.   Dana Wingate[7], b. August 1, 1861.

     5.   Elizabeth Homer[7], b. June 16, 1864.

7.   *George[6]*, b. November 28, 1820.
     m. Nov. 30, 1854, Clarinda Frost, (b. March 3, 1832),
     dau. of John and Hannah (Morrill) Frost.   Lived in
     Stratham, and had :

     1.   Isabel C.[7], b. March 2, 1858.

     2.   George Frederick[7], b. July 1, 1859, d. June 23, 1883.
          D. C. 1878

8. *Henry Pickering* [6], b. June 22, 1823.

    m. Jan. 1, 1855, Sarah Ann Pearson, (b. Feb. 28, 1833).
Lived in Stratham, Exeter and Hampton, and had :

  1. Henry Pickering [7], b. March 1, 1856, d. April 18, 1874.

  2. Mary Shannon [7], b. January 12, 1858.

  3. Elizabeth March [7], b. December 7, 1859.

  4. John Paine [7], b. March 30, 1862.

  5. Sarah Pearson [7], b. June 13, 1864.

  6. Oliver Shannon [7], b. August 25, 1870.

  7. Charles [7], b. September 21, 1872, d. November 5, 1876.

  8. Edith [7], b. November 9, 1876.

9. *Samuel Dana* [6], b. December 23, 1826, d. July 5, 1867.

    m. Feb. 8, 1854, Orianna Mitchell, (b. Feb. 8, 1834),
dau. of Lewis and Fannie Dearborn (Wedgewood)
Mitchell, of Exeter. She m. (2) Oct. 21, 1873, James
Munroe Lovering, (b. Oct. 12, 1817, d. Aug. 24, 1885).
Samuel Dana [6] and Orianna Wingate lived in Exeter, and
had :

  1. James Dana Paine [7], b. April 2, 1855.

      m. June 7, 1883, Helen Woodbury Locke, of Ports-
mouth, (b. Jan. 23, 1860), dau. of Woodbury and
Jane Locke. Publisher of "The Exeter Gazette."
He had :

      (*a*) Helen [8], b. May 25, 1885.

  2. Charles Edgar Lewis [7], b. Feb. 14, 1861.

      m. Sept. 9, 1885, Mabel Nickerson, (b. June 24,
1865) dau. of John Freeman and Susan Sophia
(Robinson) Nickerson, of Boston, Mass. H. U.
1883. Engaged on the staff of the " Boston Daily
Journal ", 1883.

10. *Joseph Charles Augustus* [6], b. Nov. 16, 1830.

    m. Oct. 19, 1860, Mary Green (b. May 3, 1836, d. Nov. 3,
1876). Bowd. Col. 1851. For many years United
States Consul at Swatow and Foo Chow, China.

5. ELIZABETH [5], b. April 15, 1783, d. unm. Sept. 14, 1829.

VII. JOHN⁴, b. July 4, 1741, d. March 4, 1742.

VIII. JOHN⁴ (Dr.), b. June 25, 1743, d. s. p. July 26, 1819.
m. Sarah Webster. He was a surgeon in the Continental
Army, and was an intimate friend of the brave Koskiusko
with whom on parting he exchanged miniatures. [It is
said that the miniature presented to John⁴ is now in the
possession of some member of the family]. John⁴ was
appointed by Congress to accompany Gen. Lafayette to
his home in France, and while there he remained the General's guest. Dr. John⁴ lived and died in Hallowell, Me.

IX. WILLIAM⁴, b. July 9, 1745, d. Nov. 30, 1821.
m. Mehetable Bradley, (b. Oct. 23, 1747, d. July 22, 1796)
dau. of William and Mehetable (Emerson) Bradley, and gd.
dau. of Joseph and Hannah (Heath) Bradley. The Bradley family was connected also with the Wingates by marriage with Moses⁵, son of William⁴, and with Sarah⁴, dau.
of Rev. Paine³. William⁴ and Mehetable lived in Haverhill, Mass., and had eleven children :

1. PAINE⁵, b. Dec. 20, 1767, d. Feb. 20, 1833.
m. Aug. 1792, Mary Pecker, of New Salem. Lived in Haverhill, Mass., and had five children :

   1. *James⁶*, b. June 11, 1793, d. s. p.
   m. Ann Hersey, of Hingham, Mass., and lived in Haverhill, Mass.

   2. *Paine⁶*, b. Mar. 24, 1795.
   m. and lived in New York and Penn.

   3. *Mary⁶*, b. Feb. 22, 1797. Unm.

   4. *Priscilla⁶*, b. Aug. 24, 1799. Unm.

   5. *Mehetable Bradbury⁶*, b. Feb. 22, 1802, d. unm. at Haverhill, Mass.

2. MOSES[5] (Hon.), b. Oct. 25, 1769, d. June 15, 1870.

    m. (1) Mehetable Bradley (b. April 9, 1774, d. Nov. 5, 1807), dau. of Peter Bradley and gd. dau. of Daniel and Elizabeth (Ayer) Bradley, and great gd. dau. of Joseph and Hannah (Heath) Bradley; (2) Sarah Smith, of Pelham, N. H. (b. July 18, 1785, d. Aug. 15, 1820). Lived in Haverhill, Mass. [See sketch Chapter VII]. Moses[5] had two children by his first wife, and four by his second:

1. Peter[6], b. Nov. 30, 1793, d. Aug., 1876.
    m. Evelina ———, of Philadelphia.

2. Mehetable[6], b. Nov. 29, 1795, d. unm. Mar. 11, 1817.

3. Moses[6], d. aged 12.

4. Charles[6] (Rev.) b. Feb. 20, 1815.
    m. Lucy F. Stone, (b. Feb. 15, 1732) dau. of Alpheus F. Stone, M. D., of Greenfield, Mass. Was for some years a merchant in Philadelphia; was admitted to Holy Orders Dec. 15, 1858, and since 1875 has been Rector of the Church of St. John the Evangelist, Haverhill, Mass.

5. Maria[6], b. Feb. 12, 1817, d. Nov. 25, 1835.

6. James[6], b. April 24, 1820, d. June 12, 1851.
    Lived in Haverhill, Mass.

3. MEHETABLE[5], b. Aug. 29, 1772, d. May 24, 1846.
    m. Dec. 31, 1792, Thomas *Woodbury*, of Montreal, Can., and had six children:

1. Clarissa[6].

2. Mehetable[6].

3. Sarah[6].

4. Elisha[6].

5. Nancy[6].

6. Edward[6].

4. SARAH[5], b. Sept. 20, 1774, d. Mar. 3, 1857.
   m. Nov. 27, 1792, Abner *Kenrick*, of Haverhill, Mass., and
   had seven children :

   1.   Sarah[6].
   m. Joseph *Dolloff*, of Exeter.

   2.   William Wingate[6].

   3.   Mehetable Bradley[6], b. 1798.
      m. (1) Moses *Ayer*; (2) Mason *Whipple*, both of Ha-
      verhill, Mass., and had, by her first husband :

      1. Caroline[7].
         m. (1) Edward *Emerson*, of Waltham, Mass.; (2)
         —— ——; (3) —— ——, and had by her first
         husband :
         (*a*) Charles F.[8]

      2. Edwin F.[7], b. 1819.
         m. Elizabeth Gage, and had, besides two who died
         young :
         (*a*) Florence[8]
         (*b*) Isabel[8]

   4.   James[6].
      Lived in Maine.

   5.   Anna Frances[6], d. unm.

   6.   Francis[6],
      m. Minerva Crowde.

   7. *Mary*[6].
      m. George W. *Sargent.*

5. WILLIAM[5], b. June 9, 1777, d. unm. April 12, 1796, at sea.

6. ABIGAIL[5], b. August 12, 1779, d. unm. July 28, 1861.

7. FREDERIC[5], b. January 11, 1782, d. November 16, 1864.
m. Jan. 12, 1806, Hannah Page, of Augusta, Me., (b. April 10, 1784, d. March 28, 1864). They lived in Augusta, Me. He left Haverhill, Mass., for Augusta, Me., in 1804. He was a maker of clocks, an article seldom seen in those days. The first clock Mr. Wingate sold was to Ezekiel Page. Mr. Page had never had a clock. He wanted one, but did not know how to take care of it, and none of his family knew how. To remove this difficulty Mr. Wingate proposed, if he would purchase, to call weekly and wind it until the family should learn to take care of it. This offer was accepted, the clock made and set up, and the young clock-maker commenced his weekly visits. He soon found he had considerable anxiety about that clock. His visits became frequent, although the clock appeared to be keeping excellent time. In short, Mrs. Page's daughter Hannah was learning the mystery of taking care of the clock, and her tutor in the art took so much interest in teaching that the diploma of competency turned out to be a marriage certificate. Mr. Wingate always said that his first bargain was the best he ever made. He had seven children :

1. *Eliza Ann*[6], b. April 21, 1807, d. December 1, 1807.

2. *Charles Frederic*[6], b. March 1, 1809, d. March 6, 1885.

3. *Susan*[6], b. December 30, 1811.
m. Sept. 16, 1835, Daniel *Waldron*, of Augusta, Me., (b. July 3, 1809, d. Nov. 1873), and had :

1. Susan Wingate[7], b. June 9, 1838.

2. Daniel Wingate[7] (Rev.), b. November 11, 1840.
m. Sept. 4, 1867, Mary A. Waite, of Braintree, Mass. Lived in Boston, where he was for many years City Missionary. Had :
(*a*) ———[8] (dau.), b. Dec. 25, 1869, d. Dec. 27, 1869.
(*b*) Mary Russell[8], b. October 23, 1871.

3. Anna Sheafe[7], b. March 31, 1848.
m. April 16, 1884, E. *Gould*, of Augusta, Me.

4. Emma Alberta [7], b. October 2, 1851.
    m. Sept. 24, 1873, John A. *Raymond*, of East Wey-
    mouth, Mass., and had :
    (*a*)   Frederick Wingate [8], b. October 14, 1874.
    (*b*)   Emma Watterman [8], b. May 10, 1876.
    (*c*)   Alberta Waldron [8], b. June 24, 1878.
    (*d*)   Robert Bates [8], b. November 8, 1880.
    (*e*)   Walter Lee [8], b. October 29, 1884.

4. Hannah Elizabeth [6], b. Jan. 15, 1815, d. Nov. 24, 1884.

5. Emmeline [6], b. January 10, 1817, d. May 4, 1870.
    m. Jan. 10, 1866, Dr. J. W. *Toward*.

6. Franklin [6], b. January 8, 1820, d. June 16, 1863.

7. Caroline Augusta [6], b. March 27, 1823, d. May 4, 1824.

8. FRANCIS [5], b. August 13, 1784, d. January 19, 1843.
    m. (1) Rebecca Dolloff (d. Aug. 13, 1820) ; (2) Rebecca
    Goodwin, (d. April 3, 1832), of Kennebunk.   Lived in Ports-
    mouth and Westbrook, Me., and had eleven children, eight by
    first wife :

1. George [6], b. December 8, 1805, d. March 29, 1885.
    m. Sarah Wise, of Portsmouth, and lived in that city.
    They had :

    1. George Edwin [7].
        He entered the United States Navy as Acting Ensign
        in 1863 ; served on a blockading squadron during
        the Rebellion ; transferred to the regular navy at the
        end of the War ; was commissioned as Lieutenant
        Commander July 13, 1870 ; torpedo service 1872 ;
        R. S. New Hampshire 1874 ; commanding Ajax
        (iron-clad), N. A. Station, 1875-76 ; Adams, S. A.
        Station, 1877-78 ; stationed at nitre station, Malden,
        Mass., 1884.

2. James Woodbury [7].

    m. Nov. 12, 1863, Carrie E. Senter. Sailmaker U. S. N. Lived in Portsmouth, and had:

    (*a*) Annie [8], b. December 26, 1867.

2. *Eliza Ann* [6], b. September 16, 1807.

    m. Sept. 9, 1832, Ephraim R. *Knox*, of Portsmouth, [who m. (2) Eliza Jane Dixon], and had:

    1. Charles Henry [7], b. June 9, 1833.

    2. ————— [7] (son), b. April 17, 1835, d. April 17, 1835.

    3. Charlotte Ann [7], b. November 22, 1837.

    4. Harriet Maria [7], b. March 21, 1839.

    5. Charles Henry [7], b. January 17, 1842.

    6. John Hill [7], b. October 30, 1844.

        m. Oct. 29, 1869, Abbie A. Gotham, and had:

        (*a*) Susie Ricker [8], b. January 26, 1874.

        (*b*) Ralph Wingate [8], b. March 31, 1885.

    7. Mary Ellen [7], b. September 7, 1847.

3. *Francis* [6], b. Sept. 8, 1809, d. at sea.

4. *Mary Jane* [6], b. March 9, 1812.

    m. July 12, 1835, Silas *Moody*, of Dover, (b. 1811, d. April 22, 1875), and had seven children, of whom two were living in 1885:

    1. Charles Wingate [7], b. Jan. 23, 1838.

        m. ——— ———, and lived in Worcester, Mass.

    2. James Henry [7], b. April 18, 1840.

        m. Nov. 26, 1885, Flora Fleming, of Manlius, N. Y., and lived in Dover.

5. *James Henry* [6], b. Nov. 25, 1813, d. Aug. 10, 1857.

    m. (1) Esther Merrill d. s. p.; (2) Mrs. Charlotte Kelburn, of New York.

6. *Joseph Dolloff*[6], b. Feb. 1, 1816, d. Oct. 18, 1846.
    m. Elizabeth Merrill, of Parsonsfield, Me., (d. Dec. 5, 1842), and had :

   1. Cora E.[7], b. April 18, 184–.
      Adopted by James H.[6] Wingate.   Lived in Boston.

   2. Forrest[7], b. Oct., 1842, d. Nov. 15, 1842.

7. *Martha Maria*[6], b. July 22, 1818.
    m. Joseph *McNeil*, and had two children.

8. *Edward Bradley*[6], b. Aug. 7, 1820.
    m. Sarah Rigdon, dau. of Sidney Rigdon.   Lived in Friendship, N. Y.

9. *John Foster*[6], b. July 28, 1823, d. in Brunswick, Me., while preparing for the ministry.

10. *Rebecca Wiley*[6], b. Dec. 8, 1825.

11. *Charlotte Jackson*[6], b. March 26, 1829.

9. SUSANNA[5].
    m. Asa *Davis*, of Hallowell, Me., and removed to Iowa. They had seven children :

   1. *William Bradley*[6], b. ———, d. unm.

   2. *Susan Wingate*[6].

   3. *John Wingate*[6].

   4. *Moses Moody*[6].

   5. *Mehetable Wingate*[6].

   6. *Emily Augusta*[6].

   7. *Julia Maria*[6].

10. HARRISON[5], b. Aug. 7, 1788, d. July 15, 1869.

m. (1) Chloe Smith; (2) Sarah Smith, of Belgrade, Me.
Lived in Charlestown —— and had nine children:

1. *Harrison*[6], b. ——, d. 1844.
Drowned in Mobile harbor.

2. *Caroline*[6], b. June 17, 1815.
m. March 31, 1845, Joseph *Moore*, of Mobile, Ala., and
had:

1. Caroline[7], b. April 15, 1851.
m. Aug. 24, 1876, Clarence E. *Kelley*, Principal of
Haverhill, Mass., High School, and had:
(*a*) Lucy Jeannette[8].
(*b*) Wingate[8].
(*c*) Henry[8].
(*d*) Clarence Moore[8].

2. Hannah[7], b. June 17, 1855, d. unm., Sept. 16, 1878.

3. *Sarah*[6].

4. *Maria*[6].
m. 1844, Phineas Sprague *Blair*, of Cambridgeport,
Mass., and had:

1. Alfred Blair[7].
Lived in Boston.

5. *George*[6].
m. Louisa ——, and lived in Philadelphia.

6. *Frederick Augustus*[6].

7. *Edward*[6], b. 1830.

8. *Napolean*[6], b. Feb. 17, 1833.

9. *Abigail*[6], b. Dec. 22, 1835.

11. ANNA[5], b. June 21, 1792, d. Oct. 11, 1807.

X. JOSHUA⁴, (Col.), b. March 3, 1747, d. Oct. 11, 1844.
m. Hannah Carr, (b. Oct., 1758), dau. of Deacon James Carr.
About 1794 he removed to Hallowell, Me., and was an active
merchant there for many years. He afterwards held the
office of Post-master for a number of years. He lived to a
remarkable old age, becoming, however, totally blind in his
later years. Up to the time of his death he wore small
clothes and knee buckles. He was "universally respected
for his industry, integrity and a faithful discharge of all the
social and Christian duties." When Deacon James Carr
withdrew from the Congregational Society to join the Baptists,
Joshua⁴ and his family seceded also. When Joshua⁴ moved
to Maine most of the passages thither were made by vessel,
but Mrs. Wingate, not liking the sea voyage, undertook the
journey in a chaise. Finding, however, the roads so very
rough her husband was obliged to have a servant on each side
of the vehicle to keep it upright and pry it out of occasional
mud-holes. Joshua⁴ purchased a large tract of farming land
in the town of Windsor. He had six children :

1. JOSHUA⁵, (Gen.), b. June 28, 1773, d. Nov. 6, 1843.
   m. Nov. 17, 1799, Julia Cascaline Dearborn, (b. Oct. 10,
   1781, d. Feb. 11, 1867), daughter of the Revolutionary
   patriot, Major General Henry Dearborn, and sister of Gen.
   H. A. S. Dearborn, of Roxbury, Mass. Joshua⁵ graduated
   at Harvard 1795, and in early life was associated with his
   father in mercantile pursuits. When Major Gen. Dearborn
   was appointed, in 1801, Secretary of War under Pres.
   Jefferson, Mr. Wingate accompanied him to Washington and
   was for several years second to Secretary Dearborn in the
   War Department. But his health was impaired by the Southern climate, and therefore he was appointed Collector of
   Customs at Bath, Me., which office he resigned in 1822, and
   removed to Portland, Me., where he resided (excepting a
   few years at Hallowell, Me.), until his death. He was a
   Brigadier General of the militia, and a member of the Convention which formed the constitution of the State of Maine
   in 1819, being upon the important committee which drafted
   that constitution. He was also President of the U. S. Branch

Bank at Portland during its existence. He served in the State Legislature a number of years. In 1820-21 he was one of the Presidential Electors of Maine and cast his vote for James Monroe. He was candidate for Governor of Maine twice, in 1821 and 1822, but failed of election. From 1827 to 1831 he was a member of the United States Congress. His wife survived him. They had:

1. *Julia Octavia*[6], b. Aug. 7, 1800, d. Feb. 13, 1877.
    m. Sept. 20, 1820, Charles Quincy *Clapp*, of Portland, Me., (d. March 2, 1868), and had two sons and two daughters:

    1. Julia Elizabeth Dearborn[7], b. July 4, 1821.
        m. Aug. 23, 1843, John Bryce *Carroll*, of Va., (d. Oct. 15, 1868). Lived in Portland, Me., and had:
        (*a*) Octavia C.[8], b. Jan. 17, 1846.
        (*b*) Charles Asa Clapp[8], b. April 19, 1847, d. May 11, 1865.
        (*c*) George Wingate[8], b. Oct. 10, '49, d. April 8, '65.
        (*d*) John Hicks[8], b. July 21, 1852.

    2. Georgianna Wingate[7], b. Nov. 30, 1822.
        m. Nov. 10, 1845, Winthrop Gray *Ray*, and lived in New York. Had:
        (*a*) Mary Gray[8], b. Oct. 20, 1846.
        (*b*) ———[8] (dau.), b. ———, d. aged 1 day.

    3. ———[7] (son; twin), b. ———, d. same day.

    4. ———[7] (son; twin), b. ———, d. same day.

2. *George Raleigh Dearborn*[6], b. April 4, 1807, d. unm. Apr. 24, 1826. Bowd. Col.

3. JOHN[5], b. 1776, d. unm. 1814.
    Was an officer in the U. S. Army; secretary to Hon. John Jay on his mission to Algiers to treat with the Bey for the suppression of piracy carried on by the subjects of that State. Died at Fort Sackett's Harbor.

3. JAMES[5], b. Jan. 15, 1778, d. aged 84.
    m. Ann Pope, dau of Capt. John Pope, U. S. N., and sister of
    Commodore Pope.   Was merchant at Hallowell, Me., and
    Post-master at Portland.   Afterwards moved to Windsor
    Farms.   They had four children :

 1. Algernon Sidney[6], b. 1807, d. 1847.
      m. Emma Glazier, and had :

      1. George Raleigh[7].

      2. Cassie[7].

      3. James[7].

      4. Thomas Tingey[7].

      5. Annie L.[7].

      6. Margaretta[7].

 2. Charles J.[6]
      m. (1) Mary P. Robinson, of Augusta, Me. ; (2) Mary
      T. Obrien of Thomaston, Me.   Lived in Waterville and
      Bangor, Me., and had one son by each wife :

      1. Charles W.[7]
          m. Katie Allen, dau. of Dr. H. G. Allen, of Dresden.
          Lived in Boston and had :

          (*a*)   Mary Kittie[8].

      2. William Henderson[7], b. Aug. 10, 1863.

 3. Mary Ann[6], d. in infancy.

 4. Julia Cascaline[6], b. June, 1805, d. May, 1885.
      m. Robert *Pope* (d. July, 1870), and had :

      1. Elizabeth[7].

      2. Emily[7].

      3. Robert[7].
          m. ———— and had :
          (*a*)   Robert W.[8].
          (*b*)   Ellis[8].

4. SALLY [5], b. June 24, 1782, d. 1864.
    m. William H. *Page*, and had :

    1. *Lucretia M.*[6], b. March 19, 1812, d. 1844.
        m. Hon. Jonathan P. *Rogers*, and had :
        1. Howard [7], b. 1836, d. December 26, 1872.
        2. Georgia [7], b. ———, d. May 7, 1847.

    2. *Adelaide Wingate* [6].
        m. Capt. W. A. *Noward*.

    3. *William Henry* [6].
        m. Mary E. McLellan, and had :
        1. Ella Wingate [7], b. May 6, 1844.
            m. Dr. T. L. *Ireland*, and had :
            (*a*) John Oakley [8], b. January 12, 1876.
            (*b*) Mary Wingate [8], b. March 16, 1877.
            (*c*) Howard Rogers [8], b. December 6, 1879.
            (*d*) Adelaide Page [8], b. March 7, 1881.

5. JOSEPH F.[5], b. June 29, 1786.
    m. Margaret Tingey, dau. of Commodore Tingey, of Washington, D. C., and had :

    1. *Virginia* [6].
        m. Com. Thomas *Craven*, U. S. Navy.

    2. *Tingey Henry* [6], (Lieut.).
        m. ——— Skinner. U. S. Navy.

    3. *Julia* [6].

    4. *Sidney* [6].
        m. ———.

6. MARY CARR [5], b. March 19, 1797, d. 1868.
    m. William A. *Woodbridge*.

XI. ABIGAIL⁴, b. March 27, 1749, d. August 28, 1807. m. Henry *Ingalls*, of Haverhill, Mass., and had three children:

1. THOMAS⁵.

2. ABIGAIL⁵.
   m. Capt. ————.

3. MARY⁵.
   m. 1806, Count Francis de *Vepart*, an exile from Guadaloupe in the time of the French Rebellion, and is the person referred to in Whittier's poem, "The Countess." [See Chapter VII].

XII. JOSEPH⁴, b. July 17, 1751, d. Sept. 18, 1828. m. Judith Carr, dau. of Elder James Carr. He was born in Amesbury, Mass., and lived there many years; all his children were born in Amesbury. About 1800 he came with his family to Maine and settled at Hallowell. He was called "Farmer" Wingate because he owned and cultivated a large farm in Hallowell. His wife's father first brought the "Baptist persuasion" into the family, Joseph⁴ severing his connection with the church of his father. Joseph⁴ had ten children:

1. SARAH⁵, b. 1777, d. Nov. 20, 1845.

2. JOSEPH⁵, b. July, 1779, d. Aug. 26, 1845.
   m. Sept. 18, 1803, Hannah Pecker (b. 1785–86, d. June 25, 1821), dau. of Deacon Pecker, of Parson Wingate's church, Amesbury. Joseph⁵ was a farmer. He moved to New Sharon, Me., some time before 1806. He had seven children:

   1. Abigail Weld⁶, b. June 26, 1806, d. s. p. Nov. 12, 1875. m. 1842 Peter *Atherton*, of Hallowell, Me.

   2. Sophia⁶, b. Oct. 2, 1808. m. Jonathan *Hallett*, of Waterville, Me.

3. *Henry F.*[6], b. Jan. 13, 1811.
     m. Laura A. Leadbetter, (d. 1885), of Hallowell, Me.;
     lived in Hallowell and Houlton, Me., and had:

     1. Hannah F.[7], b. Nov. 10, 1847, d. July 21, 1850.

     2. Joseph H[7], b. Sept. 23, 1850.
          m. Feb. 7, 1883, Lizzie Q. Webber.

4. *William Abbot*[6], b. Dec. 26, 1812, d. Oct. 15, 1879.
     m. April 13, 1837, Eliza White, of Winterport Me., (b.
     Dec. 9, 1813), dau. of John and Sarah White. Moved
     to Boston and had:

     1. Sarah Eliza[7], b. Sept. 20, 1839, d. April 21, 1842.

     2. Abbot P.[7], b. Aug. 3, 1844, d. May 23, 1866.

     3. William Tobey[7], b. Jan. 27, 1847, d. July 15, 1865.

5. *George*[6], b. Jan. 19, 1815, d. Sept. 1879.
     m. Abigail B. Ricker, of Cherryfield, Me. He moved to
     Cherryfield and had besides three children who died in
     infancy:

     1. Harriet S.[7], b. Oct. 17, 1844.
          m. Dec. 2, 1868, Edwin C. *Wakefield*, of Cherry-
          field, Me., and had:
          (*a*) Ida E.[8], b. Sept. 15, 1869.

     2. Edward R.[7], born Mar. 28, 1852.

     3. Mary A.[7], b. Oct. 13, 1855.

6. *Nathan M.*[6], b. Nov. 14, 1816, d. unm. April 25, 1844.

7. *Sarah*[6], b. Dec. 17, 1818; d. Oct. 22, 1848.
     m. Henry *Nason*, of New York, and had:

     1. Harry[7].

     2. Joseph W.[7]

     3. Sarah[7].
          m. George *Innis*, dentist in New York city.

3.   JUDITH[5], b. April 22, 1782, d. July 24, 1820.

m. Sept. 25, 1805, Nathan *Moody*, (b. at Newbury, Bayfield parish, Mass., Sept. 11, 1768 ; D. C. 1795 ; came to Hallowell, Me., July, 1796).   They had two children :

1.   Mary Elizabeth[6], b. July 25, 1806, d. Sept. 1, 1822.

2.   Caroline Judith[6], b. April 22, 1809, d. Nov. 19, 1853.

m. Oct. 21, 1828, Willham *Stickney*, of Hallowell, Me. (b. April 17, 1799), and had :

1.   William Moody[7], b. Aug. 16, 1829, d. Jan. 19, 1854.

2.   David Moody[7], b. Nov. 5, 1831, d. July 11, 1851.

3.   Joseph Wingate[7], b. Nov. 5, 1833.

m. Sept. 24, 1856, Harriet Harding of Union, Me., (b. May 24, 1832).   Lived in Hallowell, Me. and in Chelsea, Mass., and had :

(*a*)   Caroline Barrett[8], b. Feb. 13, 1858.

(*b*)   William[8], b. Apr. 29, 1868.

(*e*)   Henry Harding[8], b. May 20, 1870.

4.   Caroline Elizabeth[7], b. June 19, 1838, d. Apr. 24, 1880.

m. Jan. 14, 1869, George Henry *Hoyt*, of Bradford, Mass., (b. June, 1833), and had :

(*a*)   George Humphrey[8], b. Jan. 18, 1870.

4.   BETSEY[5], b. 1785, d. Feb. 21, 1826.

m. Daniel *Haines*, of Hallowell, Me. (his father from Concord, N. H.) and had twelve children.

5.   PAINE[5], b. 1787, d. Jan. 12, 1849.

m. (1) Mary Page, of Augusta, Me. ; (2) Charlotte Swan, of New Sharon, Me., (d. Jan. 14, 1855).   Had four children, two by each wife :

1.   Fred[6].

Lived in Illinois.

2.   Albert[6].

Lived in Illinois.

3.   Paine[6].

m. Eliza Wing, and had :

1.   Albert[7].

2.   Charlotte[7].

Lived in Manchester, Me.

4.   Elizabeth[6].

m. William *Sampson*.

6. FRANCIS[5], b. Jan. 5, 1789, d. May 14. 1848.

　　m. Jan. 14, 1823, Martha Savary, of Bradford, Mass. (b. Oct. 26, 1799, d. Feb. 24, 1862), grandau. of Eliphalet Rollins, of Bradford, lived in Hallowell, Me., and had two children :

　　1. Mary Savary[6], b. Aug. 6, 1825, d. Nov. 24, 1862.

　　　　m. Sept. 10, 1849, Dr. Moses Charles *Richardson*, (D. C. 1841), of Hallowell, Me., and had two children :

　　　　1. Charles Francis[7], b. May 29, 1851.

　　　　　　D. C. 1871. An Editor of the Independent, New York, 1872–1877 ; of the Sunday School Times, Philadelphia, 1878–1880 ; of Good Literature, New York, 1880–1882. Winkley Professor of Anglo-Saxon and English, Dartmouth College 1882. Author of " A Primer of American Literature," 1878, " The Cross " (poem), '1879 ; and " The Choice of Books," '81 ; also Editor of " The College Book," '78.

　　　　2. George Wingate[7], b. Mar. 2, 1854, d. Mar. 6, 1854.

　　2. George Francis[6], b. August 27, 1827.

　　　　m. Aug. 6. 1861, Emma A. Myers, of Manchester, Me., (b. Nov. 11, 1840). Lived in Hallowell, Me., and had :

　　　　1. Edward Francis[7], b. Dec. 25, 1862, d. Aug. 7, 1863.

　　　　2. Mary Mona[7], b. December 25, 1863.

　　　　3. Florence Martha[7], b. February 18, 1866.

　　　　4. Francis Savary[7], b. December 7, 1868.

7. WILLIAM ABBOT[5], b. 1791, d. May 1, 1817.

　　m. Elizabeth Lily, of Newburyport, Mass., and had one child :

　　1 Mary A.[6]

　　　　m. William *Nason*, of Hallowell, Me., and moved to Chicago.

8. ABIGAIL[5], b. 1795, d. October 4, 1819.

9. FREDERICK[5].

　　m. (1) Nancy ᴄᴏᴏ.r, of Hallowell, Me., d. s. p. ; (2) Miss Wingate, of Sebec, Me. Moved to Illinois. By second wife he had one child :

　　1 George[6].

10. MARY[5], b. 1799, d. January 4, 1816.

JOHN¹.
JOSHUA² (Col.).
SARAH³.

m. Dr. Edmund *Toppan*, and had five children :

I.   SARAH⁴, b. April 12, 1728.
     m.   (1) Jabez *Smith*; (2) Col. John *Webster*.

II. ANNA⁴, b. May 18, 1730, d. August 14, 1745.

III. MARY⁴, b. September 15, 1732, d. May 22, 1751.

IV. CHRISTOPHER⁴ (Col.), b. Jan. 18, 1735, d. Feb. 28, 1818.
     m. Sarah Parker, (b. about 1746, d. July 26, 1837), dau. of
     Hon. William and Elizabeth (Grafton) Parker, of Ports-
     mouth. Lived in Hampton. Was Representative to the
     State Legislature for a number of years between 1762 and
     1789, and Delegate to the Convention to revise the Consti-
     tution, Aug. 8, 1791. [For sketch of Col. Christopher⁴,
     see N. E. Mag., Jan., 1886]. They had four children :

  1.   ABIGAIL⁵, b. May 1, 1770, d. unm. September 11, 1866.
       Lived in Hampton.

  2.   SARAH⁵, b. May 18, 1775, d. June 22, 1857.
       m. Oct. 22, 1795, Rev. Dr. Nathaniel *Thayer*, of Lancaster,
       Mass., and had :

     1.   John Eliot⁶.
          Banker in Boston.

     2.   Nathaniel⁶, b. September 11, 1808.
          Banker in Boston. Donated "Thayer Hall" to Harvard
          College.

     3.   Christopher Toppan⁶ (Rev.).
          Lived in Beverly, Mass.

3. EDMUND [5], b. September 25, 1777, d. July 29, 1849.

m. June 22, 1799, Mary [5] Chase, (b. Nov. 15, 1776, d. Dec. 2, 1857), dau. of Stephen [4] and Mary (Frost) Chase, and granddaughter of Rev. Stephen and Jane [3] (Wingate) Chase. H. U. 1796. Practiced law in Portsmouth in 1799. Removed to Deerfield in 1800, and then to Hampton 1803. Representative in the State Legislature, 1809-18-22-26. Selectman 1808. Postmaster of Hampton for a number of years. Had six children :

1. *Christopher Stephen* [6] (Hon.), b. June 16, 1800, d. s. p. October 3, 1861.

m. April 10, 1827, Ann Elizabeth Salter, (b. April 5, 1799, d. Feb. 1, 1868). Was Mayor of Portsmouth.

2. *Elizabeth Grafton* [6], b. July 27, 1802, d. March 17, 1835.

3. *Mary Chase* [6], b. March 17, 1804.

4. *Edmund Willoughby* [6], b. Sept. 14, 1808, d. May 17, 1846.
m. May 17, 1832, Abigail March Pickering, of Greenland.

5. *Sarah Jane* [6], b. August 27, 1810, d. February 17, 1816.

6. *Sarah Jane Parker* [6], b. September 7, 1822.
m., Sept. 16, 1851, as second wife, Rev. Samuel Jones *Spalding*, and had :

1. Mary Toppan [7], b. December 22, 1856.

2. Abbie Toppan [7], b. March 23, 1860.

3. Edmund Samuel [7], b. January 5, 1865.

4. MARY ANN [5], b. October 27, 1780, d. October 15, 1817.
m. Oct. 30, 1803, Hon. Charles Humphrey *Atherton*, of Amherst, N. H., and had :

1. *Charles Gordon* [6].
Lawyer in Nashua. U. S. Senator and Representative.

V. EDMUND [4], b. 1739, d. February 9, 1740.

JOHN¹.
JOSHUA² (Col.).
MARY³.

m. Timothy *Pickering*, and had nine children :

I. SARAH⁴, b. January 28, 1730, d. November 21, 1826.
m. Capt. John⁴ *Clarke*, (b. Feb. 16, 1718-19, d. Jan. 7, 1800),
son of Josiah and Mary³ (Wingate) Clarke. He was "master
of a ship in ye London trade," and lived in Salem, Mass.
They had five children :

1. JOHN⁵ (Rev.), b. April 13, 1755, d. April 2, 1798.
m. June 7, 1780, Esther Orne, (b. April 13, 1758, d. Sept. 25,
1848), dau. of Timothy and Rebecca (Taylor) Orne. He
graduated at Harvard College, 1774 ; was pastor of the First
Church in Boston, as successor to Dr. Chauncy. They had
five children :

1. *Harriet*⁶, b. March 24, 1781, d. April 2, 1782.

2. *John*⁶, b. July 26, 1782, d. unm. February 5, 1784.

3. *Esther Orne*⁶, b. October 10, 1784, d. June 4, 1822.
m. Sept. 4, 1806, James *Fillis*, and had :

1. Lucy W.⁷, b. July 26, 1807, d. May 18, 1809.

2. John L. Clarke⁷, b. Oct. 27, 1808, d. Oct. 11, 1885.
(Name changed to John L. Clarke,—dropping the
Fillis).
m. February, 1833, Elizabeth Matilda Sheperd.
Lived in Chicago, Ill., and had :
(*a*) Matilda Fairfax⁸, b. 1833.
(*b*) Charles Chauncy⁸, b. September 23, 1836, d.
September 6, 1838.
(*c*) Esther Orne⁸, b. September 4, 1839.
m. April 29, 1882, Fred Ward *Putnam*, (b.
April 16, 1839). He lived in Cambridge as
Curator of the Peabody Museum.
(*d*) Charles Chauncy⁸, b. December 11, 1840, d,
July 3, 1851.

(*e*) Harriet Mack[8], b. September 29, 1843.

(*f*) Louisa Belcher[8], b. July 22, 1849.

  m. Nov. 5, 1873, Andrew Smith *Church*, of
  Chicago, Ill., (b. 1826). They had :

  1. Louisa[9], b. 1874.

  2. John Clarke[9], b. 1876.

  3. Howard[9], b. 1877.

(*g*) Florence[8], b. January 5, 1851.

4. *Charles Chauncy*[6], b. April 3, 1789, d. unm. Oct. 14, 1838.

5. *Harriet*[6], b. March 12, 1792, d. November 21, 1848.
  m., Nov. 27, 1820, as second wife, Elisha *Mack*, (b. May
  25, 1783, d. Dec. 9, 1852), and had :

  1. Esther C.[7], b. September 25, 1821, d. Dec. 24, 1884.

  2. Harriet Orne[7], b. January 31, 1827, d. March 15, 1879.

2. SARAH[5], b. September, 1758, d. unm. May, 1766.

3. ELIZABETH[5] [Betsy N.], b. Nov. 1763, d. unm. Oct. 4, 1810.

4. MARY[5], (twin), b. July, 1761, d. September, 1762.

5. ANN[5], [Nancy], (twin), b. July, 1761, d. September 9, 1788.
  m. June 28, 17—, Francis *Cabot*, (b. June 19, 1757, d. 1832).
  Merchant and brother of George Cabot. They had five
  children :

  1. *Francis*[6], b. November 17, 178–, d. May 9, 1786.

  2. *John Higginson*[6], b. August 17, 1782, d. unm. Nov. 9, 1846.
  Lived many years in France.

  3. *Marianne*[6], b. May 2, 1784, d. July 25, 1809.
  m. (1) April 11, 1803, Nathaniel Clarke *Lee*, of Salem,
  (b. May 30, 1772, d. Jan. 14, 1806. H. U. 1791. Merchant) ; (2) Francis[6] *Blanchard*, (b. Jan. 31, 1784, d.
  June 26, 1813, at Wenham. H. U. 1802). By her first

husband she had one son, and by her second, one
daughter :

1. John Clarke⁷, b. April 9, 1804, d. November 19, 1877.
    m. July 29, 1826, Harriet Paine Rose, (b. Feb. 5,
    1804, d. Aug. 14, 1885). He founded the banking
    house of Lee, Higginson & Co., Boston. Lived in
    Salem and had :

    (*a*) John Rose⁸, b. April 25, 1827.
           m. Nov. 11, 1856, Lucy M. Howard, (b. Nov.
           16, 1832), and had :
           1. Arthur Howard⁹, b. Sept. 15, 1857.
           2. Lucy Howard⁹, b. Sept. 8, 1859.
           3. Lillian Howard⁹, b. May 16, 1862.
           4. John Clarke⁹, b. Dec. 2, 1864.
           5. George Winthrop⁹, b. Feb. 27, 1867.

    (*b*) Marianne Cabot⁸, b. Oct. 11, 1828.
           m. Nov. 23, 1848, Samuel Endicott *Peabody*,
           (b. April 19, 1825), and had :
           1. John Endicott⁹, b. Jan. 6, 1853.
               m. June 15, 1878, Gertrude Lawrence, (b.
               Feb. 19, 1855 ; d. May 2, 1883), and
               had :
               1. Marianne¹⁰, b. July 6, 1879.
               2. Harold¹⁰, b. Dec. 7, 1880.
           2. Francis⁹, b. Sept. 1. 1854.
               m. Jan. 13, 1881, Rosamond Lawrence,
               (b. May 17, 1856), and had :
               1. Rosamond¹⁰, b. Oct. 7, 1881.
               2. ———¹⁰.
           3. Endicott⁹, b. May 31, 1857.
               m. June, 1885, his cousin.
           4. Martha Endicott⁹, b. Sept. 23, 1863.
           5. George Lee⁹, b. May 16, 1865.

    (*c*) George Cabot⁸, b. March 21, 1830.
           m. Dec. 10, 1857, Caroline W. Haskell, (b.
           Jan. 4, 1835). Lived in Newton, Mass.,
           and had :
           1 Rose⁹, b. Jan. 20, 1860.

2. Alice Haskell[9], b. July 29, 1861 ; d. Feb. 14, 1884.

   m. Oct. 27, 1880, Theodore *Roosevelt*, of New York, (b. Oct. 27, 1858), and had :

   1. Alice[10], b. Feb. 12, 1884.

3. Harriet Paine[9], b. May 4, 1863.

4. Caroline Haskell[9], b. Jan. 15, 1866.

5. Isabella Mason[9], b. Sept. 15, 1869.

5. George Cabot[9], b. Mar. 2, 1871.

(*d*) Harriet Rose[8], b. Nov. 23, 1831.

(*e*) William Paine[8], b. Apr. 19, 1833.

   m. Mar. 5, 1858, Hannah Greely Stevenson (b. Feb. 19, 1834, d. s. p. July 27, 1865):

(*f*) Rose Smith[8], b. Jan. 24, 1835.

   m. Oct. 19, 1854, Leverett *Saltonstall* (b. Mar. 16, 1825). He was born in Salem, Mass., graduated at Harvard in 1844, studied two years in the Harvard Law School, and was admitted to the bar in 1850. In 1860 he was a candidate for Congress on the Constitutional Union and Democratic ticket but was defeated. Was Overseer of Harvard, and has held other offices political and social. Was appointed Collector of the Port of Boston by President Cleveland. Mr. Saltonstall belonged to the old Saltonstall family of Salem, which is one of the three oldest in the State of Massachusetts. Sir Richard Saltonstall, who came over from England with Governor Winthrop, was one of the six patentees of the colony. Hon. Leverett Saltonstall, Sr., the father of the subject of this sketch, was the first Mayor of Salem. Leverett and Rose Smith[8] Saltonstall had :

   1. Leverett[9], b. Nov. 3, 1855, d. Feb. 14, 1863.

   2. Richard M.[9], b. Oct. 28, 1859.

    3.   Rose Lee⁹, b. June 17, 1861.

         m. Nóv. 6, 1884, George Webb *West*, (b. May 17, 1850).

    4.   Mary Elizabeth⁹, b. Oct. 17, 1862.

         m. June 30, 1884, Louis Agassiz *Shaw* (b. Sept. 18, 1861). Lived in Brookline, Mass.

    5.   Philip L.⁹, b. May 4, 1867.

    6.   Endicott P.⁹, b. Dec. 25, 1872.

(*g*)   Francis Henry⁸, b. Dec. 23, 1836.

         m. Oct. 17, 1871, Sophia Edgell Willson (b. Mar. 1, 1845).

(*h*)   Charles Jackson⁸, b. Feb. 10, 1839.

         m. June 29, 1864, Mary Ann Berry (b. Aug. 18, 1842).

(*i*)   Josephine Rose⁸, b. Aug. 27, 1841, d. Aug. 19, 1842.

(*j*)   Josephine Rose⁸, b. Dec. 21, 1843.

         m. Dec. 18, 1867, William Gurdon *Saltonstall*, of Boston, and had :

    1.   Robert⁹, b. Jan. 3, 1870.

    2.   Lucy Sanders⁹, b. Mar. 19, 1871.

    3.   John Lee⁹, b. May 23, 1878.

    4.   Rosamond⁹, b. Mar. 8, 1881.

2.   Elizabeth Cabot⁷, b. May 27, 1809, d. June 14, 1842. m. Hon. Robert Charles *Winthrop* (b. May 12, 1809). Robert C. Winthrop was the son of Lieut. Gov. Thomas L. Winthrop, and a descendant in the sixth generation of Gov. John Winthrop. He graduated at Harvard in 1828, studied law with Daniel Webster, was a member of the Massachusetts Legislature, and a member of Congress, 1841–42 and 1843–50, being speaker in 1847–49. Delivered the official oration at the laying of the corner stone of the Washington Monument, Washington, D. C., in 1848, and wrote the official oration delivered at

its completion in 1885. Was U. S. Senator by executive appointment to fill the unexpired term of Daniel Webster, 1850–51, and held many other offices of public trust. He married, for second wife, Laura Derby, widow of Arnold F. Wells, for third wife, widow of Nathaniel Thayer. Elizabeth Cabot[7] and her husband lived in Boston and had :

(a)   Robert Charles,[8] b. Dec. 7, 1834.

        m. (1) Oct. 15, 1857, Frances Pickering Adams (b. May 11, 1835, d. April 23, 1860) ; (2) Elizabeth Mason, (b. Oct. 1. 1844). Lived in Boston. By second wife he had :

        1. Robert Mason[9], b. Mar. 7, 1873.

        2. Clara Bowdoin[9], b. March 12, 1876.

        3. Margaret Tyndall[9], b. Feb. 23, 1880.

(b)   Eliza Cabot[8], b. May 13, 1838. Lived in Boston.

(c)   John[8], b. June 20, 1841.

        m. Mar. 30, 1864, Isabella Cowpland Weyman (b. June 21, 1841). Lived in Stockbridge, Mass.

4. *Frederick*[6], b. Feb. 20, 1786, d. June 16, 1869.

  m. 1821, Marianne Cabot, (b. Feb. 7, 1802). He was a merchant in Boston. They had :

  1. Frederick Samuel[7], b. June 19, 1822.

      m. Oct. 20, 1847, Mary Hersey Lincoln (b. Jan. 9, 1817), and had :

      (a)   Lincoln[8], b. Oct. 18, 1849.

      (b)   Frederick E.[8], b. Jan. 10, 1852.

      (c)   Francis McC.[8], b. Sept. 19, 1853, d. Sept. 6, '59.

      (d)   Meriel[8], b. Oct. 9, 1855, d. June 18, 1866.

      (e)   John Winslow[8], b. Oct. 19, 1857.

      (f)   Theodera[8], b. July 15, 1862.

2. Marrianne[7], b. Nov., 1823, d. May, 1826.

3. Francis[7], b. June 16, 1825.

    m. Nov. 12, 1856, Louisa Higginson (b. April 13, 1832), lived in Brookline, Mass., and had :

    (*a*)   Marian[8], b. Sept. 24, 1857.

    (*b*)   Francis Higginson[8], b. June 28, 1859.

    (*c*)   Louisa Storrow[8], b. Nov. 16, 1860.

        m. Oct. 24, 1883, John *Richardson* (b. Oct. 22, 1857).

    (*d*)   Elizabeth Higginson[8], b. Feb. 1, 1863, d. Aug. 1863.

    (*e*)   Susan Channing[8], b. May 6, 1864.

    (*f*)   Margaret Copley[8], b. June 15, 1866.

    (*g*)   Frederick Pickering[8], b. June 15, 1868.

    (*h*)   Stephen Perkins[8], b. Sept. 20, 1869.

    (*i*)   Philip Wentworth[8], b. June 17, 1871, d. July, 1871.

    (*j*)   Amy Wentworth[8], b. June 17, 1872.

4. Mary Elizabeth[7], b. Dec. 23, 1827.

5. Arthur[7], b. Mar., 1829, d. Mar., 1830.

6. John Higginson[7], b. Feb., 1831.

    H. U. 1850.

7. Susan Copley[7], b. Nov., 1833, d. May, 1834.

8. William Furness[7], b. Jan. 17, 1835.

    m. Nov. 18, 1862, Caroline Baker Whitney (b. April 8, 1838).   Lived in Boston.

9. Robert[7], b. Oct., 1837, d. Sept., 1840.

10. Follen[7], b. Oct. 29, 1839.

    m. Sept. 20, 1865, Caroline Sturges Channing (b. April 13, 1846) and had :

    (*a*)   Chilton[8], b. Oct. 11, 1866.

    (*b*)   Walter Channing[8], b. Nov. 15, 1867.

    (*c*)   Follen[8], b. April 14, 1869.

    (*d*)   Harold[8], b. April 22, 1870.

    (*e*)   John Higginson[8], b. April 10, 1877.

5. *Eliza*[6], b. Sept. 1788, d. unm. May, 1807.

II. MARY[4], b., Mar. 29, 1733, d. Jan. 30, 1805.

> m. (1) Oct. 17, 1751, Rev. Dudley *Leavitt*, of Salem, Mass. (b· 1720, d. Feb. 7, 1762, H. U. 1739) ; (2) Nathaniel Peaslee *Sargeant*, of Haverhill, Mass. (b. Nov. 2, 1731, d. Oct. 1791), Chief Justice Supreme Court. She had by her first husband four children :

1. DUDLEY[5] (Dr.), b. Oct. 1, 1752, d. unm.

2. MARY[5], b. Feb. 9, 1755, d. Oct. 6, 1778.

> m. Nov. 6, 1774, Dr. Joseph *Orne* (b. June 4, 1749, d. Jan. 28, 1786). He was the son of Jonathan and Elizabeth (Putnam) Orne, Elizabeth Putnam being the dau. of William Putnam, brother of Israel Putnam, and Jonathan Orne being the son of Josiah and Sarah (Ingersoll) Orne. [Joseph Orne m. (2) Theressa Emery]. Mary[5] had two children :

> *1. Josiah[6]*, b. Feb. or April 14, 1778, d. unm. Oct., 1806.
> He was captain of the ship "Essex," and was said to have been killed by pirates or Arabs in the Red Sea.

> *2. Mary[6]*, b. Nov. 13, 1775, d. Dec. 14, 1806.
> m. Sept. 16, 1798, Ichabod *Tucker*, of Haverhill, Mass., (b. April 17, 1765, d. Oct. 22, 1846). He was a son of Benjamin and Martha (Davis) Tucker, and m. (2) Esther Orne (Paine) Cabot, widow of Joseph Cabot, and dau. of Dr. William and Lois (Orne) Paine.

3. SARAH[5], b. Oct. 9, 1757, d. Sept., 1820.

> m. (1) Isaac *White*, "lost at sea,"——, he was the son of John White who was brother of Benjamin who was father of Rebecca who m. Col. T. Pickering——, (2) Jonathan *Payson*. Sarah had by her first husband two children, by her second, two children :

> *1. Sarah[6]*, b. July 23, 1777, d. Dec. 14, 1846.
> m. March 3, 1805, John[5] *Pickering*, of Salem, Mass., (b. Feb. 7, 1777, d. May 5, 1846). They had :

1. Mary Orne⁷, b. Dec. 7, 18—.
    Lived in Salem, Mass.

2. John⁷, b. Nov. 8, 1808, d. Jan. 20, 1882.
    m. Oct. 22, 1850, Mehitable Cox, (b. March 9,
    1815, d. May 21, 1879). Lived in Salem, Mass.
    H. U. 1830. Had:

    (*a*)   Sarah White⁸, b. June 20, 1852.

    (*b*)   Mary Orne⁸, b. June 28, 1854.
            Lived in Salem, Mass.

    (*c*)   John⁸, b. May 24, 1857.
            H. U. 1878.

3. Henry White⁷, b. May 27, 1811.
    m. Feb. 24, 1835, Frances Dana Goddard, (b. May
    1, 1810. d. May 7, 1880), dau. of Nathaniel God-
    dard of Boston. H. U. 1831. Lived in Boston
    and had:

    (*a*)   Rebecca White⁸, b. January 10, 1836.
            m. Sept. 12, 1866, John G. *Walker*, U. S. N.,
            (b. March 20, 1835), and had:

            1. Frances Pickering⁹, b. August 16, 1867.

            2. James Wiloan Gemmes⁹, b. Sept. 22, 1868.

            3. Susan Grimes⁹, b. May 9, 1871.

            4. Henry Pickering⁹, b. July 15, 1872.

            5. Alice Pickering⁹, b. June 25, 1874, d. August
                10, 1874.

            6. Elizabeth Grimes⁹, b. January 2, 1876, d.
                January 5, 1880.

            7. Sarah Cochran⁹, b. July 16, 1878.

    (*b*)   Frances G.⁸, b. Nov. 13, 1841, d. May 28, 1865.

    (*c*)   Henry G.⁸, b. June 1, 1848.
            Lived in Boston. H. U. 1869.

2. Mary Henley[6], b. May 5, 1779, d. June 25, 1862.
m. Samuel *Gile*, of Milton, (b. July 23, 1778, d. Oct. 16, 1836). They had :

1. Mary Pickering[7], b. February 15, 1808.
m. 1841, Lewis B. *Tucker*, of Milton.

2. Samuel[7], b. August 2, 1809, d. October, 1827.

3. ———[7], d. in infancy.

4. ———[7], d. in infancy.

3. Nancy[6], b. April, 1787, d. April 18, 1866.
m. Nathaniel *Adams*, of Portsmouth and of Salem, Mass., (b. January, 1785, d. Jan. 4, 1861).

4. Elizabeth L.[6], b. January 26, 1789, d. February 15, 1864.
m. March 11, 1810, Henry *Goddard*, merchant of Portsmouth and of Portland, Me., (b. Nov. 23, 1785, d. Dec. 8, 1871). They had :

1. John[7], b. February 28, 1811, d. March 27, 1870.
m. 1831, Lydia Leavitt Johnson, (b. Oct. 2, 1811), and had :

(*a*) John Henry[8], b. Oct. 23, 1832, d. May 17, 1835.

(*b*) Eliza Payson[8], b. Jan. 7, 1834, d. Jan. 27, 1863.
m. Aug. 19, 1861, Rev. Aug. F. *Beard*, and had :

1. Eliza Isabel[9], b. June 19, 1862.

(*c*) Annie W.[8], b. April 17, 1836, d. July 1, 1838.

(*d*) Annie[8], b. November 9, 1838, d. Feb. 1, 1839.

(*e*) John Henry[8], b. March 9, 1841.
m. June 25, 1872, Mildred Dyer, (b. March 22, 1850).

(*f*) Charles William[8], b. December 10, 1843.

(*g*) Annie White[8], b. April 7, 1846.
m. Nov. 18, 1869, Albert *Thompson*, of Cape Elizabeth, near Portland, Me., (b. Jan. 8, 1843), and had :

1. Mary Ella[9], b. October 2, 1870.

(*h*) Ella⁸, b. April 22, 1848, d. Sept. 16, 1852.
(*i*) Mary Jane⁸, b. April 30, 1850, d. April 2, 1870.
(*j*) Ella E.⁸, b. Dec. 12, 1852, d. March 20, 1870.

2. Elizabeth White⁷, b. May 25, 1812, d. April 27, 1884.
     m. March 5, 1835, William W. *Thomas*, of Portland,
     (b. Nov. 7, 1803), and had :
     (*a*) Henry Goddard⁸, b. April 5, 1837.
            m. July 17, 1861, Ellen R. Webster, (b. Nov.
            25, 1839), and had :
            1. Mary E.⁹, b. May 27, 1863.
                 m. October, 1882, William N. *Blorr*, and
                 had :
                    1. William Thomas¹⁰, b. Sept. 29, 1883.
            2. Louise W.⁹, b. November 18, 1866.
            3. ———⁹, (a dau.), b. 1868, d. 1868.
            4. Henry G.⁹, b. August 22, 1869.
            5. ———⁹, (a dau.), b. 1870, d. 1870.
            6. Ellen W.⁹, b. December 12, 1873.
     (*b*) William Widgery⁸, b. August 26, 1839.
     (*c*) Elias⁸, b. May 6, 1842.
            m. Nov. 4, 1869, Helen M. Brown, of Wash-
            ington, (b. Sept. 10, 1846), and had :
            1. Elias⁹, b. March 15, 1871.
            2. William W.⁹, b. April 18, 1873.
            3. Helen B.⁹, b. April 2, 1876.
     (*d*) John Pickering⁸, b. October 6, 1844.
            m. Dec. 21, 1881, Susan Clifford Ross, (b.
            April 24, 1857).
     (*e*) Eliza Payson⁸, b. Dec. 22, 1847, d. Mch 4, 1876.
            m. Dec. 17, 1873, Edward C. *Jordan*, of Port-
            land, Me., and had :
            1. Edward Clarence⁹, b. October 26, 1874, d.
                 April 4, 1875.
     (*f*) Mary Goddard⁸, b. August 21, 1856, d. April
            14, 1863.

3. Mary Pickering⁷, b. May 25, 1814, d. unm. February
     20, 1876.

4. Henry Warren⁷, b. December 3, 1816.

     m. May 8, 18—, Mary Perley Gordon, (b. Oct. 11, 1825), and had :

     (*a*) Charles William[8], b. January 16, 185–, d. June 25, 1851.

     (*b*) Elizabeth White[8], b. Dec. 2, 1858, d. July 5, 1861.

5. Charles William[7], b. December 29, 1825.

     m. (1) Sept. 20, 1852, Caroline R. Little, (b. April 7, 1831, d. Sept. 18, 1853) ; (2) Nov. 10, 1858, Rowena Caroline Morrill, (b. April 24, 1839), and had :

     (*a*) Benjamin L.[8], b. Aug. 8, 1853, d. Jan. 23, 1854.

     (*b*) Anson Morrill[8], b. September 1, 1859.

     (*c*) Henry[8], b. July 13, 1861.

     (*d*) Morrill[8], b. October 7, 1865.

     (*e*) Rowena[8], b. February 6, 1869.

     (*f*) Eliza Payson[8], b. June 14, 1872.

     (*g*) Ellen[8], b. April 19, 1874, d. February 25, 1875.

     (*h*) Charles William[8], b. November 26, 1879.

4. ELIZABETH L.[5], b. September 16, 1759, d. October 20, 1782.

    m. Oct. 27, 1776, William *Pickman*, (b. March 12, 1748, d. Nov. 5, 1815 ; H. U. 1766). They had three children :

   1 *William*[6], b. October 18, 1777, d. unm. Dec. 13, 1798.

   2. *Dudley Leavitt*[6], b. May 21, 1779, d. November 4, 1846.

     m. Sept. 6, 1810, Catherine Saunders, (b. Aug. 29, 1784, d. May 18, 1823). He was a merchant, and lived in Salem, Mass. They had :

     1. Lucy Grafton[7], (name changed to Catherine Saunders[7]), b. July 9, 1811.

         m. May 30, 1832, Richard S. *Fay*, (b. 1806, d. Aug. 9, 1865), lived in Boston, and had :

         (*a*) Richard S.[8], b. February 28, 1833, d. 1881.

             m. Elizabeth Francis Bowditch, of Boston, (b. June 17, 1836), lived in Boston, and had :

             1. Dudley Bowditch[9], b. January 31, 1860.

                m. Catherine Gray.

         (*b*) Catherine[8], b. June 15, 1837.

             m. Sidney *Everett*, son of Edward Everett, lived in Boston, and had :

1. Sidney Brooks⁹, b. November 5, 1868.
2. Leo⁹, b. July 25, 1871.
3. Lilian⁹, b. June 30, 1873.
4. Hildegarde⁹, b. November 30, 1877.

(*c*) Elizabeth P.⁸, b. Jan. 8, 1841, d. Sept. 4, 1880.
m. Nov. 10, 1868, Henry H. *Parker*, and had :
1. Richard Fay⁹, b. Sept. 9, 1869.
2. Henry Montfort⁹, b. November 25, 1870.
3. Augustia Hamilton⁹, b. August 9, 1875.

(*d*) William Peckman⁸, b. July 5, 1843, d. March
25, 1879.
m. Oct. 12, 1870, Sarah Abbott, dau. of Jos.
G. Abbott, of Boston, and had :
1. Richard Sullivan⁹, b. July 9, 1871.
2. Catherine⁹, b. September 9, 1872.
3. Edward Henry⁹, b. September 13, 1876.

2. Elizabeth Leavitt⁷, b. Sept. 22, 1814, d. Sept. 18, '53.
m. Mar. 17, 1847, as second wife, Richard Saltonstall *Rogers* (b. Jan. 13, 1790, d. June 11, 1873).
He was the son of Nathaniel and Abigail (Dodge)
Rogers. They had:

(*a*) Dudley Pickman⁸, b. Aug. 30, 1848, d. May 12,
1873. H. U. 1869.

(*b*) George Willoughby⁸, b. April 8, 1850.
m. Sept. 1, 1874, Josephine Francis Lord,
dau. of J. A. and Eliza A. Lord, and had :
1. Dudley Pickman⁹, b. Oct. 8, 1875.

(*c*) Elizabeth Pickman⁸, b. Sept. 17, 1853.
m. Alfred *Pound*, and had :
1. Alfred Dudley Pickman Rogers⁹, b. Aug.
29, 1879.
2. Elizabeth Amelia Leavitt Pickman⁹, b.
May 5, 1880, d. Sept. 23, 1880.
3. Elizabeth Josephine Charlotte Pickman⁹,
b. Nov. 8, 1881.
4. Louisa Catherine Saltonstall Pickman⁹, b.
April 28, 1883.
5. John Mather C. Farley⁹, b. May 20, 1884.

3. William Dudley[7], b. Jan. 6, 1819.

> m. June 12, 1849 Caroline Silsbee, lived in Boston and had :
>
> (a) Dudley Leavitt[8], b. Dec. 30, 1850.
> H. U. 1873.
>
> (b) Fanny[8], b. May 29, 1857, d. Oct. 5, 1880.
> m. Oct. 31, 1877 William .F. *Wharton* of Boston (b. April 28, 1847, H. U. '70) and had :
> 1. William P.[9], b. Aug. 12, 1880.

3. Elizabeth[6], b. Feb. 11, 1782, d. March 29, 1850.

> m. Nov. 18, 1805, Daniel *Abbott*, lawyer of Dunstable, N. H. (b. Feb. 25, 1777, d. Dec. 3, 1853, H. U. 1797), and had :

1. , William Pickman[7].

2. William P.[7], b. May 15, 1811.

> m. (1) April 2, 1845, Abby Ann Chandler (b. 1817, d. May 22, 1850) ; (2) Feb. 20, 1855, Harriet Mead Henderson (b. Dec. 29, 1820). Lived in Boston, and had :
>
> (a) Daniel[8], b. April 2, 1847, d. Oct. 20, 1853.
> (b) William H.[8], b. Dec. 26, 1855.
> (c) Henry P.[8], b. Aug. 21, 1857.
> (d) Daniel Abbott[8], b. June 1, 1859, d. May 3, '67.
> (e) George Chandler[8], b. Mar. 12, 1861, d. May 21, 1861.
> (f) Catherine E.[8], b. Aug. 22, 1862.

3. Charles Dudley[7], b. Sept. 1813, d. 1847.

> m. May 23, 1838, Laurinda Holbrook, of Nashua, and had :
>
> (a) Mary Elizabeth[8], b. Feb. 22, 1843.

4. Catherine Pickman[7], b. Aug. 19, 1819.

> m. (1) June 3, 1840 Charles James *Fox*, of Nashua, (b. Oct. 23, 1811, d. Feb. 17, 1846) ; (2) May 4, 1853, as second wife, Samuel *Dinsmore* (b. May 5, 1799, d. Feb. 24, 1869), and had :
>
> (a) Charles William[8], b. March 29, 1843.
> m. 1883, Alice Brown. H. U. 1864.

III. LYDIA⁴, b. Feb. 27, 1735–36, d. Oct. 21, 1824.

    m. March 15, 1758, as second wife, George D. Williams, of Salem, (probably b. Feb. 10, 1731, d. June 11, 1797. His first wife was Hannah Hathorne, b. April 5, 1730, d. Oct. 30, 1756). Lydia⁴ and George Williams had thirteen children :

1. LYDIA⁵, b. Dec. 30, 1758, d. March 12, 1759.

2. SAMUEL⁵, b. March 30, 1760, d. Jan. 15, 1841.
    H. U. 1780. He was a merchant. Lived in London.

3. HENRY⁵, b. Nov. 2, 1761, d. unm. Feb. 15, 1832.

4. LYDIA⁵, b. Sept. 23, 1763, d. April 30, 1826.
    m. Jan. 24, 1786, Theodore *Lyman* (b. Jan. 8, 1753, d. May 24, 1839). He was a merchant in Boston ; died at Waltham. (He m. in Kennebunkport, Me., Sarah Emerson by whom he had four children). Lydia⁵ and Theodore Lyman had five children :

    1. *George Williams*⁶, b. Dec. 4, 1786, d. Sept. 24, 1880.
        m. (1) May 31, 1810 Elizabeth Gray Otis, (b. May 3, 1791, d. Dec. 20, 1824), dau. of Harrison Gray Otis ; (2) May 3, 1827, Anne⁶ Pratt (b. May 9, 1798, d. March 16, 1875). He was a merchant in Boston. Joined his father in trade, but turned his attention to cotton manufacture, and was prominent among the founders of the city of Lowell. He took an earnest interest in agriculture, and was an active member of the Massachusetts Society for the Promotion of Agriculture. By his first wife he had six children, by his second four :

        1. George Theodore⁷, b. April 25, 1811, d. Oct. 11, 1819.
        2. Arthur Wellesley⁷, b. March 28, 1813, d. Feb. 24, 1826.
        3. ————⁷, b. May 8, 1815, d. May 8, 1815.
        4. Elizabeth Otis⁷, b. July 29, 1817, d. June 12, 1847.
            m. April 18, 1844, Francis *Boott*, of Boston, (b. June 24, 1813, H. U. 1831), and had :
            (*a*) Francis⁸, b. May 10, 1845, d. Aug. 26, 1845.
            (*b*) Elizabeth O. L.⁸, b. April 13, 1846.

5. Mary Ellen[7], b. Sept. 8, 1819, d. May 29, 1875.

 m. (1) June 18, 1840, James Amory *Appleton*, of Boston, (b. Oct., 1818, d. June 29, 1843); (2) Feb. 16, 1856, Charles S. *Arnold*, of Savannah, (b. 1824, d. March 4, 1856). By her first husband she had:

 (*a*) George Lyman[8], b. Nov. 25, 1841.

   m. Oct. 20, 1870, Louisa Arnold, (b. Sept. 18, 1851), and had:

  1. Mary[9], b. July 12, 1871.

6. George Theodore[7], b. Dec. 23, 1821.

 m. April 17, 1845, Sally Otis, (b. Oct. 4, 1825), dau. of James W. Otis, of N. Y. H. U. 1842. He had:

 (*a*) George Gray[8], b. Oct. 28, 1846, d. Nov. 4, 1883.

   m. Jan. 21, 1871, in California, Millie Parker, (b. July 9, 1850), and had:

  1. George Parker[9], b. Nov. 6, 1871.

  2. Frank Marion[9], b. Feb. 4, 1873.

  3. Harrison Gray[9], b. Aug. 17, 1874.

  4. James Otis[9], b. Dec. 13, 1882.

 (*b*) James Otis[8], b. Oct. 7, 1847, d. June 1, 1881, at sea.

 (*c*) Francis Marion[8], b. March 9, 1849, d. July 25, 1868.

 (*d*) Charles[8], b. April 27, 1850.

 (*e*) Alice[8], b. Jan. 14, 1852.

   m. April 29, 1879, in New York, William Platt *Pepper*, of Philadelphia, (b. Sept. 20, 1837), and had:

  1. Emily[9], b. Feb. 13, 1880.

  2. Alice Marion[9], b. Aug. 29, 1881.

  3. Martha Otis[9], b. Dec. 29, 1883.

 (*f*) Elizabeth G[8], b. Jan. 17, 1858.

7. William Pratt⁷, b. April 8, 1828, d. April 16, 1864.
    m. Oct. 12, 1854, Abby Mauran Church Humphrey,
    of Providence, R. I., (b. Oct. 30, 1831), and had :
  (*a*)   Mary Williams⁸, b. Nov. 9, 1855, d. Jan. 16,
        1864.
  (*b*)   Olivia Mauran⁸, b. Nov. 27, 1858, d. Feb. 9,
        1864.
  (*c*)   William P.⁸, b. March 24, 1860.

8. Arthur Theodore⁷, b. Dec. 8, 1832.
    m. April 8, 1858, Ellen Bancroft⁷ Lowell, (b. Nov.
    1, 1837), dau. of J. A. Lowell. H. U. 1853. Lived
    in Boston and had :
  (*a*)   Julia⁸, b. Jan. 30, 1859.
  (*b*)   Arthur⁸, b. Aug. 31, 1861.
  (*c*)   Herbert⁸, b. May 17, 1864.
  (*d*)   Ella⁸, b. Feb. 26, 1866.
  (*e*)   Susan Lowell⁸, b. Feb. 8, 1869, d. Sept. 14, 1878.
  (*f*)   Mabel⁸, b. Jan. 15, 1872.
  (*g*)   Roger⁸, b. Feb. 17, 1876, d. Feb. 17, 1876.
  (*h*)   Ronald Theodore⁸, b. July 8, 1879.

9. Sarah P.⁷, b. Feb. 4, 1835.
    m. April 23, 1861, Philip Howes *Sears*, of Boston.
    (b. Dec. 30, 1823, H. U. 1844), and had :
  (*a*)   Annie Lyman⁸, b. March 10, 1862.
  (*b*)   Mary Pratt⁸, b. Aug. 21, 1864.
  (*c*)   Richard⁸, b. July 19, 1867.
  (*d*)   Frank⁸, b. Oct. 31, 1869.
  (*e*)   Evelyn Georgiana⁸, b. March 9, 1875.

10. Lydia Williams⁷, b. April 29, 1837.
    m. April 24, 1862, Robert Treat *Paine*, of Bos-
    ton, (b. Oct. 28, 1835, H. U. 1855), and had :
  (*a*)   Edith⁸, b. April 6, 1863.
  (*b*)   Fanny⁸, b. Jan. 13, 1865.
  (*c*)   Robert Treat⁸, b. Aug. 9, 1866.
  (*d*)   Florence⁸, b. Sept. 30, 1868, d. July 17, 1872.
  (*e*)   Ethel⁸, b. March 24, 1872.
  (*f*)   George Lyman⁸, b. July 29, 1874.
  (*g*)   Lydia Lyman⁸, b. Sept. 6, 1876.

2. *Theodore*[6], (Gen.), b. February 17, 1792, d. July 18, 1849.
m. May 16, 1821, Mary Elizabeth Henderson, of New
York, (b. March 26, 1799, d. Aug. 5, 1836). He graduated at Harvard in 1810, studied law, served in both
branches of the Legislature, became Brigadier General
of the militia, and was Mayor of Boston in 1832-35.
He had:

1. Julia[7], b. February 10, 1822, d. February 5, 1835.

2. Henderson[7], b. January 21, 1823, d. June 8, 1824.

3. Mary Henderson[7], b. April 30, 1825, d. Dec. 31, 1839.

4. Cora[7], b. February 25, 1827.
m. June 10, 1848, Gardiner Howland *Shaw*, of Boston, (d. May 1, 1867, at Toulon, France). Had:

  (*a*) Amy[8], b. October 15, 1850.
m. May 27, 1873, John Collins *Warren*, of
Boston, (b. May 4, 1842), and had:

    1. John Collins[9], b. Sept. 6, 1874.

    2. Joseph[9], b. March 16, 1876.

  (*b*) Francis[8], b. November 27, 1854.
m. April 19, 1883, Mary Peabody Sears, (b.
March 29, 1859), and had:

    1. Cora Lyman[9], b. January 28, 1884.

  (*c*) Henry Russell[8], b. April 25, 1859.
m. Sept. 20, 1883, Grace L. Rathbone, of
Albany, N. Y.

5. Theodore[7], b. August 23, 1833.
m. Nov. 28, 1856, Elizabeth Russell, (b. Nov. 2,
1836), dau. of George R. Russell. Lived in Brookline, Mass., and had:

  (*a*) Cora[8], b. March 9, 1862, d. July 20, 1873.

  (*b*) ———[8], (a son), b. 1873.

  (*c*) Theodore[8], b. November 23, 1874.

  (*d*) Henry Russell[8], b. November 7, 1878.

3.   *Charles*⁶, b. October 9, 1799, d. April 5, 1881.

m. April 4, 1827, Susan Powell Warren, (d. July 4, 1856), dau. of Dr. John C. Warren, of Boston. H. U. 1819. Had:

    1.   Charles⁷, b. January 18, 1828, d. September 7, 1833.

    2.   Charles Frederic⁷, b. Oct. 21, 1833, d. July 19, 1880.
m. February 28, 1867, Annie Grant, (b. May 29, 1876), dau. of Patrick Grant. They had:

      (*a*)   Annie⁸, b. July 10, 1868.

      (*b*)   Charles Frederick⁸, b. November 23, 1871.

    3.   Florence⁷, b. November 8, 1837.

4.   *Mary*⁶, b. October 9, 1802.

m. June 13, 1826, Samuel A. *Eliot*, of Boston and Cambridge, (b. March 5, 1798, d. Jan. 26, 1862). He graduated at H. U. 1817, was Mayor of Boston 1837-39 ; was a Senator and Representative in the Massachusetts State Legislature ; was elected a Representative from Massachusetts in the Thirty-First Congress, (in place of Robert C. Winthrop appointed Senator), as a Whig, and served from August, 1850, to March, 1851 ; was for eleven years Treasurer of Harvard College. Had:

    1.   Mary Lyman⁷, b. March 10, 1827.
m. Nov. 22, 1854, Charles Eliot *Guild*, of Boston, (b. Nov. 3, 1827, H. U. 1846). Had:

      (*a*)   Robert Wheaton⁸, b. Sept. 29, 1855, d. June 9, 1880.

      (*b*)   Henry Eliot⁸, b. July 19, 1859.

      (*c*)   Eleanor⁸, b. November 6, 1860.

      (*d*)   Charles Eliot⁸, b. July 15, 1862.

      (*e*)   Katherine Eliot⁸, b. September 7, 1866.

    2.   Francis⁷, b. September 27, 1829, d. June 4, 1832.

3. Elizabeth Lyman[7], b. December 8, 1831.

    m. May 26, 1859, Stephen Hopkins *Bullard*, of Boston, (b. Sept. 18, 1818, at Richmond, Va., d. July 7, 1873), and had :

    (*a*)   Mary Lyman[8], b. August 12, 1860.

    (*b*)   John Eliot[8], b. October 2, 1861.

    (*c*)   Ellen Twistleton[8], b. February 25, 1865.

    (*d*)   Theodore Lyman[8], b. June 10, 1867.

    (*e*)   Stephen Eliot[8], b. May 14, 1871.

4. Charles W.[7], (LL. D.), b. March 20, 1834.

    m. (1) Oct. 27, 1858, Ellen Derby Peabody, (b. June 22, 1836, at Dayton, O., d. March 13, 1869), dau. of Ephraim Peabody, D. D., of Boston ; (2) Oct. 30, 1877, Grace Mellen Hopkinson, (b. Aug. 16, 1846). H. U. 1853. He was appointed President of Harvard College 1869. By first wife he had :

    (*a*)   Charles[8], b. November 1, 1859.

    (*b*)   Francis[8], b. May 18, 1861, d. October 9, 1861.

    (*c*)   Samuel Atkins[8], b. August 24, 1862.

    (*d*)   Robert Peabody[8], b. July 8, 1866, d. Dec. 8, 1867.

5. Catherine Atkins[7], b. April 27, 1836, d. June 6, 1882.

    m. June 21, 1871, Prof. Francis B. *Storer*, of Harvard College, (b. March 27, 1832).

6. Frances Anne[7], b. May 22, 1838.

    m. July 9, 1863, Rev. Henry Wilder *Foote*, (b. June 2, 1838, H. U. 1858, Pastor of King's Chapel, Boston). They had :

    (*a*)   Mary[8], b. November 6, 1864.

    (*b*)   Frances Eliot[8], (twin), b. February 2, 1875.

    (*c*)   Henry Wilder[8], (twin), b. February 2, 1875.

    (*d*)   Dorothea[8], b. November 3, 1880.

7. ——[7], (a dau.), b. Dec. 10, 1840, d. Dec. 18, 1840.

5. *William*[6], b. June 1, 1805, d. Dec. 7, 1819.

5. TIMOTHY⁵, b. July 15, 1765, d. Feb. 19, 1846.
    H. U. 1784. He was a merchant in Boston.

6. MARY⁵, b. July 15, 1767, d. Aug. 26, 1864.
    m. Nov. 17, 1792, William *Pratt*, of Boston, (b. March 15,
    1759, d. May 6, 1844).   He was a merchant, born in Derby,
    England.   Had eight children :

    1. *Mary⁶*, b. Aug. 17, 1793, d. Dec. 14, 1881.

    2. *Samuel Williams⁶*, b. Dec. 6, 1794, d. Sept. 24, 1795.

    3. *Anne⁶*, b. May 9, 1798, d. March 16, 1875.
        m. May 3, 1827, as second wife, George Williams⁶ *Lyman*
        (b. Dec. 4, 1786, d. Sept. 24, 1880).

    4. *Elizabeth⁶*, b. March 20, 1800, d. March 18, 1855.

    5. *George Williams⁶*, b. May 27, 1802, d. Jan. 13, 1876.
        m. May 3, 1831, Mary Barrow White, of Salem (b. Mar.
        27, 1811), and had :
        1. George Williams⁷, b. Feb. 2, 1832, d. May 25, 1865,
            in Florence, Italy.
        2. William⁷, b. Aug. 5, 1834.
            m. Oct. 4, 1865, Anita P. Jones, of Boston, (b.
            Sept. 3, 1846).
        3. Robert Marion⁷, b. Nov. 10, 1837.
        4. Joseph White⁷, b. Jan. 25, 1845, d. Feb. 20, 1845.

    6. *William⁶*.
        H. U. 1824.

    7. *Sarah Pickering⁶*, b. Jan. 12, 1807, d Nov. 22, 1866.

    8. *Lydia⁶*, b. May 30, 1809, d. June 3, 1809

7. JOHN⁵, b. Aug. 16, 1769, d. unm. June 19, 1839.
    Lived in Northboro', Mass.

8. STEPHEN⁵, b. Oct. 8, 1771, d. Feb. 5, 1838.
    m. July 14, 1799, Alice Orne (b. April 21, 1769, d. May 21,
    1856).   He was a farmer in Northboro'.   They had five child-
    ren :

1. *Mary* [6], b. July 3, 1800, d. Oct. 12, 1833.

　m. Sept. 9, 1822, Capt. Edward *Orne* of Salem, (b. April
　3, 1791, d. April 7, 1845), and had :

　1. Henry Augustus [7], b. June 19, 1823, d. April 29, 1863.
　　　m. (1) Elizabeth Putnam (d. March 27, 1846) ;
　　　(2) Jan. 25, 1849, Anne Fiske (d. Nov. 7, 1851) ;
　　　(3) Sept. 6, 1855, Anne Merrill, of Pittsfield. He
　　　had by second wife one child, by third wife four
　　　children :
　　　(*a*) Susan Gertrude [8], b. Sept. 16, 18—, d. June
　　　　7, 1851.
　　　(*b*) Alice Clapp [8], b. June 20, 1856.
　　　(*c*) Henry Merrill [8], b. Jan. 25, 1859.
　　　(*d*) Stephen Williams [8], b. July 16, 1861.
　　　(*e*) Lillie Maria [8], b. Aug. 19, 1863.

　2. Charles Williams [7], b. May 8, 1827.

　3. Mary Elizabeth [7], b. May 4, 1831.

　4. Alice [7], b. Oct. 4, 1833, d. Nov. 7, 1854.

2. *Anne* [6] (or Nancy) b. March 25, 1803, d. Feb. 27, 1826.

3. *Elizabeth* [6], b. May 25, 1805, d. Apr. 25, 1849.

　m. Sept. 20, 1830, Benjamin Derrick *Whitney*, of Bos-
　ton, (b. Nov. 10, 1807, H. U. 1828). Had :

　1. Annie Williams [7], b. Oct. 1, 1832, d. Feb. 20, 1864.
　　　m. Aug. 15, 1861, Jeffries *Wyman*, (d. Sept. 4,
　　　1874 ; H. U. 1833). Had :
　　　(*a*) Jeffries [8], b. Feb. 3, 1864.

　2. Mary [7], b. Sept. 9, 1834.

　3. Elizabeth [7], b. Aug. 18, 1836.

　4. Alice Orne [7], b. Jan. 10, 1839.

　5. Stephen Williams [7], b. Mar. 23, 1841.
　　　H. U. 1861.

　6. Emily [7], b. Sept. 8, 1843.

　7. Benjamin [7], b. Sept. 10, 1846, d. Nov. 26, 1858.

　8. Charles Henry [7], b. April 16, 1849, d. Dec. 5, 1867.

*4. Susan*⁶, b. March 11, 1808, d. July 13, 1811.

*5. George Henry*⁶, b. April 15, 1811.
    m. Dec. 21, 1835, Frances Elizabeth Simes, (b. Aug. 18,
    1804). Lived in Northboro'. Had:

    1. Mary Susan ⁷, b. Feb. 21, 1838, d. Nov. 28, 1882.

    2. Ellen⁷, b. Nov. 30, 1839.

    3. Frances Elizabeth⁷, b. Jan. 6, 1847, d. Aug. 18, 1869,

9. ELIZABETH ⁵, b. April 25, 1774, d. May 28, 1808.
    m. April 17, 1799, Dr. Moses *Little*, (b. July 3, 1766, d.
    Oct. 13, 1811, H. U. 1787). He was a physician in Salem.
    They had three children :

    *1. Elizabeth*⁶, b. Feb. 15, 1800, d. March 5, 1820.

    *2. Henry*⁶, b. Sept. 21, 1802, d. March 31, 1826.

    *3. Francis*⁶, b. Aug. 31, 1805, d. June 21, 1828.

10. FRANCIS⁵, b. June 17, 1776, d. June 22, 1847.
    H. U. 1796. Lived in Boston.

11. ANNE⁵, b. Feb. 9, 1779, d. April 22, 1821.
    m. May 19, 1816, Loammi *Baldwin*, (d. June 30, 1838).
    He was a lawyer in Boston, graduated H. U. 1800, and
    married a second time. Anne ⁵ and Loammi Baldwin had :

    *1. Samuel Williams*⁶, b. April 17, 1817, d. Dec. 29, 1822.

12. ———⁵, b. Feb., 1783, d. June 18, 1783.

13. CHARLES WILLIAMS ⁵, b. Jan. 10, 1784, d. unm. Aug. 10, 1841.
    He was a merchant.

IV. ELIZABETH[4], b. Nov. 12, 1737, d. Oct. 12, 1823.

> m. Nov. 7, 1757, as second wife, John *Gardner*, of Salem,
> (b. July 4, 1731, d. Oct. 27, 1805). "She was distinguished
> for the strength of her understanding and the energy of her
> character; she was a great reader, and possessed much
> information." Her husband was born in Danvers, Mass.,
> and died of apoplexy in Wenham. He m. (1) Mary Gale,
> of Marblehead, who was born in 1728 and died, about one
> year after marriage, March 24, 1755. Elizabeth[4] and John
> Gardner had three children:

1. ELIZABETH[5], b. Feb. 9, 1759, d. June 24, 1816.

   > m. June 3, 1781, Samuel *Blanchard*, (b. Feb. 29, 1756, d.
   > May 4, 1813). He was a surgeon in the army, and a
   > merchant in Salem, Mass., and Baltimore, Md. He died at
   > Wenham. They had four children:

   1. Henry[6], b. July 9, 1782, d. unm. Dec. 24, 1826.

   > He was in his brother Francis's class at Harvard, but
   > left on account of ill health. He spent two or three
   > years in France; became a merchant in Salem; after-
   > wards supercargo two or three times to India and
   > elsewhere; died in Lexington, Mass.

   2. Francis[6], b. Jan. 31, 1784, d. June 26, 1813.

   > m. Aug. 29, 1808, as her second husband, Marianne
   > (Cabot) Lee, (b. May 2, 1784, d. July 25, 1809), widow
   > of Nathaniel C. Lee and daughter of Francis Cabot.
   > He graduated at Harvard College in 1802, studied law
   > with Judge Charles Jackson, became his partner in the
   > law business, and was distinguished for his good sense
   > and legal acquirements which were considered extra-
   > ordinary for his age. He died, of consumption, at
   > Wenham.

   3. George Frederick[6], b. Dec. 24, 1786, d. July 17, 1787.

   4. Lucy[6], b. May 10, 1793, d. s. p. June 16, 1816.

   > m. March 24, 1814, Charles Henry *Orne*, (b. April 1,
   > 1789, d. Dec. 25, 1816, in Salem). He was the son of
   > William Orne.

2. JOHN⁵, b. Aug. 31, 1760, d. Oct. 10, 1792, in Charleston, S. C.

3. SAMUEL PICKERING⁵, b. May 14, 1767, d. Dec. 18, 1843.
    m. Sept. 19, 1797, Rebecca Russell Lowell, (b. May 17, 1779, d. May 11, 1853), dau. of Judge John Lowell, LL. D. He graduated at Harvard 1786, went to Charleston, S. C. that same year and engaged in mercantile pursuits with his brother there; afterwards came to Boston. They had six children :

    1. *Elizabeth Pickering*⁶, b. March 11, 1799, d. June 8, 1879.
        m. May 25, 1820, Hon. John C. *Gray*, of Boston, (b. Dec. 26, 1793).

    2. *Mary Lowell*⁶, b. Jan. 12, 1802, d. Aug. 3, 1854.
        m. Jan. 11, 1826, Hon. Francis C. *Lowell*, of Boston, (b. Jan. 5, 1803, d. Sept. 8, 1874. Had :

        1. Francis Cabot⁷, b. Sept. 8, 1827, d. July 2, 1830, in Waltham, Mass.

        2. George Gardner⁷, b. March 29, 1830, d. Feb. 6, 1885.
            m. April 4, 1854, Mary Ellen Parker, (b. Aug. 21, 1832), and had :
            (*a*) Francis Cabot⁸, b. Jan. 7, 1855.
                   m. Nov. 27, 1882, Cornelia Prime Baylies, (b. Aug. 5, 1859).
            (*b*) Anna Parker⁸, b. Aug. 21, 1856.
                   m. June 19, 1879, Abbott Lawrence⁸ *Lowell*, (b. Dec. 13, 1856).

        3. Mary⁷, b. July 26, 1833.
            m. July 15, 1856, Algernon *Coolidge*, of Boston. (b. Aug. 22, 1830), and had :
            (*a*) Algernon⁸, b. Jan. 24, 1860.
            (*b*) Francis L.⁸, b. Nov. 20, 1861.
            (*c*) Sidney⁸, b. March 8, 1864.
            (*d*) Ellen W.⁸, b. Jan. 24, 1866.
            (*e*) Mary L.⁸, b. Aug. 14, 1868.

        4. Georgina⁷, b. Jan. 10, 1836.

5. Edward J.[7], b. Oct. 18, 1845.

m. (1) Jan. 14, 1868, Mary W. Goodrich (b. Jan. 1, 1846, d. April 5, 1874); (2) June 19, 1877, Elizabeth Gilbert Jones. By first wife he had ·

(a) Alice [8], b. Feb. 25, 1869.

(b) Guy [8], b. Aug. 6, 1870.

(c) Frederick E.[8], b. Mar. 30, 1874.

3. *John Lowell* [6], b. February 8, 1804, d. July 24, 1884.

m. Oct. 4, 1826, Catherine E. Peabody, (b. June 23, 1808, d. Sept. 21, 1883), dau. of Joseph and Elizabeth (Smith) Peabody. H. U. 1821. He began apprenticeship with Ropes and Ward, Sept. 20, 1821, and lived in Boston. They had :

1. Catherine Rebecca [7], b. Aug. 1, 1827, d. April 7, 1833.

2. Joseph Peabody [7], b. August 2, 1828, d. June 11, 1875.

m. Nov. 14, 1860, Harriet Sears Amory. (b. Sept. 27, 1835, d. Nov. 26, 1865), and had :

(a) Joseph Peabody [8], b. September 17, 1861.

(b) William Amory [8], b. December 3, 1863.

(c) Augustus Peabody [8], b. November 5, 1865.

3. George Augustus [7], b. September 30, 1829.

m. Nov. 8, 1854, Eliza Endicott Peabody, (b. Oct. 4, 1834, d. Jan. 13, 1876), lived in Boston. Had :

(a) George Peabody [8], b. November 19, 1855.

m. June 11, 1884, Esther Burnett, (b. July 7, 1859), dau. of Joseph Burnett, of Southboro, Mass.

(b) Catherine Elizabeth [8], b. February 27, 1857, d. October 22, 1865.

(c) Ellen [8], b. February 24, 1860.

m. June 3, 1884, Augustus P. *Loring*, of Beverly, Mass.

(d) Samuel Pickering [8], b. July 21, 1864, d. October 26, 1865.

(e) John Lowell [8], b. June 28, 1867.

(f) William Endicott [8], b. August 1, 1868, d. June 15, 1870.

(g) Olga Eliza [8], b. October 21, 1869.

4. Elizabeth⁷, b. Dec. 6, 1834, d. April 17, 1839.

5. Samuel Pickering⁷, b. June 28, 1836, d. Sept. 13, '41.

6. John Lowell⁷, b. Nov. 26, 1837.
    m. April 10, 1860, Isabella Stewart of New York,
    (b. Mar. 1839), and had :
    (*a*) John Lowell⁸, b. June 18, 1863, d. Mar. 15, '65.

7. Albert⁷, b. Feb. 8, 1840, d. Sept. 12, 1841.

8. Julia⁷, b. Aug. 4, 1841.
    m. Dec. 18, 1860, Joseph Randolph *Coolidge* of
    Boston (b. Dec. 29, 1828), and had :
    (*a*) Joseph Randolph⁸, b. May 17, 1862.
    (*b*) John Gardner⁸, b. July 4, 1863.
    (*c*) Archibald Cary⁸, b. March 6, 1866.
    (*d*) ———⁸, b. Jan. 11, 1868, d. Jan 11, 1868.
    (*e*) Harold Jefferson⁸, b. Jan. 22, 1870.
    (*f*) Julian⁸, b. Sept. 28, 1873.

9. ———⁷ (a daughter), b. Feb. 6, 1843, d. Feb. 21, '43.

10. Eliza Blanchard⁷, b. May 28, 1846.
    m. Oct. 15, 1868, Francis *Skinner*, of Boston (b.
    Sept. 3, 1840), and had :
    (*a*) Francis⁸, b. Nov. 17, 1869.
    (*b*) Gardner⁸, b. Aug. 26, 1871, d. April 24, 1876.

4. *Sarah Russell⁶*, b. Sept. 20, 1807.
    m. July 3, 1837, as second wife, Hon. Horace *Gray*
    (b. Aug. 25, 1800, d. July 31, 1873), and had :

1. John Chipman⁷, b. July 14, 1839.
    m. June 4, 1873, Anna L. Mason (b. Oct. 4, 1854),
    dau. of Rev. Chas. Mason, of Boston, and had :
    (*a*) Roland⁸, b. April 1, 1874.
    (*b*) Eleanor Lyman⁸, b. May 25, 1876.

2. Russell⁷, b. June 17, 1850.

5. George[6], b. Sept. 15, 1809, d. Dec. 19, 1884.

    m. Oct. 18, 1838 Helen Maria Read (b. May 16, 1819), dau. of James Read of Boston. He went to college but did not graduate ; began in Lowell and Gardner's store, Boston, July 21, 1828. They had :

    1. Helen Read[7], b. Sept. 21, 1839.

        m. May 30, 1867, James Freeman *Curtis* (b. March 12, 1839), son of Theodore B. and Laura Greenough Curtis. They had :

        (*a*) Francis Gardner[8], b. Mar. 9, 1868.

        (*b*) Laura Greenough[8], b. Jan. 11, 1871, d. May 10, 1875.

        (*c*) Alfred[8], b. Jan. 31, 1876.

        (*d*) Mary[8], b. April 19, 1878.

    2. Francis Lowell[7], b. June 4, 1841, d. Feb. 10, 1861.

    3. Elizabeth[7], b. June 28, 1843.

        m. Oct. 23, 1867, Charles W. *Amory* of Boston, (b. Oct. 16, 1842), and had :

        (*a*) William[8], b. Sept. 19, 1869.

        (*b*) Clara Gardner[8], b. Jan. 3, 1872.

        (*c*) George Gardner[8], b. June 22, 1874.

        (*d*) Dorothy[8], b. July 17, 1878.

    4. Clara[7], b. Feb. 8, 1845.

        m. Dec. 10, 1872 Shepherd *Brooks*, of Boston, (b. July 23, 1837), and had :

        (*a*) Helen[8], b. Dec. 30, 1875.

        (*b*) Gorham[8], b. June 19, 1881.

        (*c*) Rachel[8], b. Jan. 5, 1883.

6. Francis Lowell[6], b. Dec. 28, 1811, d. July 5, 1812.

V. JOHN[4], b. Mar. 2, 1739–40, d. unm. Aug. 22, 1811.

    H. U. 1759. Register of Deeds for twenty years. Representative from Salem to Massachusetts Legislature, and Speaker of the Massachusetts House. Judge of Court of Common Pleas.

VI. LOIS⁴ (twin), b. April 19, 1742, d. Feb. 4, 1815.

m. May, 177–, John _Gooll_ (d. 1776). He was a Scotch
merchant from Paislee, Scotland. Lived in Salem, Mass.
They had two children :

1. SARAH⁵, b. Nov. 28, 177–, d. Nov. 22, 1864.

m. Oct. 28, 1795, Samuel _Putnam_, of Boston (b. April 13,
1768, d. July 3, 1853). He graduated at Harvard 1787 ; was
a Judge of the Superior (or Supreme) Court ; was the son of
Gideon Putnam. They had eight children :

1. _Samuel Raymond⁶_, b. March 2, 1797, d. Dec. 24, 1861.
m. April 25, 1832, Mary Lowell (b. Dec. 3, 1810), dau.
of Rev. Dr. Chas. Lowell, pastor of the West church,
Boston. H. U. 1815. He was a physician in Boston
and had :

1. Alfred Lowell⁷, b. Mar. 13, 1833, d. Oct. 2, 1855.

2. Georgina Lowell⁷, b. Oct. 21, 1835.

3. William Lowell⁷, b. July 9, 1840, d. Oct. 22, 1861.
Was mortally wounded at Balls Bluff, Oct. 21, 1861.

4. Charles Lowell⁷, b. Jan. 29, 1845, d. Sept. 10, 1847.

2. _Hannah⁶_, b. June 21, 1799, d. Aug. 4, 1872.
m. Dec. 9, 1822, Thomas Poynton _Bancroft_, of Boston,
(b. Dec. 20, 1798, d. Mar. 16, 1852), and had :

1. Elizabeth Ives⁷, b. Nov. 8, 1823, d. Sept. 23, 1851.

2. Sarah Ellen⁷, b. Jan. 17, 1826, d. May 6, 1837.

3. Thomas Poynton⁷, b. Jan. 5, 1829, d. May 30, 1838.

4. Samuel Putnam⁷, b. Nov. 23, 1834, d. Nov. 30, 1850.

5. Ellen⁷, b. May 22, 1838.

6. Robert Hale⁷, b. April 21, 1843.
H. U. 1865.

3. _Louisa⁶_, b. Oct. 4, 1801, d. Oct. 7, 1876.
m. Sept. 3, 1821, Joseph Augustus _Peabody_, of Salem,
(b. Aug. 7, 1796, d. June 18, 1828), son of Joseph and
Elizabeth (Smith) Peabody. They had :

1. Elizabeth Smith[7], b. July 31, 1822, d. Dec. 13, 1869.
m. Jan. 15, 1845, Caleb William *Loring*, of Boston
and Beverly (b. July 31, 1819, H. U. 1839), had:

(*a*) Katherine P.[8], b. May 21, 1849.

(*b*) William C.[8], b. Aug. 24, 1851.
m. Sept. 25, 1883, Susan M. Lawrence (b.
Feb. 4ᵢ 1852), dau. of Amos A. Lawrence.
H. U. 1872.

(*c*) Louisa P.[8], b. Jan. 15, 1854.

(*d*) Augustus P.[8], b. Dec. 7, 1856.
m. June 3, 18–4, Ellen Gardner. H. U. '78.

2. Sarah Louisa[7], b. Nov. 6, 1823, d. 1832.

3. Catherine[7], b. Oct. 12, 1826, d. Jan. 8, 1847.

4. Josephine Augusta[7], b. June 12, 1828.
m. Nov. 6, 1851, William Gardner *Prescott*, (b. Jan.
27, 1826, H. U. 1844), and had:

(*a*) Edith[8], b. April 20, 1853.
m. Sept. 2, 1874, Roger *Walcott*, of Boston,
(b. July 13, 1847, H. U. 1870), and had:

1. Huntington F.[9], b. Nov. 29, 1875, d. Feb.
19, 1877.

2. Roger[9], b. July 25, 1877.

3. William Prescott[9], b. May 1, 1880.

4. Samuel Huntington[9], b. Nov. 9, 1881.

(*b*) William Hickling[8], bᵢ Feb. 22, 1855, d. Oct. 2,
1864.

(*c*) Linzee[8], b. Nov. 27, 1859.

(*d*) Catherine Elizabeth[8], b. Feb. 19, 1863.

4. Mary Ann[6], b. Aug. 20, 1803, d. April 10, 1845.
m. June 4, 1840, as second wife, Charles Greeley *Loring*,
of Boston, (b. May 2, 1794, d. Oct. 8, 1867, H. U. 1812).
He married again.

5. *Charles Gideon*⁶, (Dr.), b. Nov. 7, 1805, d. Feb. 5, 1875.
    m. May 28, 1835, Elizabeth Cabot Jackson, of Boston,
    (b. July 2, 1808, d. Feb. 25, 1875), dau. of Dr. James
    Jackson. Graduated at Harvard in 1824. Was a
    physician in Boston. Had :

    1. Elizabeth Cabot⁷, b. Feb. 19, 1836.

    2. Sarah⁷, b. Sept. 7, 1839, d. July 22, 1841.

    3. Annie C.⁷, b. May 14, 1842.

    4. Charles Pickering⁷, b. Sept. 15, 1844.
        H. U. 1865.

    5. James Jackson⁷, b. Oct. 3, 1846.
        H. U. 1866.

6. *Elizabeth Cabot*⁶, b. Nov. 11, 1807, d. Feb. 12, 1881.
    m. April 2, 1829, as second wife, John Amory *Lowell*,
    of Boston, (b. Nov. 11, 1798, d. Oct. 31, 1881, H. U.
    1815). Had :

    1. Augustus⁷, b. Jan. 15, 1830.
        m. June 1, 1854, Katherine B. Lawrence. H. U.
        1850.   Lived in Brookline, Mass., and had :
        (*a*) Percival⁸, b. March 13, 1855.
               H. U. 1876.
        (*b*) Abbott Lawrence⁸, b. Dec. 13, 1856.
               m. June 19, 1879, Anna Parker Lowell, (b.
               Aug. 21, 1856). H. U. 1877.
        (*c*) Katherine⁸, b. Nov. 27, 1858.
               m. Dec. 5, 1882, Alfred *Roosevelt*, of New
               York, and had :
               1. Elfrida⁹, b. Dec. 22, 1883.
        (*d*) Roger⁸ (twin), b. Feb. 2, 1862, d. Aug. 31,
               1863.
        (*e*) Elizabeth⁸ (twin), b. Feb. 2, 1862.
        (*f*) May⁸, b. May 1, 1870, d. May 1, 1870.
        (*g*) Amy⁸, b. Feb. 9, 1874.

2. Elizabeth Rebecca[7], b. Feb. 27, 1831.
   m. Oct. 5, 1868, Francis Peleg *Sprague*, (b. Feb. 17, 1832–3, H. U. 1857).

3. Ellen Bancroft[7], b. Nov. 1, 1837.
   m. April 8, 1858, Arthur Theodore[7] *Lyman*, of Boston, (b. Dec. 8, 1832, H. U. 1853).

4. Sara Putnam[7], b. June 24, 1843.
   m., as second wife, George Baty *Blake*, of Brookline and Boston, (b. Dec. 13, 1838, d. June 17, 1884, H. U. 1859). Had:
   (*a*) John Amory Lowell[8], b. Oct. 2, 1879.

7. *Sarah Gooll*[6], b. June 1, 1810, d. Dec. 10, 1880.
   m. March 20, 1832, Francis B. *Crowningshield*, of Boston, (b. April 23, 1809, d. May 8, 1877, H. U. 1829). Had:

1. Mary[7], b. Jan. 17, 1833, d. May 6, 1834.

2. Sarah[7], b. Dec. 22, 1834, d. Nov. 24, 1840.

3. Benjamin Williams[7], b. March 12, 1837.
   m. Dec. 15, 1866, Katherine M. Bradley, of Boston, (b. Jan. 3, 1844). H. U. 1858. Had:
   (*a*) Bowdoin Bradlee[8], b. Oct. 13, 1867.
   (*b*) Francis B.[8], b. April 22, 1869.
   (*c*) Benjamin Williams[8], b. April 21, 1871.
   (*d*) Katherine Bradlee[8], b. Nov. 6, 1874.
   (*e*) Emily[8], b. June 18, 1879.

4. Alice[7], b. Nov. 22, 1839.
   m. March 17, 1864, Josiah *Bradlee*, of Boston, (b. Dec. 17, 1837, H. U. 1858). Had:
   (*a*) Sarah Crowningshield[8], b. Feb. 5, 1865.
   (*b*) Frederick Josiah[8], b. March 28, 1866.
   (*c*) James Bowdoin[8], b. Jan. 31, 1873.
   (*d*) Francis Crowningshield[8], b. April 20, 1881.

5. Louisa⁷, b. Jan. 7, 1842.
   m. Oct. 8, 1860, Francis Edward *Bacon*, (b. July 2, 1835), and had :
   - (*a*)   Mary Louisa⁸, b. Nov. 9, 1861, d. Jan. 22, 1862.
   - (*b*)   Alice Crowningshield⁸, b. Jan., 1863, d. Aug. 27, 1863.
   - (*c*)   Francis Edward⁸, b. April 19, 1864.
   - (*d*)   Susan Gorham⁸, b. July 26, 1866.
   - (*e*)   Alice Putnam⁸, b. Nov. 29, 1869.
   - (*f*)   Louis⁸, b. June 29, 1872.

6. Francis⁷, b. June 8, 1845, d. April 23, 1847.

7. Emily⁷, b. Nov. 9, 1847, d. May 18, 1879.

8. *John Pickering*⁶, b. Jan. 21, 1813, d. Jan. 4, 1867.
   m. Oct. 10, 1842, Harriet Upham, (b. April 20, 1820), dau. of Phineas Upham.   They had :

   1. Mary Upham⁷, b. July 13, 1843.
      m. July 9, 1866, Charles F. *Fearing*, of New York, (b. July 31, 1840).

   2. Harriet⁷, b. Feb. 8, 1845.
      m. Oct. 23, 1872, Horace John *Hayden*, of New York, (b. Sept. 11, 1840.   H. U. 1860).   Had :
      - (*a*)   Mary Putnam⁸, b. Oct. 16, 1873.
      - (*b*)   John Putnam⁸, b. June 2, 1875.
      - (*c*)   Harold⁸, b. Oct. 5, 1876.

   3. John Pickering⁷, b. July 3, 1847.

   4. Sarah Gooll⁷, b. March 19, 1851.

2. ANDREW⁵.

VII.   EUNICE⁴, (twin) b. April 19, 1742, d. Jan. 7, 1843.
   m. May 23, 1765, Hon. Paine⁴ *Wingate*, (b. May 14, 1739, (O. S.), d. March 7, 1838).   They had five children.   [See Paine⁴, Paine³, Joshua².].

VIII. TIMOTHY[4], (Col.), b. July 6, 1745, d. Jan. 29, 1829.
m. April 8, 1776, Rebecca White, (b. July 18, 1754, in Bristol, England, d. Aug. 14, 1828), dau. of Benjamin and Elizabeth (Miller) White. Timothy[4] Pickering graduated at Harvard in 1763, was admitted to the bar in 1768, was on the Committee of Correspondence and was a Colonel of Militia at the opening of the war; joined Washington with his regiment in the Fall of 1776, and was Adjutant-General of the army and afterwards Quarter-Master General. After the war he settled in Philadelphia. He was a delegate to the Pennsylvania Convention for considering the United States Constitution, was in the cabinet of Washington and Adams, Post Master General 1791-95, U. S. Sec. of War 1795, U. S. Sec. of State 1795-1800. In 1801 he returned to Massachusetts. U. S. Senator from 1803 to 1811, and Representative in U. S. Congress from 1814 to 1817. Lived in Salem, Mass., and had ten children:

1. JOHN[5], b. Feb. 7, 1777, d. May 5, 1846.
m. Mar. 3, 1805, Sarah[6] White, (b. July 23, 1777, d. Dec. 14, 1846), dau. of Isaac and Sarah (Leavitt) White. He graduated at Harvard in 1796, was a lawyer of Salem, and an eminent philological scholar.

2. TIMOTHY[5], b. Oct. 1, 1779, d. May 14, 1807.
m. Dec. 29, 1804, Lurena Cole, (b. Sept. 28, 1781, d. April 22, 1860), dau. of Zebulon Cole, of Farmington, Conn. H. U. 1799. Had:

　　1. Charles[6], (Dr.), b. Nov. 10, 1805, d. Mar. 17, 1878.
　　m. Feb. 25, 1851, Sarah Stoddard Hammond, (b. Oct. 7, 1811). He graduated at Harvard in 1823 and was a physician in Boston.

　　2. Edward[6], b. Oct. 2, 1807, d. Nov. 21, 1876.
　　m. Oct. 20, 1841, Charlotte Hammond, (b. July 7, 1819). H. U. 1824. Lived in Boston. Had:

　　　　1. Ellen Hammond[7], b. Aug. 19, 1842, d. July 13, 1861.
　　　　2. Edward Charles[7], (Prof.), b. July 19, 1846.
　　　　m. March 9, 1874, Elizabeth W. Sparks, (b. May 1

1849), dau. of Jared Sparks. He graduated at
Harvard in 1865, became Director of the Observa-
tory and Phillips Professor of Astronomy at Harvard. Member of the Royal Astronomical Society
of London.

3.   William Henry[7], b. Feb. 15, 1858.

m. June 11, 1884, Anne Atwood Butts, (b. Jan. 29,
1861).

3.   HENRY[5], b. Oct. 8, 1781, d. May 9, 1838.

4.   CHARLES[5], b. May 25, 1784, d. May 12, 1796.

5.   WILLIAM[5], b. Feb. 16, 1786, d. June 16, 1814.

6.   EDWARD[5], b. Sept. 12, 1787, d. Oct. 10, 1793.

7.   GEORGE[5]. b. Aug. 7, 1789, d. April 23, 1826.

8.   OCTAVIUS[5], b. Sept. 2, 1791, in Wilkesbarre, d. Oct. 29, 1868.

m. Dec. 29, 1836, Jane Pratt, (b. July 28, 1799, d. March 16,
1869), dau. of Joseph Pratt, of Exeter, Eng. H. U. 1810.
Lived in Boston. Had one child :

1.   Henry[6], b. Feb. 4, 1839.

m. Oct. 11, 1864, Mary Goddard Wigglesworth of Boston, (b. Oct. 11, 1838). H. U. 1861. Lived in Boston.

9.   MARY[5], b. Nov. 21, 1793, d. March 22, 1863.

m. April 12, 1813, Benjamin Ropes *Nichols*, of Boston, (b.
May 18, 1786, d. April 30, 1848. H. U. 1804). They had
six children :

1.   Mary Pickering[6], b. March 8, 1814, d. April 3, 1814.

2.   Lucy Orne[6], b. June 23, 1816, d. April 24, 1883.

m. May 25, 1836, J. Ingersoll *Bowditch*, of Boston, (b.
Oct. 15, 1806), and had :

1.   Mary Pickering[7], b. Aug. 17, 1838, d. Sept. 7, 1838.

2.   Henry Pickering[7], b. April 4, 1840.

m. Sept. 9, 1871, Selma Knauth, of Leipzig, Germany, (b. Feb. 4, 1853), and had :

(*a*)   Ethel[8], b. Jan. 29, 1873.

(*b*)   Fanny[8], b. May 19, 1874.

(*c*)   Theodora[8], b. Sept. 2, 1878.

(*d*)   Selma[8], (twin), b. Oct. 31, 1880.

(*e*)   Eliza I.[8], (twin), b. Oct. 31, 1880.

(*f*)   Harold[8], b. June 8, 1883.

3. Charles Pickering[7], b. Sept. 30, 1842.
    m. June 7, 1866, Cornelia Rockwell, of Pittsfield
    and Lenox, Mass., (b. Oct. 7, 1841), and had :
    (*a*)   Cornelia[8], b. June 12, 1867.
    (*b*)   Lucy Rockwell[8], b. Aug. 24, 1868.
    (*c*)   Catherine P.[8], b. April 13, 1870.
    (*d*)   Edith[8], b. April 29, 1872, d. Sept. 14, 1872.
    (*e*)   Ingersoll[8], b. May 31, 1875.

4. William[7], b. Jan. 30, 1845, d. Feb. 14, 1845.

5. Charlotte[7], b. Feb. 28, 1846.

6. Lucy[7], b. March 10, 1850.
    m. Aug. 30, 1875, Richard *Stone*, of Boston, (b.
    May 23, 1840), and had :
    (*a*)   Robert Bowditch[8], b. Jan. 6, 1877.
    (*b*)   Mary Gray[8], b. Nov. 25, 1878.
    (*c*)   Malcolm Bowditch[8], b. Jan. 14, 1881.
    (*d*)   Ingersoll Bowditch[8], b. March 18, 1883.

7. Eliza Ingersoll[7], b. Nov. 25, 1852.

8. Alfred[7], b. Sept. 6, 1855.
    m. Jan. 8, 1880, Mary L. Rice, of Boston, (b. July
    6, 1854), and had :
    (*a*)   Mary Ingersoll[8], b. April 4, 1881.
    (*b*)   Mary Orne[8], b. Dec. 6, 1883.

3. *Charlotte Elizabeth*,[6] b. Aug. 29, 1821, d. July 29, 1840.

4. *Benjamin White*[6], b. April 7, 1823.

5. *Mary*[6], (twin) b. Jan. 29, 1829.

6. *Elizabeth*[6], (twin) b. Jan. 29, 1829.
    m. Oct. 6, 1863, Cyrus Frederick *Knight*, (b. March 28,
    1831). Lived in Pa. Had :

  1. Mary[7], b. Jan. 28, 1865.

  2. Herbert[7], b. April 15, 1866.

  3. Arthur[7], b. May 1, 1867.

  4. Margaret[7], b. May 23, 1869.

  5. Elizabeth[7], b. Aug. 4, 1871.

10. ELIZABETH⁵, b. Nov. 21, 1793, d. Aug. 11, 1819.
 m. Aug. 12, 1816, Hammond *Dorsey*, (a Maryland planter,
who d. Feb. 7, 1823). They had two children :

*1. Elizabeth*⁶, b. May 27, 1817, d. June 17, 1817.

*2. Mary Elizabeth Pickering*⁶, b. Oct. 10, 1818.
 m. Oct. 23, 1838, Thomas *Donaldson*, of Baltimore,
(b. May 8, 1815, d. Oct. 4, 1877), and had :

 1. Caroline⁷, b. Aug. 18, 1839, d. June 12, 1877.
  m. Oct. 20, 1863, as third wife, Foxhall Alexander
Parker, U. S. N., (b. Aug. 5, 1822, d. June 10,
1879). Had :
  (*a*) Mary Dorsey⁸, b. Aug. 4, 1865.
   m. Edward Lloyd *Winder*, (b. June 4, 1858).
  (*b*) Thomas Donaldson⁸, b. May 17, 1867.
  (*c*) LeRoy⁸, b. March 28, 1869.
  (*d*) Robert Bogardus⁸, b. June 26, 1870.
  (*e*) John Donaldson⁸, b. Nov. 16, 1873.
  (*f*) Henry Pickering⁸, b. June 24, 1875.
  (*g*) Sara Jay⁸, b. June 19, 1876.

 2. Mary⁷, b. Nov. 29, 1840.

 3. Elizabeth P.⁷, b. Nov. 16, 1842.

 4. Thomas⁷, b. Aug. 15, 1844.

 5. Lucy⁷, b. Aug. 26, 1846.

 6. Ellen⁷, b. Feb. 22, 1848.

 7. John Johnston⁷, b. April 21, 1850.
  Lived in Baltimore.

 8. Frank⁷, b. Dec. 30, 1851, d. April 8, 1853.

 9. Fanny⁷, b. March 25, 1854.

 10. Frederick Brune⁷, b. April 22, 1857.

 11. Ethel⁷, b. Oct. 19, 1860.
  m. June 13, 1883, Robert Sage *Sloan*, (b. Oct. 23.
1859), and had :
  (*a*) Donaldson⁸, b. April 21, 1884, in Oswego, N. Y,

IX. LUCIA[4], b. Nov. 12, 1747, d. Oct. 31, 1822.

    m. June 17, 1766, as second wife, Israel *Dodge* (b. Feb. 21, 1739–40, d. Oct. 3, 1822). He was a distiller in Salem. They had eight children :

1. LUCIA[5], b. June 16, 1768, d. s. p. Mar. 24, 1812.
    m. Oct. 27, 1799, as second wife, Jonathan *Gardner* (b. 1755, d. Sept. 26, 1821). He was a merchant in Salem, Mass.

2. ISRAEL[5], b. Nov. 2, 1770, d. Sept. 9, 1803.

3. CALEB[5], b. Aug. 1, 1773, d. Jan. 1, 1798.

4. HENRY[5], b. June 27, 1775, d. Feb. 11, 1794.

5. PICKERING[5], b. April 6, 1778, d. Aug. 16, 1833.
    m. Nov. 5, 1801, Rebecca Jenks (b. Feb. 19, 1781, d. March 30, 1851). He was a merchant in Salem. They had eight children :

    1. Mary Jenks[6], b. Aug. 25, 1802, d. Sept. 15, 1802.

    2. Pickering[6], b. April 24, 1804, d. Dec. 28, 1863.
        m. (1) Mar. 28, 1826, Anna Storer Colman, (b. Nov. 20, 1808, d. Sept. 16, 1849) ; (2) June 9, 1853, Eliza Webb Gilman. By first wife he had five children ; by second, two :

        1. Charles Henry[7], b. Feb. 3, 1827, d. 1846.

        2. Ellen Barry[7], b. May 14, 1829, d. 1854.

        3. Edward Pickering[7], b. Aug. 6, 1831, d. 1854.

        4. George Storer[7], b. April 6, 1838, d. Aug 24, 1840.

        5. Georgiana S.[7], b. Nov. 23, 1841, d. Mar. 21, 1865.
            m. Oct. 28, 1863, Edward *Mellen*, and had :
            (*a*) Mary Colman[8], b. Sept. 3, 1864.

        6. Frank Pickering[7], b. Aug. 31, 1856.

        7. Rebecca Gilman[7], b. Jan. 20, 1861.

3. *Mary Jenks* [6], b. July 27, 1806, d. Sept. 23, 1807.

4. *Mary Jenks* [6], b. Sept. 17, 1807, d. Sept. 20, 1833.
    m. Mar. 21, 1831, George W. *Jenks* (b. June 13, 1804).

5. *Lucy Pickering* [6], b. Mar. 17, 1810, d. Aug. 6, 1840.
    m. Dec. 16, 1833, S. Fiske *Allen* (b. July 14, 1807, d.
    Oct 8, 1876).   He married again.   They had :

    1. Pickering Dodge [7], b. May 20, 1838, d. June 2, 1863.

6. *Catherine Elizabeth* [6] b. Aug. 17, 1816.
    m. Sept. 20, 1837, Wm. A. *Lander* (b. 1816), and had :

    1. Lucy Allen [7], b. June 29, 1839.

    2. William [7], b. Feb. 3, 1842, d. April 10, 1849.

    3. Catherine [7], b. May 3, 1844, d. June 21, 1844.

    4. Mary [7], b. Nov. 19, 1845, d. July 12, 1863.

7. *Rebecca Anne* [6], b. Dec. 21, 1819.
    m. May 15, 1838, John Henry *Silsbee* (b. July 17, 1815),
    and had :

    1. William Hodges [7], b. Jan. 26, 1841.

    2. Alice Dodge [7], b. Oct. 30, 1843.
        m. Dec. 1, 1864, Dr. Hall *Curtis*, of Boston, (b.
        July 7, 1834), and had :
        (*a*)   John Silsbee [8], b. Oct. 18, 1865.
        (*b*)   Frances Mixter [8], b. Mar. 28, 1870.

    3. Walter J. [7], b. June 20, 1847, d. July, 1868.

8. *Eliza Devereaux* [6], b. Sept. 18, 1824, d. Nov. 28, 1826.

6. ELIZABETH [5], b. Oct. 11, 1780, d. Sept. 25, 1783.

7. CATHERINE[5], b. Oct. 9, 1782, d. Mar. 24, 1818.

m. Nov. 9, 1806, John *Stone* (b. July 9, 1781, d. Nov. 22, 1849), son of E. and Sarah (Hubbard) Stone. He was a distiller. He married a second wife. Catherine[5] and John Stone had four children :

1. Lucy Pickering[6], b. Aug. 11, 1807, d. Sept. 17, 1808.

2. John Hubbard[6], b. Sept. 9, 1809, d. Nov. 17, 1862.

m. Aug. 31, 1837, Eliza Jane Flint, (b. March 20, 1816), and had :

1. Henry Radcliffe[7], b. May 20, 1841.

2. Catherine Dodge[7], b. May 19, 1848.

3. Frank[7], b. Jan. 14, 1853.

4. Lucia Pickering[7], b. Feb. 24, 1855, d. Aug. 20, 1856.

5. Arthur Robinson[7], b. March 15, 1861.

3. Lucy Pickering[6], b. June 30, 1815.

m. (1) June 6, 1839, John *Robinson*, of Salem, (b. Aug. 29, 1796, d. April 24, 1846) ; (2) June 1, 1857, as second wife, Dr. Samuel *Johnson*, (b. Dec. 8, 1790). She had by her first husband :

1. ————[7], (a daughter), b. May 15, 1845, d. same day.

2. John[7], b. July 13, 1846.

m. Oct. 21, 1869, Elizabeth Rollins Kemble, (b. Aug. 10, 1850), and had :

(*a*) Mary Kemble[8], b. Nov. 17, 1870.

(*b*) Lucy Pickering[8], b. May 5, 1872.

4. Henry Orne[6], b. March 7, 1818.

m. Nov. 12, 1844, Mary Baldwin Low, (b. March 26, 1817), and had :

1. Mary Isabella[7], b. June 24, 1850.

8.   ELIZA[5], b. Dec. 14, 1785, d. Nov. 19, 1828.
m. March 6, 1809, Humphrey *Devereaux*, of Salem, (b. Aug.
6, 1779, d. June 1, 1867). They had two children :

1. George Humphrey[6], b. Dec. 1, 18—, d. Oct. 24, 1878.
m. Dec. 19, 1832, Charlotte Story Forrester, (b. Sept. 4,
1811, d. April 27, 1873), dau. of John and Charlotte
(Story) Forrester. Had :

1.   George Forrester[7], b. Sept. 2, 1833.
m. Dec., 1860, Mary A. Niecewanger.

2.   John Forrester[7], b. March 12, 1835.

3.   Arthur Forrester[7], b. April 27, 1836, d. March, 1883.
m. Dec. 25, 1860, Clara A. Rich, (b. Nov. 11, 1838).
He was a Colonel of the 19th Regiment ; went out
as Lieut.-Col. under Hicks. Their children :
(*a*)   Clara Wass[8], b. Nov. 25, 1861, d. Sept. 16, 1862.
(*b*)   Bertha Bohun[8], b. July 11, 1864.
(*c*)   Humphrey D.[8], b. Aug. 3, 1865.
(*d*)   Louise Latham[8], b. Jan. 6, 1867.
(*e*)   Charlotte[8], b. Dec. 16, 1868, d. March 6, 1870.
(*f*)   Arthur Forrester[8], (twin), b. Jan. 4, 1870, d.
Jan. 6, 1870.
(*g*)   George Humphrey[8], (twin), b. Jan. 4, 1870, d.
Jan. 5, 1870.
(*h*)   Arthur Forrester[8], b. Jan. 19, 1871.
(*i*)   Frances Marion[8], b. July 8, 1873.
(*j*)   Guy Hathorne Story[8], b. Jan. 30, 1877.

4.   Charles Upham[7], b. June 27, 1838.
m. 1867, Jane Dewey Ensign, and had :
(*a*)   Robert[8], b. June 4, 1868.

5.   Walter Forrester[7], b. Sept. 7, 1841.

6.   Marianne Silsbee[7], b. Sept. 21, 1843.

7. Edward Forrester[7], b. Oct. 5, 1845.

8. Charlotte Forrester[7], b. Dec. 22, 1847.
     m. Dec. 14, 1876, Francis Q. *Story*.

9. Frank F.[7], b. Feb. 14, 1849.

10. Eliza Dodge[7], b. Feb. 6, 1856.

2. *Marianne Cabot*[6], b. Feb. 6, 1812.
     m. Nov. 9, 1829, Nathaniel *Silsbee*, Jr., of Salem and
     Boston, (b. Dec. 28, 1804, d. June 7, 1881, H. U.
     1824), son of Hon. N. Silsbee. Had :

  1. Nathaniel Devereux[7], b. Oct. 22, 1830.
       m. Oct. 22, 1856, Mary Stone Hodges, (b. Dec. 8,
       1836), and had :

     (*a*) Eliza White[8], b. Sept. 27, 1857.
             m. Aug. 23, 1876, Winslow Lewis *Montgomery*,
             (b. Sept. 8, 1848), and had :

         1. Hugh Devereux[9], b. April 18, 187–.

         2. Marian Silsbee[9], b. Dec. 6, 1879.

     (*b*) Nathaniel[8], b. Feb. 9, 1859.

     (*c*) Rosamond White[8], b. Nov. 16, 1863.

     (*d*) George Devereux[8], b. Dec. 30, 1865.

  2. George Devereux[7], b. Oct. 29, 1832, d. Aug. 18, 1843.

  3. Eliza Devereux[7], b. Oct. 23, 1835, d. Mar. 20, 1837.

  4. Marianne Devereux[7], b. Sept. 11, 1837, d. Mar. 10,
       1838.

  5. Mary Crowninshield[7], b. April 7, 1840.
       m. June 12, 1861, Frederick A. *Whitwell*, of Boston,
       (b. March 10, 1820), and had :

     (*a*) Frederick Silsbee[8], b. March 12, 1862.
             H. U. 1884.

     (*b*) Natalie Silsbee[8], b. July 2, 1863.

  6. ———[7], (a son), b. March, 1841, d. March, 1841.

  7. William Edward[7], b. Sept. 27, 1845.
       H. U. 1867.

JOHN [1].
JOSHUA [2], (Col.)
JOSHUA [3].
m. Dorothy Frees and had six children :

I. ANNA [4].

m. Nathan *Mordough*, of Wakefield, and had ten children :

1. ANNA [5].

m. John *Huggins*, and had five children.

2. ABIGAIL [5].

m. John *Glidden*, and had eight children.

3. Mary [5].

m. Elijah *French*, and had seven children.

4. DOLLY [5].

m. Jonathan *Quimby*, and had five children.

5. LYDIA [5].

m. Samuel *Tibbets*, and had seven children.

6. ELIZABETH [5].

m. Seth *Fogg*, and had eight children.

7. MARGARET [5].

m. Joshua *Titcomb*, and had eight children.

8. ROBERT [5].

m. (1) Hannah Stratton ; (2) Abigail Nichols, and had three children by each wife.

9. JAMES [5].

m. Temperance Wentworth, aud had seven children.

10. NATHAN [5], b. ———, d. aged 22.

II. JOSHUA[4], b. ——, d. s. p.

    m. Hannah Veazie. Lived in Stratham.

III. JOHN[4], (Col.).

    m. Mary Philbrick, of Hampton. Lived in Wakefield and was Selectman of the town. He had eight children :

1. MARY[5], b. April 24, 1769.

    m. Nathan *Watson*, of Brookfield, and had eight children.

2. JOSHUA[5], b. April 30, 1771.

    m. March 28, 1810, Sally Ricker and had four children.

3. DOLLY[5], b. Oct. 25, 1774.

    m. Jan. 25, 1796, William *Randall*, and had seven children.

4. LOVE[5], b. July 23, 1776.

    m. Jonathan *Sanborn*, and had four children.

5. SARAH[5], b. Nov. 26, 1778.

    m. May 15, 1804, James *Shaw*.

6. JOHN[5], b. Aug. 29, 1780.

    m. Sept. 27, 1804, Abigail Sanborn, of Brookfield, and had eight children. Went to Canada.

7. JAMES[5], b. Aug. 2, 1783.

    m. twice. m. (1) March, 1806, Polly Shaw, in Tamworth; (2) a widow Philbrook of Freedom. Some of his children went to New York.

8. BETSEY[5].

    m. Aug. 30, 1807, John *Fellows*, and had three children.

IV. DOROTHY[4].

    m. David *Wiggin*, of Greenland, and had four children.

V. LOVE[4].

    m. —— *Frost*.

VI. JAMES[4]. d. young, unm., in the West Indies.

JOHN[1].

JOSHUA[2], (Col.).

JANE[3].

m. Rev. Stephen *Chase* and had seven children:

I.　ABRAHAM[4], b. March 25, 1734, d. March 25, 1734.

II.　STEPHEN[4], b. Feb. 22, 1735; d. Dec. 1, 1739.

III.　JOSHUA[4], b. March, 1738.
　　　m. Anna Swett.

IV.　JANE[4], b. Jan. 7, 1740.
　　　m. Samuel *Wallace* and had children.

V.　STEPHEN[4], b. June 22, 1742; d. March 31, 1805.
　　　m. Mary Frost, (b. Jan. 29, 1752; d. Sept. 15, 1819), dau.
　　　of Joseph Frost, of Newcastle, and his wife Margaret
　　　(Cotton), of Springfield, Mass., and grand-daughter of Hon.
　　　John Frost who in early life commanded a British ship of
　　　war and was of the Governor's Council in 1727. Stephen[4]
　　　graduated H. U. and was a merchant in Portsmouth. Had
　　　six children:

1.　JOSEPH[5], b. April 22, 1772; d. 1814.
　　m. Margaret Chesley, of Durham, and lived in Portsmouth.
　　Had eight children.

　　1.　Mary[6], b. 1798.
　　　　m. John *Taylor*.

　　2.　Ann Margaret[6], b. ———, d. unm. 1845.

　　3.　Stephen[6], bapt. Aug. 1, 1802, d. unm. early in life.
　　　　Was lost at sea.

　　4.　Joseph[6], b. about 1804, d. unm.

　　5.　Theodore[6], b. 1807, d. 1815.

6. *Caroline Augusta*[6], b. 1809, d. Nov., 1844.

   m. Rev. ——— *Morgan*, and had :

    1. Newton[7], b. 1841, d. 1862.

      Killed at the battle of Corinth.

7. *Adelaide Smith*[6], b. 1811–12.

    m. (1) J. Lawrence *Page;* (2) Judge E. R. *Budd.*

8. *William* *(A.) L.*[6], b. 1814.

2. WILLIAM[5], b. Feb. 10, 1774, d. s. p, Aug. 30, 1834.

    m. Oct. 11, 1824, Sarah Blunt, (d. July, 1880), and lived in Portsmouth.

3. MARY[5], b. Nov. 15, 1776, d. Dec. 2, 1857.

    m. June 22, 1799, Edmund[5] *Toppan* of Portsmouth (b. Sept. 25, 1777, d. July 29, 1849), son of Christopher[4], and Sarah (Parker) Toppan, and grand-son of Dr. Edmund and Sarah[3] (Wingate) Toppan. Had six children. [See Edmund[5] Toppan].

4. HARRIETT[5], b. Aug. 14, 1778.

    m. Oliver *Crosby*, of Dover, counsellor, and had six children :

    1. Harriet[6].

      m. ——— *Morrill*, of Atkinson, Me.

    2. Oliver[6].

    3. Cornelia[6].

      m. Dr. *Barrett.*

    4. Willam[6].

    5. Henrietta[6].

      m. George *Ingersoll*, of Maine.

    6. Josiah[6].

5. SARAH[5], b. Oct. 23, 1780.

    m. Jeremiah H. *Woodman*, of Rochester (b. 1774-5, d. 1854 ; counsellor ; D. C. 1794), and had seven children :

    1. Charles William[6] (Judge).

      m.(1) 1840, Charlotte Pearce, daughter of Stephen Pearce, of Portsmouth ; (2) 1866, Frances J. Soren, daughter of Jn. J. Soren of Roxbury, Me.   He graduated D. C. 1829.

2.   *Sarah Jane*[6].
. m. Judge *Tibbets*, of Rochester. ·

3.   *Jeremiah H.*[6].

4.   *Harriett*[6].

5.   *Charlotte*[6].

6.   *Theodore Chase*[6] (Hon.), b. April 10, 1815.
m. Aug. 16, 1843, Mary Jane Darling, dau. of Deacon Henry Darling, of Bucksport, Me.   D. C. 1835.   Practiced law in Bucksport after 1839.

7.   *Samuel*[6].

6.   THEODORE[5], b. Mar. 16, 1786, d. Mar. 13, 1859.
m. April 26, 1831, Clarissa Andrews Bigelow, dau. of Tyler Bigelow, of Watertown, Mass.   Lived in Portsmouth and Boston, and had three children :

1.   *Theodore*[6], b. Feb. 4, 1832.
m. Nov. 17, 1868, Alice Bowdoin Bradlee, dau. of James Bowdoin Bradlee, of Boston.   H. C. 1853.

2.   *George Bigelow*[6], b. Oct. 1, 1835.
m. Jan. 10, 1860, Anne Lowndes, dau. of Rawlins and Gertrude (Livingston) Lowndes, of South Carolina. H. C. 1856.   Had :
1.   Stephen[7], b. Jan. 30, 1863.
2.   Gertrude Lowndes[7], b. Oct. 23, 1868.

3.   *Charles Henry*[6], b. Mar. 5, 1841, d. Feb. 27, 1849.

VI.   MARY[4], b. Oct. 19, 1744, d. Sept. 15, 1749.

VII.   JOHN[4], b. Aug. 14, 1749.
m. Abigail Toppan, of Manchester, and had two children :

1.   STEPHEN[5].
Lived in Maine and had several children.

2.   BENJAMIN[5].
Lived in Portland, Me.

JOHN[1].
JOSHUA[2], (Col.).
ABIGAIL[3].

m. John *Stickney* and had eight children :

I.   JOHN[4], b. Feb. 19, 1738, d. Dec. 5, 1803 (?)

II. ABIGAIL[4], b. Oct. 2, 1740, d. in infancy.

III. ANNA[4], b. Feb. 26, 1742, d. Oct. 27, 1827.
    m. Mar. 7, 1770, Benjamin *Johnston*, of Boston, (b. Sept. 7, 1740, d. Aug. 13, 1818). They had six children :

1. THOMAS[5], b. Mar. 27, 1772.
    m. May 5, 1793, Rhoda Atwood, and had nine children :

    1. *Rhoda*[6], b. Feb. 5, 1795.

    2. *Mary*[6], b. Jan. 15, 1798.

    3. *Thomas*[6], b. Dec. 4, 1800.

    4. *Betsey*[6], b. Mar. 22, 1803.

    5. *William*[6], b. Aug. 7, 1805.

    6. *George W.*[6], b. Mar. 15, 1808.

    7. *Harrietta*[6], b. Mar. 17, 1812.

    8. *John*[6], b. April 25, 1815.

    9. *Emily H.*[6], b. Jan. 11, 1818.

2. MARY[5], b. Sept. 3, 1773, d. Aug. 2, 1809.
    m. 1802, Dudley *Russell*, and had four children :

    1. *Mary Ann*[6], b. Nov. 16, 1802.
        m. —— *Woods*, of Newburyport, Mass.

    2. *Edward Johnston*[6], b. Feb. 18, 1805.
        Lived in Bradford, (prob. Mass.).

    3. *Caroline*[6], b. Jan. 4, 1807.

    4. *Benjamin*[6], b. Feb., 1809.

3. SARAH⁵, b. March 5, 1775, d. Oct. 9, 1776.

- 4. JOHN⁵, b. July 10, 1777.
     m. Sept., 1798, Mary Knight, dau. of Job Knight, of Glou-
     cester, Mass., and had three children:

     1. John S.⁶, b. Sept. 7, 1799.
          m. 1822, Harriet Ayers, of New Bedford, Mass.

     2. Anna Knight⁶, b. March, 1802.

     3. Mary Elizabeth⁶, b. Jan., 1803, d. 1812-13.

5. SARAH⁵, b. July 16, 1779.

6. ANN⁵, b. Sept. 2, 1781, d. Nov. 16, 1795.

IV. MARY⁴, b. Feb. 22, 1744, d. in infancy.

V. WILLIAM⁴, b. Dec. 22, 1745, d. Aug. 25, 1823.
     m. 1777, Mary Tucker, dau. of Rev. John Tucker, of New-
     bury, Mass., and had four children:

1. SARAH⁵, b. March 25, 1778, d. Sept. 14, 1845.
     m. Nov. 25, 1800, as second wife, Capt. Samuél *Prince*, of
     Boston, and had five children:

     1. William⁶, b. Sept. 4, 1801, d. unm. July 3, 1834.

     2. Frances Charlotte⁶, b. Dec. 29, 1803, d. June 9, 1846.
          m. 1825, Robert *Farley*, of Ipswich, Mass., and Boston,
          and had:

          1. Frances Ann⁷, b. ———, d. 1834.

          2. Susan Crosswell⁷, b. Oct. 25, 1832.
               m. March 13, 1815, Emilio *Sanchez y Dolz*, and had:
               (*a*) Panchita⁸, b. ———, d. about 1852.

          3. Robert⁷, b. June 30, 1839.
               m. Jane Kelly, dau. of William Kelly, and had four
               sons and three daughters.

          4. Eleanor Shattuck⁷.

3. John Tucker[6], b. May 10, 1806.
> m. Dec. 4, 1834, Lucy Maria Parker, lived in Boston, and
> had :

> 1. John Tucker[7], b. Sept. 25, 1835.
>> m. Oct. 18, 1865, Caroline Augusta Pond, dau. of
>> Moses Pond, of Boston, and had :
>> (*a*) John[8].

> 2. Lucy Maria[7], b. April 18, 1838.

> 3. Frances Charlotte[7], b. Oct. 24, 1848.

4. Theodore Sedgwick[6], b. April 6, 1809.
> Supposed to have died in the Texan War.

5. Sarah Ann[6], b. about 1815, d. about 1819.

2. ANN[5], b. Dec. 20, 1779, d. unm.

3. CHARLOTTE[5], b. Jan. 11, 1781, d. Sept. 13, 1845.
> m. Nov. 25, 1805, John *Barnard*, and had two children :

1. John[6].

2. Sarah[6].
> m. Dr. Ralph *Huse*, of Newburyport, Mass., and George-
> town, Mass., and had two children.

4. JOHN[5], b. Feb. 29, 1783, d. unm. Dec. 14, 1833.
> H. U. 1804. Was a lawyer; teacher in Fort Hill School,
> Boston ; assistant Clerk Supreme Court.

VI. THOMAS[4], b. April 7, 1748, d. Aug. 28, 1791.
> m. Abigail Blodgett. Died at Leicester, Mass.

VII. JOSEPH[4], b. May 3, 1750, d. unm. Oct. 29, 1803.
> Died at Leicester, Mass.

VIII. MARY[4], b. Nov. 24, 1752.
> m. Capt. Thomas *Jones*, of Wales, Mass., and died there.

JOHN¹.
JOSHUA², (Col.)
MARTHA³.

m. Dr. John *Weeks*, and had ten children.

I. JOSHUA WINGATE ⁴, (Rev.), b. 1738, d. 1806.

m. Sarah Treadwell, of Ipswich, Mass. H. U. 1758. Ordained in London, England, in 1763, by an Episcopal Bishop. On his return he had charge for some twelve years of St. Michael's Church, Marblehead, Mass. At his ordination he had taken the oath of allegiance to the King of England, and when the majority of his countrymen declared for Independence "his piety was stronger than his patriotism" and he refused to violate his oath. In 1775 he was driven from his home and obliged to take refuge with his brother-in-law, Rev. Jacob Bailey, Pownalboro, (now Dresden), Maine. In 1778 he returned and petitioned for permission to leave the country with his wife aud eight children, but was refused. He escaped, however, and was taken to England, where he was appointed a chaplain in Halifax, N. S., officiating also at other places. He was a learned, very intelligent and agreeable man. Had eight children :

1. JOHN⁵.

An officer in the British Army, and settled in the West Indies.

2. MARTHA W.⁵.

m. —— Stone, lived in Sidney, Cape Breton, and had :

1. —— ⁶, (dau.).

m. Rev. Hibbard *Burney*.

2. —— ⁶, (son).

Lived in Halifax, and was, in 1857, Prot. Epis. Bishop of Nova Scotia.

3. SARAH W.⁵.

m. Rev. William *Twining*, and had :

1. —— ⁶, (son).

Chaplain of the garrison at Halifax, N. S.

4. HELEN [5].

> m. (1) ———, an officer in the army, (2) ——— *Simpson*, a merchant of London.

5. J. W.[5] (Capt.).

> m. ——— and had a large family, among whom were two sons, farmers in Cape Breton, and one son, editor of a paper in Halifax.

6. C. W.[5] (Rev.).

> Episcopal minister, first at Weymouth, then in Manchester, N. S. Died in Halifax.

7. FOSTER [5], (Major).

> Major in the army. Settled in Canada.

8. JAMES [5].

> Commissary in the British army, and died young.

II. COMFORT [4], b. 1740, d. 1814.

> m. (1) March 3, 1760, Dr. Coffin *Moore*, of Stratham, (b. Feb. 25, 1739, d. 1778), son of William Moore. He was a learned and skillful physician; (2) Simon *French*. She bore seven children, five, at least, and probably all six by first husband :

1. WILLIAM [5], b. 1762.

> m. Ann Carr, of Candia, lived in Lancaster, and had five children :

> *1. Mary* [6].

> *2. John Carr* [6].

> *3. Martha* [6].

> *4. William Weeks* [6].

> *5. Ann* [6].

2. MARTHA [5], (Patty), b. ———, d. 1821.

> m. Caleb *Prince*, of Candia, son of Rev. Joseph Prince.

3.   COFFIN[5], b. Aug. 30, 1768, d. 1842.
     m. 1789, Polly Bucknam, of Lancaster, lived in Lancaster,
     and had eleven children :

     1.   Jacob B.[6].
          Died in the army about 1813.

     2.   John Weeks[6].
          Lived in Genesee Co., N. Y.

     3.   Sukey[6].
          m. Enoch *Kinny*, of Whitefield, N. H.

     4.   Polly[6].
          m. (1) Nathan *Morrel*, of Whitefield; (2) S. B. *Johnson*, of Littleton.

     5.   Edward Bucknam[6], (Dr.), b. June 12, 1801, d. 1874.
          Bowd. Col. 1828.   Lived in Chelsea, Mass.

     6.   George W.[6].
          m. —— Hicks, and died in Stewartstown.

     7.   Simon P.[6].
          Lived in Batavia, N. Y.

     8.   Joseph B.[6].
          m. Eunice McIntyre, and lived in Lancaster.

     9.   William Harvey[6].
          Lived in Massachusetts.

     10.   Adino Nye[6].
          Merchant in Boston.

     11.   Martha[6].
          m. Enoch *Rogers*, of Concord.

4.   COMFORT[5], b. Jan. 24, 1770, d. Dec. 1, 1834.
     m. Dec. 20, 1793, John *French*, of Candia, son of Simon
     French.   Had three children :

     1.   Martha[6], b. Oct., 1794.

     2.   Simon[6], b. Feb. 2, 1796.
          m. Ann B. Evans, and lived in Candia.

3. Coffin M.[6], (Deacon), b. April 6, 1799.

m. Dolly Pillsbury, and had :

1. Samuel Franklin [7], (Rev.), b. Dec. 22, 1835.

m. Dec. 22, 1804, Martha Jane Upton, dau. of George Upton, of Andover, Mass. D. C. 1863, Andover Theol. Sem. 1864 ; ord. pastor Congregational Church, Hamilton, Mass., Sept. 29, 1864, afterwards pastor at Wallingford, Vt.

2. George Henry [7], (Rev.), b. July 27, 1838.

m. —— —— ; D. C. 1863, And. Theol. Sem. 1868 ; acting pastor at Charlestown.

3. Mary [7].

m. Rev. James H. *Fitts*, pastor Congregational Church, South Newmarket.

5. JOHN WEEKS [5].

Killed by lightning in the shrouds of a vessel during a storm at sea.

6. JACOB BAILEY [5], (Dr.), b. Sept. 5, 1772, d. Jan. 10, 1813.

m. Polly Eaton, dau. of Ephraim Eaton, of Candia, and settled in Andover in 1796. In the War of 1812 was surgeon in the United States Army. He was a man of fine literary taste and musical talent. He had four children :

1. Jacob B.[6], b. Oct. 31, 1797, d. 1853.

m. —— Hill, sister of Hon. Isaac Hill, editor of the Concord, New Hampshire, Patriot. He became Hill's partner. In 1823, with John Farmer, edited the New Hampshire Gazetteer. In 1826-29 edited the New Hampshire Journal.

2. Henry E.[6].

Was a musician.

3. Mary[6], b. ——, d. about 1868.

m. Dr. Thomas *Brown*, lived in Manchester, and left a son and two daughters.

4. John W.[6].

Once editor of Bellows Falls, (Vt.), Gazette.

7. POLLY [5].

m. Jn. *Quimby*, and removed to Candia.

III. MARTHA [4], b. 1742.

    m. Capt. Benjamin *Randall*, and died two years after marriage. Had one child :

1. WILLIAM [5], b. ——— , d. aged 18.

    Died in the West Indies.

IV. MARY [4], b. Feb. 12, 1745, d. Jan. 15, 1814.

    m. (1) Adino *Nye*, of Hingham, Mass., and Georgetown, Me. ; (2) Joseph *Bracket*, of Greenland, then of Lancaster. "An excellent woman spoken of in terms of unqualified praise." By her first husband she had two children, by her second four :

1. MARY W.[5]

    m. a British officer.

2. ELIZABETH [5].

    m. ——— *Goss*, of Lancaster, and had children.

3. JAMES [5].

    Lived in Cherry Valley, N. Y.

4. ADINO NYE [5], b. about 1780.

    m. about 1810 his cousin, Mary Wiggin [5] Weeks, (b. March 4, 1787), dau. of Capt. John Weeks, of Lancaster, lived in Lancaster, and had :

    1. John [6], b. ——— , d. early in life.

    2. Adino Nye [6], (Dr.), b. July 11, 1822.

        m. March 6, 1855, Lucy A. B———. D. C. 1844. Physician in Negrofoot, Hanover Co., Virginia.

    3. James [6].

        Farmer on the homestead at Lancaster.

5. MARTHA W.[5], b. ———, d. s. p. in early life.
    m. her cousin, Hon. John W.[5] *Weeks*, (b. March 31, 1781, d.
    s. p. April 3, 1853), son of Capt. John[4] Weeks. He married
    a second time.

6. JAMES WEEKS[5].

V. SARAH[4], b. 1747, d. Nov. 22, 1818.
    m. Aug. 1762, Rev. Jacob *Bailey*, (d. 1808. H. U. 1755).
    He had been her teacher. He was an Episcopalian, or-
    dained in England, and rector of the church at Pawnalboro,
    Me., till, driven from his people in 1779 for his attachment
    to his mother country, he became rector of St. Luke's church,
    Annapolis, N. S., where he served 25 years till his death.
    His life, "The Frontier Missionary," by Wm. S. Bartlett,
    Boston, 1853, says : "He was poor, yet hospitable and kind,
    always retaining the personal regard of all who knew him."
    They had six children :

1. CHARLES PERCY[5], (Capt.), b. ———, d. 1812.
    Was a captain in the British Army and was killed at the Bat-
    tle of Chippewa in 1812.

2. REBECCA LAVINIA[5].

3. CHARLOTTE MARIA[5].

4. THOMAS HENRY[5], b. ———, d. in early life.
    m. ——— and had three children.

5. WILLIAM GILBERT[5], b. ———, d. in early life.
    m. ——— and had children. Was a lawyer.

6. ELIZABETH ANN[5].
    m. James *Whitman*.

VI. JOHN⁴ (Capt.), b. Feb. 17, 1749, d. Sept. 10, 1818.

m. Dec. 27, 1770, Deborah Bracket, dau. of James Bracket, of Greenland. He was as zealous in favor of independence as his brother was in opposition to it ; — " was Lieutenant in the Revolutionary Army, a member of the convention that adopted the constitution of New Hampshire, several years a Representative in the Legislature and an influential citizen wherever he resided." About 1783 he moved from Greenland, lived some time in Lee, and in 1787 settled in the new town of Lancaster. He fell and died very suddenly, just as he was getting into his carriage. He had seven children :

1. MARTHA⁵, b. Dec. 20, 1771, d. 1872.

m. Edward *Spalding*, of Lancaster, and had six children :

  1. Edward Cummings⁶.

  2. John Weeks⁶.

  3. William Dustin⁶.

  4. Eliza⁶.

  5. James Bracket⁶.

  6. Martha⁶.

    m. Charles *Stebbins*.

2. DEBORAH⁵, b. Feb. 29, 1776, d. 1860.

m. (1) William *Ayres* ; (2) Jacob *Emerson*, and had by her first husband one child :

  1. Deborah⁶.

    m. Myron *Chandler*.

3. ELIZABETH⁵, b. 1778, d. April 1, 1844.

m. Judge Azariah *Webb*, of Lunenburg, Vt., and had six children :

  1. Eliza⁶.

  2. Marius A.⁶.

  3. Sally Ann⁶.

  4. Martha⁶.

  5. John Wingate⁶.

  6. Lucy A.⁶.

4. JOHN WINGATE [5] (Hon.), b. Mar. 31, 1781, d. s. p. April 3, 1853.
   m. (1) his cousin, Martha W.[5] Brackett, daughter of Mary [4]
   Weeks; (2) Persis F. Everett. He was a man of superior
   talents and was from 1829 to 1833 Member of Congress from
   New Hampshire.

5. JAMES BRACKET [5], b. June 14, 1784, d. Mar. 19, 1858.
   m. Jan., 1810, Elizabeth [Betsey] Stanley (b. Aug. 4, 1785, d.
   Dec. 24, 1854). Lived in Lancaster and had seven children :

   1. James Wingate [6] (Hon.), b. July 15, 1811.
   m. (1) May 30, 1842, Martha Willard Hemenway, (b.
   1818, d. Sept. 5, 1853), dau. of Solomon Hemenway, of
   Lancaster; (2) May, 1859, Mary Elizabeth Burns, (b.
   1826, d. Feb. 2, 1878), dau. of Dr. Robert Burns, of
   Plymouth. Had children.

   2. Mary Nye [6], b. Aug. 24, 1813, d. Nov. 5, 1856.
   m. May 1, 1851, Richard H. *Eastman*. Lived in Lancaster.

   3. Sarah Stanley [6], b. Nov. 15, 1815, d. Mar. 22, 1842.
   m. Mar. 15, 1839, Edmund C. *Wilder*. Lived in Cole-
   brook.

   4. William Dennis [6]. b. Feb. 28, 1818, d. Feb. 27, 1885.
   m. July 4, 1843, Mary Helen Livingston, of Wood-
   stock, Conn., lived in Lancaster and had three children.

   5. John [6], b. June 30, 1822.
   m. June, 1851, Ellen Merrill, of Buffalo, N. Y., and lived
   in Buffalo.

   6. Martha Eliza [6], b. Dec. 10, 1824, d. June, 1872.
   Lived in Boston.

   7. Persis Fayette [6], b. Feb. 3, 1831.
   m. Jan. 2, 1854, Rev. George M. *Rice* (d. Sept. 20, '82).

6. MARY WIGGIN⁵, b. Mar. 4, 1787.

>   m. about 1810, her cousin Adino Nye⁵ *Bracket* (b. about 1780), son of Mary⁴ Weeks Bracket. (For children see Adino Nye⁵ Bracket).

7. SALLY BRACKET⁵, b. Aug. 13, 1789.

>   m. Edward F. *Bucknam,* a farmer in Lancaster, where they lived and had four children :

>   *1. Deborah⁶.*
>>   m. James *McIntire,* and lived in Northumberland.

>   *2. John W.⁶* (Dr.), b. ———, d. in early life.
>>   m. ————, and lived in Great Falls. D. C. 1860.

>   *3. Martha⁶.*
>>   m. Proctor *Jacobs,* and had :
>>   1.   Clara⁷.

>   *4. Mary⁶.*
>>   m. S. H. *Legore.*

VII.   WILLIAM⁴, b. 1751, d. Sept., 1821.

>   m. Susanna Haines, dau. of Deacon William Haines. When his friends urged him to study medicine and follow the profession of his father he declined, saying, " I could not endure the business of going from one sick bed to another, and habitually witnessing such scenes of distress." So he became a carpenter in Portsmouth until 1776, when he bought a farm in Chester, where in a quiet way he spent the remainder of his life.   He had six children :

1.   JOHN⁵, b. Sep. 14, 1773.

>   m. ————, lived in Bangor, Me., and had four children.

2.   WILLIAM⁵, b. 1775, d. young.

3. BENIN[5], b. Feb. 17, 1779.
   Lived in Bangor, Me., and had five children.

4. MARY[5], b. Dec. 14, 1782.
   m. Edward Moore *Preston*, and went West.

5. SUSAN HAINES[5], b. Aug. 26, 1788, d. Oct. 27, 1842.
   m. July 10, 1827, James *Calef* (b. April 14, 1792, d. July 25, 1858). Lived in Auburn, and had :

   1. *Charles Weeks*[6], b. April 5, 1829.
       m. April 21, 1864, Venelia M. Richards, of Quincy, Mass. Lived in Auburn.

6. NOAH[5], b. June 14, 1790, d. Mar. 20, 1875.
   m. Charlotte Quimby (b. May 25, 1800, d. June 13, 1870), dau. of Bradbury Quimby, of Chester. Lived in Chester and had eight children :

   1. *Sarah*[6], b. 1818, d. unm. 1869.

   2. *Noah H.*[6], b. 1819.
       Lived in Chester.

   3. *Charlotte*[6], b. 1821, d. unm. 1862.

   4. *William*[6], b. 1823.
       m. M. J. Moore, of Candia, and lived in Chester.

   5. *George W.*[6], b. 1826.
       m. M. Currier.

   6. *Asahel*[6], b. 1829.
       m. Mary Dustin and had four children.

   7. *Angeline*[6], b. Sept. 17, 1832.
       Lived in Chester.

   8. *Franklin C.*[6] (Dr.), b. 1835, d. unm. Mar. 28, 1864.
       D. C. 1858. Assistant Surgeon 14th N. H. Vols.

VIII. WARD COTTON⁴, (Capt.), bap. July 15, 1753.
m. Mary Barber, dau. of Jonah Barber of Exeter, where he was in 1778, a clothier, with his father-in-law. He then became a sea captain, and is said to have died of the yellow fever in the West Indies before August, 1789. He had:

1. JOHN WINGATE⁵, b. 1784, d. 1864.
m. ——— Durgin. Settled in Wakefield, but afterwards moved into Cornville, Me. They had eight children.

    1. Cotton⁶.
    Lived in Wellington, Me.

    2. Gilman⁶.

    3. John⁶, b. Feb., 1806, d. Feb. 22, 1882.
    m. 1828, Amanda Lord, dau. of James Lord. Lived in Brighton, Me., and Springfield, Mass., and had:

        1. John Milton⁷, b. Aug. 31, 1840.
        m. June, 1862, Sarah P. Shumway.

        2. Hannah⁷.
        m. F. D. *Richards*, of Ware, Mass.

        3. Jane Eliza⁷.

    4. Alvah⁶.

    5. Noah⁶.

    6. Bradford⁶,

    7. Caroline⁶.

    8. Joanna⁶.

IX. ABIGAIL⁴. b. ———, " dyed an infant."

X. JOANNA[4], b. Dec. 31, 1755, d. July 17, 1826.

m. Dec. 4, 1776-77, Levi *Folsom*, son of Col. Jere. Folsom. His father, a merchant and shipbuilder, failing in business, and the estate of her father having been expended in educating and settling nine children, they had little to commence life with except two lots of wild land in Tamworth. To this they removed eighteen months after marriage. Joanna was a great reader, with a wonderful memory, and a remarkable command of language, a generous person and an exemplary Christian. They had nine children :

1. WARD WEEKS[5], b. Sept. 4, 1778, d. June 25, 1829.

m. Nov. 15, 1802, Lydia A. Hayford (b. 1782, d. April, 1876). Lived in Tamworth and had seven children :

   1. Edward H.[6], b. 1804, d. Mar., 1826.

   2. Horatio Nelson[6], b. April 7, 1806, d. 1884.

     m. 1836, Lucinda E. Dodge, dau. of William Dodge, of Wenham, Mass., and lived in Crescent city and Hazel Dell, Iowa. Had four children :

     1. William W.[7], b. ———, d. a child.

     2. Edward L.[7].
       Lived in Crescent City, Iowa.

     3. Horatio N.[7], b. 1841, d. July, 1863.
       In the army.

     4. Levi Bracket[7].

   3. Levi B.[6], b. 1809, d. about 1844.

   4. Simeon[6], b. 1812.

     m. (1) Selina Fisk ; (2) Hannah Tarbell. Lived in Detroit, Mich., and had :

     1. Samuel Fiske[7], b. 1835.
       Lived in Council Bluffs, Iowa.

     2. Sarah Angeline[7], b. 1836.
       m. Dr. George *Fields*, of Detroit, Mich.

     3. Frank[7], b. 1839.
       m. Debbe Briscoe. Lived in Detroit, Mich.

     4. Eliza[7], b. 1840.

5. *Jeremiah*⁶, b. 1817, d. May, 1884.
 m. (1) Marcia A. Hopkins; (2) Sarah M. Blake; (3) Agnes Peterson. Lived in Michigan, and Council Bluffs, Iowa, and had four children.

6. *Lydia H.*⁶, b. 1819.
 m. L. R. *Rogers* (d. 1872), and lived in Townsend, Mass., and Boston. Had, besides others:
 1. Charles Edward⁷.
  Lived in Boston.
 2. Alfred F.⁷.

7. *Ward Weeks*⁶, b. 1822, d Sept., 1885.
 m. 1844, Matilda Stedman, lived in Taylors Falls, Minn., and had five children, including:
 1. Charles W.⁷, d. ———.
 2. Edward H.⁷, b. 1847.
  Editor of the "Taylors Falls Journal."

2. JEREMIAH⁵, b. 1780, d. Dec., 1859.
 m. 1805, Octavia Howe, (d. Sept., 1872), lived in Bloomfield, Me., and had ten children:

1. *Levi H.*⁶, b. 1806, d. April 1, 1883.
 m. Eunice Webb. Lived in Skowhegan, Me. Had five children.

2. *Joanna Weeks*⁶, b. 1808, d. Jan., 1884.
 m. (1) J. *Stevenson*; (2) Luther *Jones*, and had six children, five by first husband:
 1. Susan A.⁷.
 2. De Witt Clinton⁷.
 3. Harriet N.⁷.
  m. L. K. *Stannard*, of Taylors Falls, Minn.
 4. William H.⁷.
  Publisher of a Law Journal in St. Louis, Mo.
 5. ———⁷, b. ———, d. an infant.
 6. Charles F.⁷, (Jones).
  Lived in Skowhegan, Me.

3. Jeremiah [6], b. 1810, d. Jan., 1869.
> m. Eliza Shaw, lived in Oakdale, Minn., and had :
>
> 1. Charles A. [7]
>   Lived in Chicago.
>
> 2. Henry F. [7]
>   Lived in Kettle River, Minn.
>
> 3. William H. [7]
>   Lived in St. Paul, Minn.
>
> 4. Philander E. [7]
>   Lived in Rush City, Minn.
>
> 5. George A. [7]
>   Lived in Boston.
>
> 6. Mabel Josie [7]
>   Lived in St. Paul, Minn.

4. John H. [6], b. Dec., 1812.
> m. 1839, ———, lived in Prarie du Chien, Wis.

5. George B. [6], b. April 9, 1815.
> m. 1843, Deborah Sawyer, and lived in St. Stephen,
> N. B., and in Taylors Falls, Minn.

6. William H. C. [6], (Hon.), b. 1817.
> m. Mary Jane Wyman, lived in St. Stephen, N. B., and
> Taylors Falls, Minn. Was in the State Senate. Had
> two children :
>
> 1. Wyman H. [7]
>
> 2. Frank William [7]

7. Simeon Pease [6], b. 1819.
> m. (1) Emeline Cutts ; (2) Julia A. Barnum ; (3) Mary
> G. Douglass ; (4) Anna L. Angier, and had :
>
> 1. Harriet O. [7]
>
> 2. Julia M. [7]
>
> 3. Simeon Pease [7]
>   Lived in St. Paul, Minn.

8. *Charles B.*⁶, b. 1822.

    m. 1849, Emily Pratt, of Skowhegan, Me., and had :

    1. Charles W. H.⁷.

    2. Julia Emma⁷.

    3. Lillie May⁷.

    Lived in Colorado.

9. *Ward Weeks*⁶, b. Oct., 1824.

    m. Sidney Purget, and lived in St. Paul, Minn.

10. *Susan O.*⁶, b. ———, d. young.

3. ELIZABETH SMITH⁵, b. March 29, 1783, d. Aug. 5, 1821.

    m. Feb. 10, 1808, Samuel *Chapman*, of Tamworth, son of Job Chapman. Had five children :

1. *Jacob*⁶, (Rev.), b. March 11, 1810.

    m. (1) 1840, Mary C. Howe, (d. April, 1869) ; (2) Sept., 1871, Mary E. Lane, dau. of Charles Lane, of Stratham. D. C. 1835, and Theol. Sem. 1839, Professor in Franklin College, Lancaster, Pa., in 1846, Principal of the Academy at Harrisburg, Pa., in 1850, and later was Professor in Terra Haute Female College. Preached from 1852 in Illinois and New Hampshire, until he retired in 1879 and settled in Exeter. Has compiled the Folsom Genealogy, besides other genealogical works.

2 *Eliza F.*⁶, b. March, 1812.

    m. 1837, Deacon James J. *Chesley*, of Tamworth, and had :

    1. Betsey S.⁷.

    2. Deborah⁷.

    3. Samuel C.⁷.

    4. Hester Ann⁷.

    5. Mary⁷, d. young.

    6. Emma⁷.

    7. John Jacob⁷, d young.

3. *John*⁶, b. 1814, d. s. p. Aug., 1845.

    m. 1839, Mary P. Swazey, of Meredith. Lived in Benton, Mo.

4. *Samuel*⁶, (Dr.), b. 1816, d. unm. June 10, 1843.

5. *Mary Ann*⁶, b. 1819, d. unm. Dec., 1848.

4. JOHN WEEKS[5], b. 1785, d. unm. about 1812.
5. LEVI[5], (Col.), b. 1788, d. 1841.
   m. Lydia Dodge, (d. 1824), and had six children:
   1. *Elizabeth*[6], b. 1813.
      m. Neh. *Stanley*, and had:
      1. Neh.[7], b. ———, d. in early life.
         Was a war correspondent. "Scout."
      2. Levi[7].
         Died in the army.
      3. Joanna[7].
         m. ———, of Concord, N. H.
   2. *Joanna Weeks*[6], b. 1814, d. 1842.
      m. 1833, Hon. Larkin D. *Mason*, of Tamworth, and had:
      1. Samuel W.[7], b. May 22, 1838, d. 1868.
         Editor of a paper in Savannah, Ga.
      2. Levi Folsom[7], b. Dec., 1840, d. s. p.
         m. L. Titcomb. Was a merchant. Lived in Chicago.
   3. *John T. D.*[6], b. 1818.
      m. 1842, Asenath Whipple, and was for more than thirty
      years Postmaster in South Tamworth. Had:
      1. Lydia D.[7].
      2. Judith M.[7].
      3. Elizabeth A.[7].
      4. Helen A.[7].
      5. Joanna Weeks[7].
   4. *Martha*[6], b. ———, d. an infant.
   5. *Levi W.*[6], b. 1821.
      m. 1859, Abigail Shaw. Penn. Col. (Gettysburg, Pa.),
      1847; lawyer; lived at Taylors Falls, Minn., and had:
      1. Jacob[7].
      2. Walter[7].
   6. *Lydia D.*[6], b. 1823, d. 1836.
6. JOANNA[5], b. Sept. 29, 1790, d. Aug., 1879.
   m. 1816, Thomas *Chesley*, of Lee, and had seven children:
   1. *Levi F.*[6].
      A farmer, unm. Lived in Durham.
   2. *Martha A.*[6].
   3. *Eliza A.*[6].
      m. E. G. *Wright.*

4. *Benjamin*[6], b. ———, d. young.
5. *James Ezra*[6], b. 1827, d. June 4, 1881.
    m. 1864, Fanny Tasker, lived in Hutchinson, Minn., and had :
    1. George Edward[7].
    2. Thomas Jewett[7].
    3. Georgianna[7].
    4. ———[7].
6. *Thomas B.*[6], b. 1829.
    Farmer, unm. Lived in Lee.
7. *George E.*[6], b, 1833.
    m. 1877, Abbie H. Pettingill, and lived in Lee.

7. MARY[5], b. 1793, d. 1849.
    m. 1815, Jeremiah D. *Ballard*, lived in Tamworth, and had five children :
    1. Mary Nye[6], d. 1833.
    2. Jeremiah D.[6], b. 1820.
        m. 1847, Elizabeth Newbegin, of Parsonsfield, Me.
    3. William Ward[6], b. 1822.
        m. 1850, M. E. Webster.
    4. Susan S.[6], b. 1830.
        m. N. H. *Shaw.*
    5. Levi W.[6], b. 1833.
        m. 1870, S. A. Chase. Lived in Lewiston, Me.

8. MARTHA WINGATE[5], b. June 24, 1795, d. Dec., 1885.
    m. 1825, B. *Durgin*, and had two children :
    1. Benjamin F.[6], b. ———, d. 1864.
        m. N. Greeley. Lived in Otisfield, Me., and had :
        1. Hattie[7].
        2. Frank W.[7].
    2. Martha A.[6].
        m. J. M. *Ricker*, and had :
        1. Martha A.[7].
        2. Elizabeth E.[7].
        3. Pamelia[7].
        4. Carrie M.[7].

9. GEORGE FROST[5], b. 1797, d. 1831.
    m. M. Dow, lived in Tamworth, and had two children.

JOHN ¹.

JOSHUA ² (Col.).

LOVE ³.

m. 1748, Rev. Nathaniel *Gookin*, and had eight children :

I. ———— ⁴. *[illegible]*

II. ———— ⁴. *[illegible]*

III. ———— ⁴. *[illegible]*

IV. ELIZABETH ⁴.

    m. Oct. 3, 1779, Dr. Edmund *Chadwick*, of Deerfield, (d. Nov. 8, 1826), and had ten children :

1. HANNAH ⁵, b. Sept. 22, 1781.
   m. John *Jenkins*, and had eleven children.

2. PETER ⁵, (Col.), b. Feb. 18, 1783.
   m. Susan C. March, of Deerfield, and had nine children.

3. ELIZABETH ⁵ (Betsey), b. Sept. 17, 1784.
   m. George *Williams*, and had four children.

4. JOHN ⁵, (Hon.), b. Jan. 7, 1786.
   m. Betsey Stearns, lived in Dover and in Maine, had nine children.

5. MEHITABLE ⁵, b. Dec. 11, 1787, d. unm.

6. ALEXANDER SCAMMELL ⁵, b. May 8, 1789.
   m. Hannah Kimball, of Laconia, lived in Gardner, Me., and had six children.

7. SUSAN ⁵, b. Mar. 7, 1791.

8. GILBERT ⁵, (Col.), b. Dec. 30, 1792, d. Sept. 21, 1836. ·
   m. Sarah Eastman and had three children.

9. SIDNEY ⁵, b. Sept. 5, 1794, d. unm.

10. SARAH ⁵, (Sally), b. Mar. 26, 1798.
    m. John *Dearborn*, and had one son.

V. HANNAH⁴, b. April 22, 1754, d. Aug. 4, 1797.

m. Rev. Timothy *Upham*, (d. 1811, H. U. 1768), of Deerfield, and lived in that town. He was the first minister of Deerfield and officiated 39 years until his death. He had seven children, four of whom died in childhood :

1. NATHANIEL⁵, b. in Deerfield, June 9, 1774, d. June 10, 1829.

m. Mar. 22, 1798, Judith Cogswell (b. Mar. 9, 1776, d. April 30, 1837), dau. of Hon. Thomas Cogswell, of Gilmanton, a descendant of John Cogswell, who settled in Ipswich, Mass., in 1635. Nathaniel⁵ was a member of the State House of Representatives, the Executive Council, and of Congress from 1817 to 1823. Lived in Rochester and had eleven children :

1. Thomas C.⁶. (D.D.), b. Jan. 20, 1799, d. April 2, 1872.

D. C. 1818. Prof. Bowdoin College from 1825 to 1870 ; was author of " Mental Philosophy ", " A Treatise on the Will " and many other volumes.

2. Nathaniel Gookin⁶, (LL.D.), b. Jan 8, 1801, d. Dec. 11, '69.

D. C. 1820. Judge of Superior Court. Lived in Concord.

3. Mary⁶, b. Sept. 16, 1802.

m. (1) Hon. David *Barker*, Jr., of Rochester, (H. C. 1815, M. C.) ; (2) Ebenezer *Coe*, of Northwood.

4. Alfred⁶ (Dr.), b. July 27, 1804, d. Nov., 1877.

Dart. Med. Col. Lived and died in New York.

5. Timothy⁶ (Dr.), b. 1807, d. in Waterford, N. Y., Aug. 7, '45.

Col. Med. Col., Washington City.

6. Joseph Badger⁶, b. Dec. 11, 1808.

m. Sarah Currier, of Dover. Merchant. Collector of Port of Portsmouth.

7. Judith Almira⁶, b. Mar. 26, 1811.

m. Hon. Jas. *Bell*, (Bowd. C. 1822, counsellor at Exeter,) had five children.

8. Hannah Elizabeth⁶, b. Dec. 18, 1813, d. an infant.

9. Ruth C.⁶, b. April 15, 1815, d. May 2, 1869.

m. John M. *Berry*, of Somersworth, N. H.

10. Francis W.⁶ (D.D.), b. Sept. 10, 1817.

m. (1) Elizabeth Brewer; (2) Elizabeth R. Kendall. Bowd. Col. 1838. Prof. and Author, New York.

11. Albert Gallatin⁶ (Dr.), b. July 10, 1819, d. June 16, 1847.

Bowd. Col. 1840. Practiced in Boston.

2. TIMOTHY[5], b. Nov. 11, 1776.
   m. Eliza Adams, and had nine children. Lived in Portsmouth.

3. HANNAH[5], b. July 12, 1789, d. unm. at Canandaigua, N. Y.
   Was a distinguished teacher.

VI. DANIEL[4], (Hon.), b. March 2, 1756, d. Sept. 4, 1831.
   m. Dec. 4, 1787, Abigail Dearborn, (b. March 10, 1766),
   dau. of Dr. Levi Dearborn. Lived in North Hampton,
   N. H., and Saco, Me. He was "an active and respectable
   man." He represented North Hampton several years from
   1805, and was Counsellor for the County in 1807 and 1808.
   Was appointed to the Bench of Common Pleas, June 6,
   1809, and held his seat until the Court was abolished in
   1813. In 1814 he was again in the House, and that year
   was appointed Judge of Probate for the County of Rockingham. On the 15th of December, the Governor, J. T.
   Gilman, nominated George Sullivan as Judge of Probate.
   Two counsellors agreed to this, but three disagreed, and the
   last three nominated Mr. Gookin; the Governor agreed to
   this nomination, and Mr. Sullivan was unanimously nominated Attorney General; both were appointed accordingly.
   Judge Gookin discharged the duties of Judge of Probate
   until 1826 to acceptance, and then retired from office, having attained the age of 70. He died among his children in
   Saco, Me., at the age of 75. It was this cousin of whom
   Judge Paine Wingate[4] made the remark quoted in the sketch
   of the latter's life; [Chapter VI.]. He had four children:

1. JOHN WINGATE[5], (Capt.), b. June 27, 1785.
   m. (1) April 20, 182[1], Elizabeth Smith; (2) 1838, Mary
   Hamilton. He was a Captain in the Army of 1812; lived
   later in North Yarmouth, Me. He had nine children by his
   first wife and one by his second:

   1. *Daniel*[6], b. June 7, 1822.
   2. *John McClary*[6], b. July 24, 1823.
   3. *Seth Storer*[6], b. ———, d. young.
   4. *Seth Storer*[6], b. Nov. 29, 1825, d. young.
   5. *J. B. Thornton*[6].

6. *Nathaniel*⁶.

7. *Charles Henry*⁶.

8. *George Wingate*⁶.

9. *Mary Elizabeth*⁶, b. ——, d. young.

10. *Mary Elizabeth*⁶, b. 1840.

2. SARAH⁵, b. Dec. 3, 1792.
   m. Jan. 20, 181–, Seth *Storer*, counsellor at Saco, Me., and had two children:

   *1. Henry Gookin*⁶, (Rev.), b. Nov. 12, 1813.
   Bowd. Col. 1832. Lives at Scarboro', Me., unm.

   *2. Frederic Tristam*⁶, (Dr.), b. Aug. 15, 1815.
   m. Hannah Spring.

3. ELIZA⁵, b. July 23, 1795, d. July 27, 1854.
   m. Jan. 20, 1817, James Brown *Thornton*, merchant of Saco., Me., and had eleven children:

   *1. John Wingate*⁶, b. Aug. 12, 1818, d. June 6, 1878.
   m. May 30, 1848, Elizabeth Wallace Bowles, dau. of Stephen Jones Bowles, of Roxbury, Mass. He graduated Harvard Law School 1840, practiced law in Boston from 1840 to 1878. A. M. at Bowdoin 1860. One of the founders of the Historic Genealogical Society of Boston, and an historical and genealogical writer of great industry. He had, besides three daughters:

   1. Henry⁷, b. Oct. 3, 1865, d. June 9, 1876.

   *2. Sarah Cutts Gookin Storer*⁶, b. July 22, 1820.

   *3. Daniel Gookin*⁶, b. Sept. 20, 1822, d. an infant.

   *4. Thomas Gilbert*⁶, b. Aug. 25, 1823.
   Bowd. Col. 1844; counsellor at Biddeford, Me., and afterwards lived in Topeka, Kan.

5. *James Brown*[6], (Rev.), b. July 6, 1825.
   m. (1) Dec. 19, 1851, Katherine Mary Stoughton, of
   South Windsor, Conn., (b. Aug. 15, 1831, d. Jan. 2,
   1872).; (2) July 24, 1872, Clara Small, of Bangor, Me.,
   (b. Aug. 19, 1838). He graduated Bowdoin 1846; ordained 1851. Pastor of First Church, Scarboro', Me.
   By first wife had four children, by second, one:

    1. Eliza Gookin[7], b. Oct. 15, 1854, d. an infant.

    2. Wyllys Stoughton[7], b. Aug. 9, 1856, d. 1864.

    3. James Brown[7], b. Oct. 5, 1861.
        Bowd. Med. Sch., 1885.

    4. Mary Stoughton[7], b. July 23, 1865.

    5. John Wingate[7], b. June 7, 1873.

6. *Albert Gallatin*[6], b. Dec. 25, 1827.
   Bowd. Col. 1848; counsellor.

7. *Charles Cutts Gookin*[6], b. May 11, 1830.
   Merchant in Boston.

8. *Henry*[6], b. Aug. 8, 1832.

9. *Eliza Gookin*[6], b. June 9, 1835.

10. *Frances Ann Dudley*[6], b. Aug. 1, 1837.

11. *Frank*[6], b.———, d. young.

4. HARRIETT[5], b. July 23, 1795.
   m. Feb. 28, 1820, Tristam *Storer*, of Saco, Me., sea-captain,
   and had three children:

    1. *Sarah Abby Gookin*[6].

    2. *Eliza Thornton*[6].

    3. *Frederic Deluis*[6].

VII. MARTHA[4], b———, d. unm.

VIII. SARAH[4], b. ———, d. unm.

JOHN ¹.
JOSHUA² (Col.).
ELIZABETH³.

m. Dr. John *Newman*, and had eleven children :

I.   ELIZABETH⁴, b. ———, d. in infancy.

II.   JOHN⁴, b. ———, d. of consumption.

III.   JANE⁴.
      m. (1) Woodbridge *Cutler;* (2) —— *Ayers.*

IV.   WINGATE⁴, b. ———, d. unm.
      " A valiant naval commander."

V.   PAINE⁴.

VI.   ELIZABETH⁴, b. ———, d. unm. of consumption.

VII.   JUDITH⁴.
      m. Paul *Stevens.*

VIII.   JOSHUA⁴.
      m. ———.

IX.   MARY⁴.
      m. Capt. *Stevenson.*

X.   TIMOTHY⁴.
      m. ———.

XI.   JOANNA⁴.

APPENDIX.

APPENDIX.

THE ENGLISH WINGATES. — THE KENTUCKY WINGATES. — BOOKS OF REFERENCE.

THE ENGLISH WINGATES.

Harlington, the residence of the early Wingates of England, was a secluded village in Bedfordshire, forty miles from London and only a few miles from the great Dunstable Downs, a dreary track which was, as late as the last century, much infested by highwaymen. Harlington is now a railway station, and can boast of a daily mail to London. Sharpenhoe is not far distant.

The old Wingate Manse house in Harlington is a quaint old building with no pretension to size or stateliness, standing at the north-west angle of the four cross-roads. In 1660 it was entered, not on the south side as now, but through a heavy gateway at the front of the house, looking towards the old vicarage and church. Portions of the house are of great antiquity. Till lately there was a plate on the oldest part bearing the date 1396; this date marked a few years after the marriage of John [2] Wingate to Agnes, sole heiress of the family of Belverge, (bearing on their shield three pears of gold—*bel v ger*), who brought him that estate with others in the neighborhood. Wingate of Harlington is included in the list of gentry made by the heralds on their visitation, held in the reign and under the auspices of Henry VI. which intimates him to have belonged to the Lancastrian party. The master of the Grange was never lord of the manor, yet his estates appear to have been considerable. In the time of Charles II., Sir Francis Wingate valued the estate at about £1000 per annum — as is shown in the letter of declaration he wrote the family of Lady Anne Annesley when he sought

her hand in marriage ; he also promised to keep a coach and six. The old house had once the honor of receiving King Charles II. as guest on a flying visit, and the china bowl with blue dragons round it, out of which the king is said to have breakfasted, is still preserved as a family relic.   In the roof of one of the gables there is a curious hiding place, which may have done good service to fugitive Royalists in the stormy days of civil war.   It was in this house that the examination of John Bunyan was held, either in the hall, wider then than now, or in the great parlor, as it was called, — an apartment with panelled walls and low ceiling, having oaken crossbeams centered by a carved rose boss.

In " Memories of Seventy Years," written by one of the descendants of Sir Francis Wingate, it is stated on the authority of Lucy Aiken, great-great-granddaughter of Sir Francis, that Sir Francis was the Wingate who committed John Bunyan to Bedford Jail.   But Rev. John Brown, in his " Life of John Bunyan," holds that Sir Francis was the son of Mr. Francis Wingate, Sr., and that the latter was the magistrate who committed Bunyan.   In other words Mr. Brown would insert a generation between John[10] and Sir Francis. There are circumstances in each story that seem to uphold each statement, so it is difficult to straighten out this matter.

According to Rev. Mr. Brown, Francis Wingate, Sr. was born in 1628, and succeeded to the Harlington estate when yet a minor. His sister, Anne, married September 22, 1653, William Foster, a lawyer of Bedford, who afterwards became Chancellor of the Diocese of Lincoln, and Commissary of the Court of the Bedford Archdeaconry.   Anne died in 1659.   Francis married, while yet in his teens, Lettice Pierce, daughter of Dr. Stephen Pierce, Vicar of Hitchin. Lettice's mother, after the death of Dr. Pierce, married Dr. Lindall, who had been Dr. Pierce's curate in 1635 and was afterwards vicar of Harlington from 1643 to 1660 and onward.   Nine children were born to Francis Wingate before 1660 (and possibly others afterwards).   Lettice was the oldest, having been born in 1644–45. Francis (afterwards Sir Francis) was the eldest son and was born in 1648, died in 1690.   Charles, the ninth child was born in 1660 and was christened in honor of the King.

The biographer of John Bunyan is naturally somewhat severe upon Mr. Wingate, and possibly he overstates when he affirms that " it may be doubted whether there was another Justice in the country

HARLINGTON HOUSE. AS IT APPEARED IN THE SEVENTEENTH CENTURY. [*From an Outline Sketch in the possession of the Aikin family.*]

through, in such eager haste [to take legal steps against dissenting ministers] as was Francis Wingate." Then he adds " Perhaps he had an ancient grudge to feed. At the outbreak of the civil war his father's death made him a ward of the crown, and his mother took him to the King's Quarters at Oxford, where they remained with the Royalists from September to February, 1642. For this offence she had to compound with Parliament for such portion of her estate as she had by jointure, and pay a fine of £100 to the Committee at Goldsmith's Hall. After her subsequent marriage with Richard Duncombe she had also to take the negative oath and sign the solemn league and covenant. Possibly her son did not forget this, and when his turn came he was eager to avenge the past."

In 1675 Francis, Sr. died. Mr. Brown declares that Francis, Jr., the eldest son, is found about 1671 the chosen friend of Lord Altham, " the scapegrace son of the Earl of Anglesey." (Note). " Through the influence of this Earl, who was of the Privy council," continues Mr. Brown, " Young Francis was knighted in 1672, and, therefore during the lifetime of his father. Some years later Sir Francis married Lady Anne Annesley, the fourth daughter of Lord Anglesey. Her father was cousin to Dr. Samuel Annesley, the eminent Non-conformist minister, and therefore she was second cousin to Susannah Wesley, the mother of John ". As regards the appearance of Sir Francis, Rev. John Brown says, " There is no portrait of Wingate himself [Francis Sr.] but there is a fine portrait of his son, Sir Francis, by Sir Peter Lely ; and if father and son were at all alike, Francis Wingate's face showed strength of will and a dash of haughtiness rather than intellectual force, and indicated a considerable liking for the good things of this life."

Lucy Aiken thinks that Sir Francis " looks in his portrait very good natured but heavy enough. Lady Anne—let us hope she was of sweeter temper than she looks in hers. She was a stiff Presbyterian, her husband a jolly Episcopalian, who said somewhat bitterly

NOTE. The son of Lord Altham who succeeded to his father's title of the Earl of Anglesey was the unhappy James Annesley, whose strange adventures and cruel fate formed the subject of a novel, and also a play called " The Lost Heir." Long litigation naturally followed which ended in the extinction of the title of Earl of Anglesey, but the family were allowed to retain their Irish title of Viscount Valentia.

that when he was gone she would turn his great hall into a Conventicle. Perhaps this thought had set an edge on his zeal when in the character of a justice of the Quorum he committed John Bunyan to Bedford jail for unlicensed preaching."

On the marriage of the young Sir Francis Wingate with Lady Anne great preparations were made at Harlington for the reception of the bride. The hall and state bed-chamber were newly fitted up for the occasion, the chamber being hung with tapestry "disfiguring and representing" the judgment of Paris and other classical stories, the bed being of damask, richly adorned with fringe and gilding. But, alas! the roads down into Bedfordshire in those days were atrociously bad, the house which was to be her future home, in spite of its attempts at grandeur, seemed to her poor and small, and Lady Anne, tired and weary with her journey, sat down and burst into tears.⁓ It was an unpromising beginning to her country life but she had too much good sense to weep for long over a position she had accepted for herself. With characteristic vigor she set about those duties of life which are serious both in lowly and lofty places, and in after years was really the stay of the household.

"Sir Francis died in middle life," says Lucy Aiken, "leaving his lady with three sons and six ill-portioned daughters. The sons all possessed the estate in succession, the two eldest dying single. The third, John, a retired naval captain, just managed to make both ends meet. He was long a widower and he had no surviving child." So the estates passed to Arthur Jennings, the son of Sir Francis's fourth daughter, Anna Letitia, who had married Rev. John Jennings, the son of an ejected minister and himself the pastor of the Congregational church at Kibworth, and tutor of the Dissenting Academy there. Two other daughters of Sir Francis were Frances and Rachel, who became members of Bunyan's Church at the Old Meeting, so that the descendants of the active magistrate made up in great measure for his harsh treatment of the Bedford preacher. Frances married Thomas Woodward, one of the deacons of the Bedford church. Her two daughters, Frances and Ann, married, the first Rev. Samuel Sanderson, one of Bunyan's successors at Bedford, [came to Bedford 1739 and remained until his death, January 24, 1766]; the second Rev. James Belsham, becoming thus the mother of Thomas and William Belsham, names well known in the circles of liberal thought nearly a century ago.

In the house of Anna Letitia Jennings, Philip Doddridge lived in his student days, finding there that atmosphere of a refined and educated home life of which he speaks in his letters. Through this Mrs. Jennings we come also upon a line of Non-conformists descendants of more than merely local fame. Her only daughter, Jane, married the Rev. Dr. John Aiken and became the mother of that Dr. Aiken and Anna Letitia Barbauld who gave us " Evenings at Home," and the grandmother of Lucy Aiken, of some reputation in the literary world of the eighteenth century. Mrs. Jennings had also Arthur, John and Francis.

To Arthur Jennings came the family estate. Francis became a brewer at Bedford and was held by the goodly followers of John Bunyan to be a black sheep among them, for although an active member and trustee of the Bedford church, he actually persisted in two sinful compliances with the world. He would wear a pair of red slippers, and he would not forbid his wife, who was young and pretty, from wearing her hair in ringlets down her neck. John Jennings became a dissenting minister.

UNCONNECTED NAMES.

A family of Wingates reside in Manchester, N. H., who belong to an English branch not connected with the John[1] Wingate line of America. Their line, as far back as they can trace, runs as follows :

JOHN[1], lived in London, Eng., and was a carpenter. Had a family of six children. Three of the sons died in London but the rest of the family live there.

RICHARD[1], (brother of John[1]), b. in Morham, Co. Kent, Eng., and died in Farmington, Co. Kent. Is said to have lain in a trance eleven days. Had ten children : 1. Richard[2] ; 2. John[2] ; 3. Thomas[2] ; 4. George[2] ; 5. William[2] ; 6. Jonathan[2] ; 7. Lydia[2] ; 8. Jane[2] ; 9. Sarah[2] ; 10. Fanny[2].

THOMAS[2], (son of Richard[1]), m. Susannah Poles of the parish of Horton, Kirby, Co. Kent, and d. 1860–61. He had seven children : 1. Thomas[3] ; 2. George[3] ; 3. Jonathan[3] ; 4. Richard[3] ; 5. Betsey[3] ; 6. Lydia[3] ; 7. Fanny[3].

George[3], (son of Thomas[2]), lived in Manchester, N. H., and had six daughters and one son, the latter T. J.[4] Wingate, of Amoskeag.

Jonathan[3], (son of Thomas[2]), had a son, Richard[4], who lived in Manchester, N. H.

KENTUCKY WINGATES.

Caleb[2] Wingate went South and it is possible that the Wingate families of Kentucky, who came from Delaware, are descendants of his, but the line has not as yet been traced back and all efforts so far have proved fruitless. Two branches have been heard from and they are given in the following genealogical tables and in the letter on succeeding pages.

Four brothers, Wingates, came to Kentucky from Delaware in 1799. One, Joseph, settled in Lexington, Fayette Co., two went to Shelby Co., and the fourth, Smith, settled in Franklin Co.

I. JOSEPH.
m. Venetia Downing, and had four children :

1. ROBERT, unm.

2. REBECCA.
m. Elijah *Warner*, and had two children.

3. WILLIAM, unm.

4. JOSEPH, b. Nov. 7, 1803.
m. July 18, 1827, Deborah Stone, and had one child who died in infancy.

II. ——.

III. ——.

IV. SMITH.
m. (in Delaware, near Wilmington), Susanna Capes, dau. of a Presbyterian Clergyman and with her and their four sons and one daughter went to Kentucky. He died when his eldest son, Thomas, was 12 years old, and his youngest, Henry, was an infant. His widow married again soon after. Had :

1. THOMAS.

    m. ———, lived in Owen Co., Ky., and had two sons :—

  1. Smith.

  2. John W.

    Lived in Hickman, Ky.

2. CYRUS.

    m. ———, lived in Owen Co., Ky. and was a Representative in the State Legislature for twenty years. Had fourteen children.

3. ISAAC, b. April 5, 1791, d. June 21, 1876.

    m. 1816, Jane M. Snead, and had eleven children.

4. HENRY, b. Oct. 5, 1795, d. Oct. 4, 1862.

    m. July 4, 1819, Penelope Hart Anderson. He was a man of great dignity and sterling integrity of character. The following sketch was written by an old friend of his, Dr. Morris : "Among the citizens of Kentucky most eminent in the workings of Free Masonry we number Henry Wingate of Frankfort. Coming into the Order as early as 1815, when the Grand Lodge of Kentucky comprised but a handful of lodges, he continued in steady and active membership until his death in 1862, a period of 47 years. To be an active Mason in Kentucky in those early days was a far different matter from what it is at present. There was no other secret order in the United States, where now there are half a hundred. In sparsely-settled communities, the halls built by the Free Masons were used for religious gatherings, for political meetings, for lectures, school houses and public demonstrations generally. It follows that the leading citizens, politicians, professional men, ministers of the gospel &c., were almost to a man Free Masons. On the Grand Lodge rolls of 1815 may be seen the names of Henry Clay, Robert J. Breckenridge and other representatives of the highest classes of the State. Amongst such men a thoughtful and spiritual-minded person like Henry Wingate found early recognition. He qualified himself to be an instructor in the principles and ceremonies of Free Masonry. He was consulted on all difficult questions that arose in the workings of that institution. When the lamentable defection occurred in 1826, which grew out of the Morgan affair, and men who dreaded the effect of public

agitation upon their own political fortunes, withdrew from active participation in Masonry, Mr. Wingate held firm, and by that act gave firmness to those around him. He was, from first to last, a member of Hiram Lodge No. 4, at Frankfort, and no other lodge did so much to stiffen the yielding spirits of the brethren and encourage them to perseverance as No. 4, under the guidance of Brother Wingate. In 1842, his faithful devotion during the hours of distress was acknowledged by his election by unanimous voice, to the supreme post of Grand Master. It is needless to affirm that the labors of this high and responsible function were performed to the credit of himself and the advantage of the Order. Restricted as the present writer is to a few paragraphs, it is sufficient to say that none in the long line of eighty prominent Kentuckians who have successively held that position have done more to give *eclat* to the ancient and honorable Order than Henry Wingate. A warm and affectionate tie endured through many years and bound the present writer to him who sleeps in the beautiful hill Cemetery at Frankfort. A welcome guest to his honored home in Frankfort, he enjoyed every opportunity to study in the quietude of the domestic hearth the spring of those virtues that insured him the public esteem. In every relation of life, as a Chistian, as a citizen, as a devoted Mason, Mr. Wingate held himself in equal poise. He loved his country, and mourned deeply when the cloud of Civil War overshadowed it. Dying amidst one of the convulsions that shook his very home, he leaves behind him the fragrance of a good memory." Henry Wingate lived in Frankfort, Ky., and had eight children :

1. Lucien, b. Oct. 21, 1820, d. 1846.

> m. 1843, Elizabeth Knight, of Louisville, Ky., and had one child :

> 1. Mary Knight.

>> m. 1871, Gen. Thomas A. *Harris*, and had one child :

>> 1. Lucien.

2. Maria Louisa, b. May 18, 1822.

> m. (1) May 19, 1842, Russel *McRery*, (d. June 2, 1845) ; (2) 1848, Rev. Duncan R. *Campbell*, President

of Georgetown College, Ky. By her first husband she had one son, by her second four children :

1. Russell Wingate, b. Sept. 5, 1845.
2. Henry Wingate.
3. Mary.
4. Archibald M.
5. Duncan Robertson.

3. *Reuben Anderson*, b. about 1823, d. Jan. 28, 1863.

m. March 20, 1851, Sarah Graham, of Shelbyville, Ky., and had four children :

1. Sallie Graham.

m. Robert *Poe*, of Baltimore, (d. 1884), and had two children :

1. Josephine.
2. Edwin Wingate.

2. Edwin Bryant.

m. Alice Waddell, of Lexington, Mo., and had two children :

1. John Waddell.
2. Edwin.

3. Henry, b. ————, d. 1881.
4. Ellen.

4. *Sarah Hart*, b. Nov. 5, 1825.

m. Oct. 5, 1843, George R. *McKee*, and had three children :

1. Henry Wingate, b. ————, d. an infant.
2. Lucien, b. 1847, d. 1867.
3. Jane Duncan.

5. *Susan Mary*, b. about 1828, d. May 30, 1842.
6. *Robert Johnston*, b. Dec. 18, 1829.
7. *Henry*, b. ————, d. in his second year.
8. *Ellen*, b. June 23, 1839.

m. Jan. 9, 1861, Dr. N. J. *Sawyier*, of Cincinnati, lived in Frankfort, Ky., and had seven children :

1. Lilian.
2. Henry Wingate.
3. Paul.
4. Nat, b. ————, d. in infancy.
5. Natalie.

6. Mary Campbell.
7. Robert Wingate, b. ————————, d. in infancy.

The following extract from a letter written to Mr. John Wingate [6] Thornton, (b. 1818), gives clews which may serve at some time to aid in connecting the Southern branches to the main family. It has no connection with the record above :

St. Louis, Mo., Aug. 13, 1872.

I was born in Boone Co., Ky., Jan. 24, 1822 ; my father moved to Louisville, Ky., and thence to Illinois, where I remained but a short time.   Grandfather Wingate lived on or near the eastern shore of Maryland, was a wagon master in the Revolution and had 18 sons and 4 daughters, having been married twice.   Two of the daughters were by his first wife.   At the close of the war he was paid off in the promises of the government which proved to be worthless ; this weighed heavily upon his mind and he died shortly afterwards ; his wife did not long survive him.   My father's given name was John, and he was the oldest son ; he and a younger brother named Edward entered the service under Wayne in the campaign against the north-western Indians, the allies of the British, at the close of the Revolution.   Edward was killed at what was called the Battle of the Fallen Timber not long after having entered the service ; my father continued with the army, in which he was several times promoted, until the close of the campaign ; he then settled in Butler Co., Ohio, and married Miss Mary Dillan who bore him two girls, Mary who died young, and Casendra who became the wife of William Herod, M. C. for several years, who lived in Columbus, Ind.   My father's first wife died quite young, and some two years afterward he married the widow of John Tarrane, deceased, and the daughter of Capt. Robert Benham, one of the first settlers of Cincinnati ; by her he had 8 children all of whom are now dead except myself and brother Edward who lives in Hardin Co., Ill.   Father first settled in Hamilton, Ohio, and removed thence to Cincinnati, and kept the first hotel ever established in that city, from which place he went in the War of 1812 as Brigadier General under Gen. Harrison and served during that war.   Some time after the close of the War of 1812 he removed to Bigbone Springs or Blue Lick, Boone Co., Ky., where he built a very large house as a place of resort and also had a

trading post with the Indians ; removed thence to a farm on the Ohio river, and after several removals finally located in Illinois, Gallatin Co. His children having established themselves in 1848 he concluded to return to Louisville, Ky., having some matters to settle up there ; my mother went in advance and died in Louisville a few days after her arrival. In 1850 my father visited Hamilton, Ohio, on business and died there a few days after his arrival. At his death he was upwards of 78 years old. I have a son, Ernest R. Wingate.

R. F. WINGATE.

BOOKS OF REFERENCE.

The following books all contain allusions, of greater or less extent, to the Wingate family and are some of those consulted in the preparation of this History :

Publication of the Harleian Society, Vol. VIII, page 276.

History and Antiquities of the County of Hertford, Vol. II, 496, by Robert Clutterbuck, pub. 1815–'27.

Lives of Scottish Writers (Ninian Winzet) by D. Irving.

Life of John Bunyan, by Rev. John Brown.

Memories of Seventy Years [edited by Mrs. Herbert Martin].

Original lists, Emigration to America, by John Camden Hotten, pub. 1874.

Genealogical Register of the First Settlers in New England, by John Farmer, pub. 1829.

Genealogical Dictionary of the First Settlers in New England, by James Savage, pub. 1860.

New England Historical and Genealogical Register, Vols. IX and XIII particularly.

Provincial Papers and Town Papers of New Hampshire.

Alden's Collection of American Epitaphs.

Wentworth Genealogy, by John Wentworth, LL. D., pub. 1878.

N. H. Churches, by Robert F. Lawrence, pub. 1856.

History of New Hampshire, by Jeremy Belknap, D.D.

History of Amesbury, by Joseph Merrill, pub. 1880.

Life of Timothy Pickering, by Charles W. Upham, pub. 1873.

Genealogical Memoirs of the Chase Family, by George B. Chase, pub. 1869.

North's History of Augusta, Me.

INDEXES.

INDEX I.

DESCENDANTS WHO BEAR THE NAME OF WINGATE.

The English line is in Italics, the American in Roman letter. The figures before each name denote the year of birth, the figures after the name denote the page on which the name occurs. The names of those who died in childhood are omitted. When the exact date of birth is not known, the century is given.

INDEX II.

DESCENDANTS BEARING SURNAMES OTHER THAN WINGATE.

The English line is in Italics, the American in Roman letter. The figures before each name denote the year of birth, the figures after the name denote the page on which the name occurs. The names of those who died in childhood are omitted. When the exact date of birth is not known, the century is given.

INDEX III.

The figures before the name indicate the year of marriage, those after indicate the page on which the name occurs. Where no figures are given before, that indicates an indirect connection. The English line is denoted by Italic.

	Grafton, Elizabeth,	174
1851	Graham, Sarah,	259
1867	Grant, Annie,	194
	Patrick,	194
18	Gray, Catherine,	187
1837	Horace,	202
1820	John C.,	200
18	Greeley, N.,	242
	Greely, Daniel,	115
1841	Nancy B.,	115
1860	Green, Mary,	157
1865	Groesbeck, Martha J.,	113
1854	Guild, Charles E.,	194
18	**Haines,** Daniel,	172
17	Susanna,	234
	William,	234
18	Hale, Elizabeth S.,	111
1761	Haley, Joshua,	148
1881	Hallowell, Henry C..	150
	Ham, Ann,	33
	Jonathan,	145
	Joseph,	33
17	Mary,	33
	Moses,	141
1760	Samuel,	132
17	Susan,	145
	Tamsen,	33
1880	Hamilton, Cyrus L.,	154
1838	Mary,	245
1845	Hamlin, Sarah,	138
1841	Hammond, Charlotte,	209
1851	Sarah S.,	209
1867	Hanscom, Isaac W.,	116
17	Hanson, Hannah,	144
1813	"	124
18	Joseph,	135
1769	William,	141
1856	Harding, Harriet,	172
1847	Harriman, Hedarrah E.,	153
1871	Harris, Thomas A.,	258
18	Hartshorne, Ida,	121
1857	Haskell, Caroline W.,	178
	Hathorne, Hannah,	190
1872	Hayden, Horace J.,	208
1776	Hayes, Aaron,	104
1832	Eliza,	105
	Ezekiel,	105
1825	John,	106
	"	45
	"	50, 147
17	Jonathan,	50, 147
1796	Joseph,	104
17	Moses,	103
17	Paul,	142
17	Peter,	45, 145
	Samuel,	142
1802	Hayford, Lydia A.,	237
	Heath, Hannah,	152, 158, 159
1842	Hemenway, Martha W.,	233
	Solomon,	233
1855	Henderson, Harriet M.,	189
1821	Mary E.,	193
18	Heriman, ——,	111
18	Herod, Wm.,	260
18	Hersey, Ann,	158
18	Hicks, ——,	228
1856	Higginson, Louisa,	182
	Hill, Anne,	40
17	Ebenezer,	50
	"	51
	Jeremiah,	151
1773	Lydia,	151
17	"	148
	Isaac,	229
	Nathan,	29

	Hill, Valentine,	29
17	Hodgdon, Mary,	143
169	Israel,	33
	Shadrach,	143
17	———	50
1856	Hodges, Mary S.,	217
1838	Holbrook, Laurinda,	189
18	Hopkins, Marcia A.,	238
1877	Hopkinson, Grace M.,	195
	Horne, Rebecca,	129
	Sally,	139
18	Samuel,	131
1856	Howard, Lucy M.,	178
18	William,	111
1840	Howe, Mary C.,	240
1805	Octavia,	238
1869	Hoyt, Geo. H.,	172
	Hubbard, Sarah,	215
18	Wm. P.,	115
17	Huggins, John,	218
1854	Humphrey, Abby M. C.,	192
1879	Edgar T.,	155
18	Hurst, Ralph,	225
18	Hussey, Daniel,	130
	Hutchins, Solomon,	138
1855	Sophia W.,	138
17	**Ingalls** Henry,	170
	Ingersoll, Sarah,	183
18	———	221
18	Innis, George,	171
18	Ireland, T. L.,	169
1835	**Jackson,** Elizabeth C.,	206
	James,	206
17	Samuel,	147
17	———,	147
18	Jacobs, Proctor,	234
18	Jenkins, John,	243
1831	Jenks, George W.,	214
1801	Rebecca,	213
	Jennings, Arthur,	254
	Jennings, John,	19, 254
1831	Johnson, Lydia L.	185
1857	Samuel,	215
18	S. B.,	228
1770	Johnston, Benjamin,	223
18	———,	116
18 5	Jones, Anita P.,	196
1850	David R.,	130
1877	Elizabteh G.,	201
1848	John P.,	129
18	Luther,	238
17	Stephen,	118
17	Thomas,	225
1873	Jordan, Edward C ,	186
18	**Kelburn,** Charlotte,	163
1876	Kelley, Clarence E.,	165
18	Joseph,	122
18	Kelly, Jane,	224
	William,	224
1869	Kemble, Elizabeth R.,	215
18	Kendall, Elizabeth R.,	244
1792	Kenrich, Abner,	160
18	Kimball, Daniel W.,	122
18	Hannah,	243
18	Kinney, Enoch,	228
1871	Knauth, Selma,	210
1841	Knight, Catherine,	116
1863	Cyrus F.,	211
1843	Elizabeth,	258
	Job,	224
1798	Mary,	224
1858	Knowles, Anna M.,	105
	William,	105

286   INDEX III.

ADDENDA.

(TO SECOND EDITION.)

Since the publication of the first edition of the Wingate History, recent marriages and births, together with additional information regarding past events make it advisable to give as a second appendix the following data :

PAGE 44. In the record of baptisms at Dover, Dr. John R. Ham finds. 1729, Nov. 23, Moses and Elizabeth, twins, children of John Wingate. These, it would seem, must be children of John[3]. It is probable they died in infancy, thus accounting for their absence from other records.

PAGE 49. Moses[3] Wingate had eight children. Edmond[4] and Abigail[4] were the eldest, having both been baptized Sept. 14, 1729. Moses[4] was baptized Aug. 20, 1738, and Ebenezer[4], May 23, 1742.

PAGE 103. John[6] Hayes m. Sarah Clough (b. 1796–97, d. Feb. 27, 1885). She m. (2) Mr. Austin.

PAGE 104. Deborah[5] Wingate, b. March, 1749.

PAGE 106. Captain Joseph Grace, d. 1886, aged 88. Charles[7] Wingate, d. Oct., 1886.

PAGE. 107. Charles[7] Wingate, b. Jan. 29, 1813, m. June 1, 1837, Mary P. Robinson. D. C. 1832, lived in Brooklyn and had :

(a) Hannah S.[8], b. July 17, 1838.

(*b*)   George W.[8] (Gen.), b. July 1, 1840.

m. July 31, 1867, Susan P. Man. Served in the war. Was secretary and afterwards president of the National Rifle Association, general inspector of rifle practice in New York, president of the Amateur Rifle Club, and president of the First American International Rifle Team. Has earned the title of "The Father of Rifle Practice in America" by his writings and work, and has also been distinguished as a lawyer. Author of " On Horseback Through the Yellowstone " and other books. Had :

1.   Mary H.[9], b. June 3, 1868.

2.   Louisa M.[9], b. Oct. 18, 1869.

3.   George A.[9], b. Oct. 24, 1871.

4.   Charles G.[9], b. June 28, 1872.

(*c*)   J. Phelps[8]. b. July 23, 1843.

(*d*)   Charles F.[8], b. March 5, 1847.

m. Aug. 26, 1874, Florence Diamond.   Had :

1.   Adah B.[9], b. Aug. 28, 1875.

2.   Karl[9], b. Dec., 1876.

(*e*)   Mary Christina[8], b. April 23, 1849.

m. March 12, 1874, Charles T. Carret and had :

1.   Elise H.[9], b. Jan. 31, 1875.

2.   Edna P.[9], b. March 10, 1876.

3.   Christina J.[9], b. May 4, 1877.

4.   Francis W.[9], b. Nov. 2, 1884.

(*f*)   Lizzie[8], b. March 1853, d. an infant.

(*g*)   Rafaella M.[8], b. Sept. 12, 1856,

m. Oct. 20, 1885, Otto Drandt.

PAGE 110. Simon[6] Wingate, m. 1820, Ann Riley (b. Oct. 28, 1785, d. July, 1856).

PAGE 110. Abigail[5] Wingate, m. Oct. 5, 1780.

PAGE 117. Deborah H.[6] Wingate, m. William A. B. Cobb.

Page 118. Sarah[5] Wingate, m. as second wife, Nathan Lord (b. Jan. 26, 1756). He served in the Revolution.

Page 125. Uranus O. B.[8] Wingate, m. 1874, Georgia A. Knowles.

Page 126. Add (children of Daniel[4] Wingate) 5. Mary[5] m. ———— Horne. 6. ————[5].

Page 132. Martha[6] Titcomb, m. James C. Sewell.

Page 135. Eliza[6] (March) Barker, had: 1 George William[7]; 2. Caroline[7]; 3. Eliza[7].

Page 135. Jonas C.[6] March had one daughter, who m. Dr. Stickney and lived in the vicinity of Boston. Caroline[6] March, d. unm. Sarah Ann[6] (March) Freeman had: 1. Charles[7]; 2. George[7]; 3. Helen[7]; 4. Mary[7]; 5. Fred[7]; 6. John[7]. Aaron Wingate[6] March (d. aged 33) m. Ann Tredick of Dover [She m. (2) John T. Gibbs, editor Dover Gazette] and had: 1. Henry Tredick[7]. Emily[6] (March) Barker had: 1. Charles Augustus[7]; 2. Annie Simpson[7]; 3. George Frederick[7]; 4. Jonas March[7]; 5. John[7]; 6. Emily[7]. John Plummer[6] March, m. Rachel Gross, lived in New York and had 7 or 8 children.

Page 136. Sarah Patten, b. Aug. 21, 1783, d. May, 1870. Elizaabeth Helen Goodwin, b. March 11, 1828, d. Jan. 12, 1872. Homer S.[7] Wingate, b. Dec. 25, 1853. Frank Edward[7] Wingate, b. Oct. 23, 1858. Arthur R.[7] Wingate had (a) Alice[8], b. Aug. 5, 1886.

Page 136. Add children of Aaron[6] Wingate: 5. George Frederick[7], b. April 4, 1863, d. April 24, 1864; 6, Alice Mary[7], b. Sept. 26, 1870.

Page 136. Hannah E.[6] Wingate, b. July 9, 1828, m. Ebenezer T. Gerrish (d. 1871) of West Lebanon and had: 1. Annie D.[7]; 2. Charles W.[7]; 3. Edith[7]; 4. Fannie[7].

Page 136. (Also on page 132), Jeremiah[5] Wingate should be Jeremy Belknap[5] Wingate, d. March 27, 1864. Nancy[5] Wingate, d. April 9, 1864.

Page 142. Ann[3] Wingate, m. (1) Francis Drew.

Page 154. Sarah E.[7] Parkman, m. Sept. 15, 1855, Erasmus Little-

field (b. April 1833), and had (*a*) Edgar E.[8], b. Dec. 25, 1856, who m. May 4, 1883. He changed his last name to Parkman.

PAGE 154. Oscar Leslie[8], (last name changed from Littlefield to Parkman) m. May 21, 1885, Ella T. Ames of Lynn, Mass.

PAGE 155. George W.[7] Parkman, m. Aug. 19, 1866, Melissa F. Robinson (b. Aug. 19, 1844.)

PAGE 155. Laura J. B.[7] Parkman, m. (2) Oct. 4, 1885, Joel M. Parkman, (b. July 3, 1854,) of Palmyra, Me.

PAGE 155. John W.[7] Clark, m. 1853, Martha E. S. Philbrick (b. July 6, 1835, d. Jan. 30, 1878).

PAGE 155. Jessie H. P.[8] Clark, b. June 26, 1856, m. Oct. 21, 1879, Edgar T. Humphrey (b. March 19, 1857).

PAGE 156. John P.[6] Wingate, m. May 16, 1839, Mary Olivia Folsom (b. May 17, 1815).

PAGE 156. John H. Gilbert, b. Jan. 9, 1817. Clarence A. Wonson, b. March 9, 1839.

PAGE 156. Dana W.[7] Baker, m. Sept. 7, 1886, Fannie E. French of Danville, N. H.

PAGE 157. Samuel Dana[7] Wingate. Went to California on the first ship that started during the mining excitement. Was there several years and then returned to Exeter and entered into the dry goods business. For a number of years was register of Probate for Rockingham County. Was notary public and in the pension business with Judge Joseph F. Wiggin. Represented Exeter in the State Legislature, in 1864–'65.

PAGE 157. Charles E. L.[7] Wingate had (*a*) Mabel[8], b. Nov. 30, 1886.

PAGE 169. Adelaide W.[6] Page, m. Capt. W. A. Howard.

PAGE 169. Tingey Henry[6] Wingate should be Henry Tingey[6]. He m. Frances Martha Skinner of Charlestown, Mass.. and had : 1. Margaret[7] ; 2. Henry Tingey[7] ; 3. Frances[7].

PAGE 173. Charles F.[7] Richardson, m. April 12, 1878, Elizabeth Miner Thomas, of Wilkesbarre, Penn., (b. April 12, 1857).

PAGE 184. Mary O.[7] Pickering, d. Oct., 1886, in her 81st year.

ANECDOTICAL.

A sketch of Gen. John Wingate, referred to on Page 260, can be found in Pioneer Biography, Vol 2, by James McBride. That states that John Wingate was born in New York, 1773-'74, and died April 14, 1851. He m. (1) before 1795, Mary Dillon, (2) May 24, 1809, Mrs Emma Torrence. Was under Gen. Wayne in frontier battles with the Indians during 1791-'95.

A humorous tradition is told regarding Hon. Paine[4] Wingate. He had a keen perception of the ridiculous that would not allow him always to keep his countenance when anything laughable occurred. One Sunday, while he was preaching, a dog entered the house of worship, and spying in a corner the lunch baskets and pails of the congregation (in those days they brought their noon meal so as not to be obliged to walk the long distance home between services) proceeded to supply himself with the delicacies there reserved. Mr. Doggy, however, came to grief. In trying to reach the milk in a can he got his head through the opening, but could not get it back. With a howl he started on the run blindly through the church, the milk meanwhile pouring over his head. The sight was so ludicrous that the preacher himself burst out laughing in the midst of his sermon. Afterwards he was so mortified at this that he would not again appear in the pulpit, and so abandoned preaching. So the story runs.

Eunice[4] Pickering Wingate, wife of Hon. Paine[4] Wingate, one day remarked to a friend, so it is said, " You know Lois and I are twins. It is generally the case that when there are twins one of them possesses a great part of the intellectuality while the other has much less. Now Lois, I'm afraid, would never set the river on fire ! "

Tradition records that Hon. Paine[4] Wingate received a call at his home in Stratham from President Washington when the latter was on his way between Exeter and Portsmouth. It is also told that Hon. Paine[4] Wingate carried the first umbrella ever carried in Hampton, and that his appearance with the thing over his head caused great astonishment as well as question regarding such action by a minister of the gospel.

Mrs. Caroline W.[6] Baker possesses the sand box used by Hon. Paine[4] Wingate in Congress. Mrs. James M. Lovering has the table that Sally Piper had when she married John[5] Wingate, and the platter that Sally Piper's mother (or grandmother) on the paternal side possessed. Charles F.[7] Richardson has the commission as Justice of the Peace of Joseph[4] Wingate, dated June 29, 1792, and signed by Gov. John Hancock.

6

CPSIA information can be obtained
at www.ICGtesting.com
Printed in the USA
BVHW042134111221
623834BV00022B/574